The Legacy of Polish Jewry

By the Same Author

The Will and Testament of the Biala Rabbi

A Guide to Hassidism

The Slave who Saved the City

The Jewish Literary Treasures of England and America

A Guide to Life

The Legacy of
Polish Jewry

A History of Polish Jews in the Inter-War
Years 1919-1939

Harry M. Rabinowicz

New York · Thomas Yoseloff · London

© 1965 by A. S. Barnes and Co., Inc.
Library of Congress Catalogue Card Number: 65-11349

Thomas Yoseloff, Publisher
8 East 36th Street
New York 16, New York

Thomas Yoseloff Ltd
18 Charing Cross Road
London W.C.2, England

6238
Printed in the United States of America

Dedicated
to the revered memory of
BENZION MARGULIES
1890–1955

Contents

Contents

List of Illustrations

The following illustrations appear as a group after page 128.

List of Illustrations

Introduction

Ninety per cent of all the Jews in Europe and America today, and 80 per cent of world Jewry originated in Eastern Europe. It was Poland which produced the pietists, the Hebraists, the Yiddishists, the pioneers, the men of letters and the men of action, the men whose faith moved mountains, and the men whose hands drained marshes. This was the main center of *Chassidism,* the movement that rekindled and reclaimed the Jewish people. And it was here that the pale wistful dream of Zion became the tangible tough reality that was Zionism.

The three and a quarter million Jews of inter-war Poland lived in close-knit communities. Although there were no specific ghettos, the Jews invariably clustered together, building their fragile defences against menacing neighbors. Differences of morals and mores set them apart from their non-Jewish neighbors and they fought to preserve their identity. In general, they were determined not to purchase civic equality at the price of assimilation, and, by an overwhelming majority, clung to traditional Judaism with whole-hearted devotion.

This was a complex and kaleidoscopic *Kehilla, Chassid* and Bundist, *Mitnagged* and Marxist, each with the fire of his own passionate beliefs, intermingled on the Polish scene to clash again and again. Only when survival was at stake did these spiritual factions forget their differences to unite in a common cause.

This was in a sense a period of religious renaissance. It marked a re-emphasis on Torah, and the re-emergence of a Shulchan Aruch Jew for whom the Torah was all-embracing and all-sufficient. It was "hard to be a Jew," but it was compensatingly "good to be a Jew." In an age of systematic persecution and licensed discrimination, the Jew managed miraculously to retain a spiritual *joie de vivre*. Only in religion, in divine service, in acts of faith, in communion with his Creator, did he find refuge and release and the strength with which to face two deathly decades. For the mood of the masses was ugly, and the full blast of its bitterness was unleashed upon the Jews. Lost in the legendary past was the myth of Poland's knightly chivalry. It was Pole against Pole, class against class, a bitterly disrupt society with but one aim in common—the total extinction of the Jews from Polish life.

Part pacifist and part freedom fighter, at once world-wise and unworldly, the Polish Jew was indeed a remarkable individual to survive under living conditions that grew increasingly unbearable. Massive were the forces of destruction that were marshalled against him. In the six years between 1939 and 1945, a millennial culture perished in a bloody blaze such as the world has never seen. Poland became the grave-yard of Polish Jewry, a central cemetery for the great Jewish communities of Europe.

Today Poland is virtually *judenrein*. As we recall with awe and anguish the martyrdom of Polish Jewry and the heroism of the Warsaw Ghetto, it is time to record the history of Polish Jewry in the years that directly preceded the holocaust. We have seen how millions of Jews died. It is equally important to see how they lived. And it is even more important that the historians and sociologists of our day and of tomorrow are possessed of the crucial and self-condemning evidence of Poland's deliberate policy of persecution of the Jews.

This work relates the story of Polish Jewry during these fateful inter-war years, outlining basic trends and sketching a general picture of the Polish scene. Inevitably, much has been omitted. Events that merit careful and meticulous analysis have been but briefly referred to. Men worthy of individual biographies have, of necessity, received only passing mention. So vast is the canvas that little short of a lifetime of collation and a massive encyclopedia could do it justice. A large Hurban literature has emerged from Israel and from the Argentine, producing a series of more than 160 volumes in Yiddish on this period. Yet, since Simon Segal's *The New Poland and the Jews,* published in 1938, very little has been written in English on this theme.

This book is based on lectures delivered under the auspices of the Extra-Mural Department of the University of London and Jews' College at North Finchley Synagogue, London. Principal sources of information, in addition to contemporary newspapers and periodicals, are listed in the Bibliography. I am deeply indebted to many people for valuable and pertinent comments. In thanking them, I stress that while they share the credit for any merit this work may have, they are not responsible for any of its shortcomings. I express my appreciation of the research facilities afforded by the Wiener Library, the Polish Research Centre and the Polish Library in London.

It is with grateful thanks that I express my indebtedness to *Yad Washem,* Jerusalem, the Yivo Institute of Jewish Research, New York, and Mr. M. Zylberberg of the Yivo office, London, for the loan of photographs, and for the assistance in procuring illustrative material for this book.

I am glad to acknowledge my thanks to my sister Miriam for the meticulous care with which she read through my manuscript. Her detailed criticism and helpful comments have greatly improved the readability of the book.

It is only fitting that I should recall the great debt of gratitude which I owe to my honored and revered mother Szaindla Brachah, at whose suggestion this work was undertaken. She departed from our midst on the 11th *Iyar* 5723. She gave me many facts from the rich storehouse of her memory. She was my mentor and inspiration, a noble daughter of Polish Jewry.

H. R.

London, April, 1964; the twenty-first anniversary of the Warsaw Ghetto uprising.

The Legacy of Polish Jewry

1

Paradise Lost

The history of the Jews in Poland can be retraced continuously, period by period, for over a thousand years. Evidence of Jewish settlement dates back to the tenth century A.C.E. and by 1939, over one-sixth of world Jewry had settled in Polish territory. It is a remarkable fact that in no other country, with the exception of the Holy Land, have the Jews lived for so long an epoch and in so large a number.

Jews began to settle in Poland before Christianity had found general acceptance in Eastern Europe. References to Jewry are found on coins of Mieszko I, first king of Poland who reigned in the mid-tenth century, and it is known that in the year 933 the Jewish community of Wronki built itself a synagogue.[1] Even etymologically the Jews associated themselves closely with their new homeland, and its name was interpreted in Hebrew either as *Polin*, "Here ye shall dwell," or *Polaniah*, "Here dwelleth the Lord."

From the South and from the East, from the land of the *Chazars* (Crimea) and most of all from the West, Jewish emigrants flowed in ceaseless streams towards Poland and Lithuania. Many factors were responsible for these mass movements: the Crusades, the expulsion from France in 1306, the Black Death (1348–1351)—for which the Jews were the inevitable scapegoats—the terrors of the fanatical fourteenth century Flagellants. Remarkably enough, a warm welcome awaited the battered wanderers. For the incoming Jews filled a definite vacuum. The Jews needed a home and the Poles needed the Jews.

Poland had not developed a native bourgeoisie. It possessed neither a balanced economy nor a balanced community. The sixteenth century dawned upon a peculiarly asymmetrical society; 11 per cent of the population, nearly 200,000 people, were noblemen, *Shlakhta*, as the ruling class was called, with neither aptitude nor inclination for commerce. In fact, noblemen were specifically forbidden to have business dealings. Only the peasants were legally entitled to engage in trade. It is of more than semantic significance that the Polish language contains no word for commerce. The term used, *Handel*, is of Germanic origin. It followed logically that the peasants needed middlemen; the town-folk needed merchants, and the nobility needed financiers. The Jews were well equipped to play these diversified roles.

As early as 1264, Boleslaw the Pious of Great Poland (1247–1279) granted the Jews inviolability of person and property. These rights and privileges were confirmed by almost all the Kings of Poland and they became part of Poland's common law. "The above Jews whom we have reserved for ourselves and the country and for our special treasury," declared the Charter, "may realise during our happy reign that they have found comfort with us."[2] The Charter allowed Jews to lend money on interest, and pro-

vided that "whoever by violence snatched a pledge from
a Jewish creditor's hand would be liable to arbitrary
punishment by the prince."[3] Jews were free to move
throughout the principality. They were exempted from
the jurisdiction of the common courts, and empowered
to settle disputes in which both plaintiff and defendant
were Jews.[4]

Both person and property were protected by law. The
Charter instituted severe penalties for killing or harming
a Jew. Violation of a Jewish cemetery was punishable by
forfeiture of all estates, desecration of a synagogue by the
imposition of the heavy fine.[5] A special addendum rendered Christians liable to fines if they withheld help from
Jewish neighbors in distress. No wonder Rabbi Moses
Isserles wrote in lyric phrases of Poland's hospitality:
"Had not the Lord left this land as a refuge, the fate of
Israel would indeed have been unbearable. By the grace
of God, both the kings and the nobles are favourably disposed towards us. In this country there is no fierce
hatred as there is in Germany."[6]

But there were bloodshot clouds on the horizon. Anti-
Jewish riots broke out in Poznan in 1390 and in Cracow
in 1407. Enemies abounded, virulent, violent. First the
Polish episcopate, and later the Jesuits, "anxious to protect the tender plant of Christianity in these regions,"
attacked the aliens. Yet neither the overt jealousy of the
ever-burgeoning Polish burghers and the German Guilds
(protected by the Magdeburg Rights), nor the inter-
mittent outbursts of the unruly Diets seriously hampered
Jewish expansion and consolidation.

At a time when Polish sovereignty extended from the
Baltic to the Black Sea, the Jews were quick to explore
the country's economic potential. Whilst, in other lands,

they were confined to money-lending and petty trading,
Jews here participated in all branches of industrial endeavour. They imported from the East and exported to
the West. Polish production increased rapidly, particularly in terms of furs and grain. In addition, Jewish
physicians were highly esteemed and frequently in the
employ of kings and noblemen.

Allied to these economic opportunities was an unusual
degree of religious freedom. On August 13, 1551, Sigismund Augustus (1548–1572) laid the foundation for
autonomous Jewish life. The Jews elected their own
Chief Rabbi who exercised wide-ranging spiritual jurisdiction, while the *Kahal* (communal board), controlled
the community from the cradle to the grave. From the
local *Kahal* stemmed an intricate structure of supervisory
organizations. First, district councils, *Guellilot,* were
created. These later became *Medinot,* provincial councils,
under the supreme governing body was the *Vaad Arba
Arazot,* "The Council of Four Lands" or "Congressus
Judaicus," embracing Little Poland (Cracow and Lublin),
Great Poland (Poznan), Ruthenia (Brest and Grodno),
and Volhynia.

Whilst the *Kahal* was regional in scope, the *Vaad* operated on a national level. It acted as the State's agent for
Jewish taxation, dealt with questions of industry and
commerce, regulated the election of the *Kahals,* and ap-
proved school curricula. "The representatives of the Council of Four Lands," remarked historian Nathan Hannover,[7]
"reminded one of the Sanhedrin, which in ancient days
assembled in the Chamber of Hewn Stones (*Lishkat
Hagazit*) of the Temple. They dispensed justice to all the
Jews of the Polish realm, issued preventive measures and
obligatory enactments (*Takkanot*), and imposed penalties
as they saw fit."

The *Vaad* issued edicts and directives on every phase and facet of life. Ostentatious functions were effectively discouraged through a series of what amounted to sumptuary laws. "In so far as people are spending too much money on unnecessarily festive meals (at marriages and circumcisions and so on), every Jewish community and settlement which has a rabbi, is expected to assemble its officers and rabbi, and to consider the number of guests which is suitable for every individual, in view of his wealth and the occasion, to invite to a festive meal." Extravagance in dress was similarly severely censured. "One is permitted to wear only two rings on a weekday, four on the Sabbath and six on holidays."

Of course the spendthrift's natural nemesis was penury and as a bankrupt he was heavily penalized. "He is to be imprisoned for a whole year and he shall not be appointed to any office for any religious work. If he already holds office he is to be deposed, and he shall not be called up to the Reading of the Law for a whole year, or until he repays all his notes to his creditors." Enactments were specific and detailed. The *Vaad* decreed that Jewish farmers for example were to be "instructed in the manner of castrating their cattle and fowls, the raising of hogs, the distilling of brandy on the Sabbath and in similar matters and laws."

For the Polish Jew, the study of the Torah was the core of his existence. *Torah iz di beste sechorah* ("The Torah is the best merchandise") runs an old folk-saying that was the expression of his credo. The life-long, life-absorbing study of the Talmud was the alpha and omega of education. This was the golden age of Polish Jewry, no less splendid than the golden age of the Jews of Spain (900–1200), or the Talmudic period in Babylon. There were great men without number, great in learning, great in

piety. *Halachic* luminaries included Rabbi Jacob Pollak (1470–1541), father of the *Pilpul* (Dialectics), Rabbi Shalom Shachna (1510–1559), Rabbi Solomon Luria (1510–1573) and Rabbi Mordecai ben Abraham Jaffa (1530–1612). The Glosses (*Haggaot*) of Rabbi Moses Isserles' the *Rema* (1525–1572) to Joseph Caro's *Shulchan Aruch*, were reverently accepted by all *Ashkenazi* Jews. Scholars from Italy, Germany and Palestine sought his guidance and deferred to his judgments. Like so many others, the youngest son of Manasseh ben Israel (1604–1657), left his native Holland for Poland "to pour water on the hands and to sit at the feet of the great ones of the Second Palestine."

It was in Poland that Yiddish was reared to rich maturity. The German dialect (middle German), uprooted from its source, absorbed Hebraic and Slavic elements as time went by. This friendly familiar amalgam of many languages became known as Yiddish, mother tongue of successive generations, a unique form of international Esperanto, second only to Hebrew in its influence on the Jewish masses of Eastern Europe.

The Jewish community paid dearly for its privileges. Every Jew was subject to a capitation tax of one Polish gulden per head, and a general tax based upon his income. In addition, he paid a "purchase tax" on most of the commodities of daily life: there was a tax on needles, a tax on liquor, a tax on meat and a substantial amount for national defence.[8] In the seventeenth century the Jews were paying annual taxes amounting to 100,000 gulden and by 1717 they were contributing 220,000 gulden a year. Yet there was still some truth in the adage that Poland was "heaven for the nobleman, purgatory for the citizen, hell for the peasant and paradise for the Jew."

Inevitably, Polish oppression of the Ukraine culminated in catastrophe. The absentee Polish landlord and his Lithuanian counterpart were not statesmen. Their concern was with the present and not the future: their policy of extortion reaped a harvest of hatred. The peasants were enslaved, burdened and abused. Between Catholic master and Greek Orthodox serf loomed barriers of faith, language and ethnic origin. The overlord landlords farmed out their land to agents who rented it to the peasantry.

With "Fire and Sword" the Cossack leader Chmielnicki (1593–1657) poured out his venom on the defenceless Jews. In the Ukraine, over one hundred thousand Jews were slain and 774 communities were all but annihilated. Only one-tenth of the Ukrainian Jewish community survived this holocaust and one-third of Polish Jewry perished. It was a genocidal devastation that ranked with the destruction of the Second Temple among the major disasters of Jewish history. The barbarities of the *Gezerot Tach* ("The Fateful Events of 1648") as the Chmielnicki massacres were known, were only to be exceeded by the Hitlerite slaughters of World War II.

As if the cup of Jewish sufferings were not full to overflowing, the infamous Blood Libels were revived. Sandomierz (1698–1710), Poznan (1736), and Zaslav (1747), were the scenes of murderous rampages. "Just as Poland cannot do without the *Liberum Veto*," it was said, "so the Jews cannot have *Matzot* without Christian blood."

"If fatherland be the first word of the Polish nobleman, liberty is his second," declared Heine. This poetic extravaganza served to underscore the tempestuous individualism that led to the disintegration of the Polish state. The instability of the "elected" monarchy was disastrously allied to the capricious *Liberum Veto*. With one phrase,

Nie pozwalam ("I do not permit it"), a veto that required neither explanation nor justification, any nobleman could not only doom the bill under discussion, but could also bring about the dissolution of the Diet and the cancellation of all bills passed by the House up to that very day. In the course of 112 years no less than forty-eight Diets dissolved. When the last of the Jagiellons, Sigismund Augustus, died in 1572 without issue, a succession of marionette monarchs were elected to the throne. "We are the electors of kings," asserted the noblemen with calculated insolence. "You may reign but you dare not rule."

These chronic constitutional weaknesses rendered the country easy prey for predatory border lords. The Three Partitions (1772–1795) erased the name of Poland from the political map of Europe and apportioned the divided territory between the triumvirate of mighty neighbors: Russia, Prussia and Austria.

During the next 120 years, the Jews shared the tribulations of the conquered country. Yearning for the vanished glories of Poland's prime, they fought in every uprising against foreign mastery. Tadeusz Kosciuszko (1746–1817), commander-in-chief of the Polish armed forces in the final struggle before the last partition of Poland in 1794, paid generous tribute to Jewish patriotism. "In defence of the Fatherland equality pays and therefore Jew, peasant, noble, priest and bourgeois are of equal merit to me." In a manifesto issued on September 17, 1794, Kosciuszko attested: "There is no better evidence that our ideal is holy and just, than the fact that the Jews who are strangers to us in their faith and habits, come to us of their own free will, sacrificing their lives . . . And it happened that on the seventeenth and eighteenth of April, 1794, when Warsaw fought with Russians, the Warsaw Jews took to the sword and fought with the enemy, showing to the whole world that if it comes to human rights they do not spare their blood."[9] Participating in the Kosciuszko campaign was a volunteer battalion of Jewish cavalry organized by Berek Joselowicz (c. 1765–1809). "I have had the happiness," wrote Berek to his coreligionists, "of being placed at the head of the regiment by my superiors. Awake then, and help to rescue oppressed Poland. Faithful brethren, let us fight for our country as long as a drop of blood is left in us! Though we ourselves may not live to see this, at least our children will live in tranquility and freedom, and will not roam about like wild beasts. Awake then like lions and leopards."[10]

It is said that when Napoleon established the Grand Duchy of Warsaw, he demanded: "How many Jews are here?" "A million," came the reply. "It is a pity," observed Bonaparte, "that you have so great a number of industrious citizens whose value you do not appreciate." At first the new regime abolished serfdom and legislated for civil equality. However, the nobility opposed the bill of civil rights and on October 17, 1809, Duke Frederick Augustus promulgated a decree to the effect that "the inhabitants of our Varsovian Duchy professing the Mosaic religion shall be barred for ten years from enjoying the political rights they were about to receive, in the hope that during this interval they may eradicate their distinguishing characteristics which mark them off so strongly from the rest of the population."[11]

The defeat of Napoleon in 1813 led to the disappearance of the Duchy of Warsaw and, at the Vienna Congress in 1815, the final partition of Poland took place. Western Poland passed to Prussia and became part of the Great Duchy of Poznan. The rest of the Duchy of Warsaw, known as Congress Kingdom, was annexed by Russia. The fall of Napoleon shattered Polish hopes for more than a century.

Although the Poles and the Jews suffered side by side, almost vying for martyrdom, not even common oppression could bridge the yawning chasm between them. During the 1830–31 rebellion led by the Polish nobility, General Josef Chlopicki debarred Jews from the National Guards, and Minister of Military Affairs General Franciszek Morawski rejected the Jewish aid so willingly offered. Polish leader Jan Orlych Szaniecki formulated an eight-point resolution calling for the abolition of labor services, the granting of property rights to the peasants, and the extension of constitutional rights to the Jews. The resolution was ignored by the Diet.[12]

Yet Jewish patriotism was not to be stifled. A. Wertheim, of the wealthy banking family, financed the rebellion and Joseph Berkowicz (1789–1846), son of Berek Joselowicz, won acceptance for himself and eight hundred and fifty Jewish volunteers. "As regards the Jews in the National Guards," writes Commander Ostrowski, "they were in every division under fire. Many Jews whom I have personally known received the Cross of Honour. I spoke with many officers and soldiers, and they all assured me that the Jews have shown themselves to be worthy descendants of King David."

In the Second Insurrection of 1863–64, many Jews died for Polish independence, and Rabbi Dov Berush Meisels (1798–1870), Chief Rabbi of Warsaw, gave fiery moral support to the insurgents. Of the twenty-five thousand Polish troops, several thousands were Jews. A handful of Jews rose to high-ranking office. Henryk Wohl was Minister of Finance. Zygmunt Lojber headed the Press Department, while Alexander Lesser (1814–84) edited the official government organ. Samuel Pozner, who fought in Garibaldi's army in Italy, was killed near Mlava in July 1863, and more than two hundred and fifty Jews were executed by their Czarist captors.

After 1848, Polish Jews under Prussian rule were granted rights of citizenship, and were classified as Germans. Prussia's aim was to Germanize the country and its Jews. The well-organized Jewish community concentrated on creating and maintaining superb welfare institutions. Then and there, the ubiquitous "Jewish question" simply did not exist. In Galicia (Austrian Poland), Jews enjoyed considerable autonomy, and on December 31, 1867, they were accorded equal status and even became eligible for the civil service. They formed 30 per cent of all Galician doctors and of 1,531 Galician lawyers, 984 were Jews.[13]

Three-fifths of old Poland remained under the Russian Czar. A policy of official state-sponsored anti-Semitism was formulated, and Jews were demoted to second-class citizens. Their pitiful condition was graphically described in a memorandum of December 10, 1890, addressed to the Czar by the Lord Mayor of London:

Pent up in narrow bounds within Your Majesty's wide Empire, and even within those bounds forced to reside chiefly in towns that reek and overflow with every form of poverty and wretchedness; forbidden all free movement, hedged in every enterprise by restrictive laws; forbidden tenure of land or all concern in land, their means of livelihood have become so cramped as to render life for them well-nigh impossible. Nor are they cramped alone in space and action. The higher education is denied them, except in limits far below the due proportion of their needs and aspirations. They may not freely exercise professions, like other subjects of Your Majesty, nor may they gain promotion in the army, however great their merit and their valour.[14]

The virus was contagious. From its breeding ground in Russia, the malevolent microbe of anti-Semitism spread fast to highly susceptible Poland. "We want to develop in our nation a drive to abolish Jewish commercial monopoly erected through the centuries," declared Jan Jelenski in an 1870 pamphlet. This ambition was re-echoed by much of the Polish populace, and was taken up with vehemence by Roman Dmowski in his book *The Thoughts of a Modern Pole* (1903). These "illiberal thoughts" expounded the Dmowski theory that assimilation "had Judaised more Poles than it had Polonised Jews." In the Russian Duma, the Polish deputies remained aloof, silent spectators, while the progressive forces sought equal rights for the Jews. Consequently, at the 1912 election to the Fourth Duma, Warsaw Jewry rejected historian Jan Kucharzhevski, anti-Semitic candidate of the National Concentration Bloc, and elected the Socialist Yaghello.[15]

During the First World War, Poland became the principal battlefield of the Eastern campaign. Six hundred thousand Jews fought under the flags of the Austrian, German and Russian armies. Six times between 1914 and 1917 Russian armies swept through Galicia and were beaten back by the Austrians. Each campaign brought death and desolation to the local population. Grand Duke Nicholas Nikolewitch, commander-in-chief of the Russian Army, found an easy and convenient scapegoat in the Jews. "The Jews are spies," and "The Jews are helping the Germans," were his slogans. Mass expulsions became the order of the day. A gasping sigh of relief rose from the soul of Polish Jewry when the Germans entered Warsaw on August 5, 1915.

For the first time Jews could venture on to the streets in safety, they even dared to visit the public parks, the Saxony and Lazienki Gardens. Despite the desperate shortage of food there were glimmers of light. Two German rabbis, Dr. Pinchas Kohn of Ansbach and Dr. Emanuel Carlebach were appointed liaison officers between the new German overlords and Polish Jewry. The German general staff even issued a weekly paper *Kol Mevassor* ("The Voice of the Herald"). Political freedom became a fact and no party, however radical, was forced underground. Nineteen of the seventy-one members of the Warsaw Municipality were Jews and four Jews sat at the Council of State established on January 6th, 1917.

The defeat of the Central Powers prepared the ground for the emergence of a free independent Poland. With the establishment of the Polish government in Lublin on November 7, 1918, Ignacy Daszynski (1866–1936) proclaimed full equality in political and civic realms for all citizens, irrespective of origin, faith and nationality. On November 10, Josef Pilsudski, returning from Magdeburg where he had been interned by the Germans during the War, assumed power in Warsaw. Eleven days later he became head of the state, and invited representatives of the Jewish community to attend a conference "with the purpose of learning their views upon the measures to be taken for setting up a Polish Government."[16] Polish Jewry whole-heartedly associated itself with the rebirth of Poland and shared the spirit of the National Anthem: "Poland is not lost forever while our lives remain; what the foe by force did sever, force shall regain."

2

Minority Rights and Wrongs

In World War I, the Poles, like the Jews, were forced to fight each other in the armies of opposing powers. Yet both Poles and Jews emerged with unexpected gains. The defeat of Turkey cleared the way for the Balfour Declaration, whilst the disappearance of the Hohenzollern, Hapsburg and Romanoff dynasties removed the major obstacles to the re-unification of Poland. As Balfour is bound up with the hopes of Israel reborn, so President Woodrow Wilson is associated with Poland's resurrection. Like the strivings of the Zionists, the campaigning of the Polish emigrants bore fruit. Chaim Weizmann in London and Ignace Jan Paderewski (1860–1941) in Washington were eloquent advocates of their separate causes. With the declaration on January 8, 1918, that "an independent Polish state should be created which should include the territories inhabited by indisputably Polish populations, which should be assured a free and secure access to the sea, and whose political and economic and territorial integrity should be guaranteed by international covenant," Wilson made the restitution of Poland one of the objectives of the allied powers.

It is significant that, even before the rebirth of Poland, its midwives were divided on the Jewish question. Paderewski pledged that "Poland will have a democratic constitution and all will be equal before the law." On the other hand, biologist Roman Dmowski bragged that he was "no preacher of liberal humanism," and constantly proclaimed his belief that the world was controlled "by secret organisations operated in the dark by International Jewry."

The emergence of the new Poland was celebrated by pogroms in 130 places and an intensive drive to oust Jews from industry and commerce. The enemy from without was replaced by the enemy from within. Alarmed by the rising tide of hatred, 489 Jewish delegates from 144 cities and towns met in Warsaw from December 26 to 30, 1918, and elected a provisional Jewish National Council. The Council demanded that the Jews be recognised as a national minority and be given the right to build their own autonomous communal life.

Polish Jewry was not alone in its fight for status and security. On June 15, 1916, Lucien Wolf (1852–1930), "foreign minister" of the Jewish people, in a memorandum on behalf of the Conjoint Foreign Committee (The Joint Foreign Committee of the Anglo-Jewish Association and the Board of Deputies of British Jews), put the issue on an international, rather than on an exclusively Polish level. Five points were stressed: qualifications for nationality, language, autonomous management of religious and educational institutions, permission to work on Sundays in predominantly Jewish areas, and the status of refugees.

The Zionist Executive in Copenhagen also petitioned for Jewish civil and religious rights, as well as independent administration of all Jewish affairs. On December 15,

1918, the American Jewish Congress adopted a seven-part Jewish Bill of Rights.

The Congress requested the Peace Conference to grant recognition to the new enlarged states only on condition that the following provisions be incorporated in their constitutions:

1. All inhabitants of the Territory of . . . including such persons together with their families, who subsequent to August 1, 1914, fled, removed or were expelled therefrom and who shall within ten years from the adoption of this provision return thereto, shall for the purposes be citizen thereof, provided however that such as have heretofore been subjects of other states, who desire to retain their allegiance to such states or assume allegiance to their successor states to the exclusion of . . . citizenship may do so by formal declaration to be made within a specified period.

2. For a period of ten years from the adoption of this provision, no law shall be enacted restricting any former inhabitant of a State which included the territory of . . . taking up residence in . . . and thereby acquiring citizenship therein.

3. All citizens of . . . without distinction as to race, nationality, or creed, shall enjoy equal civil, political, religious and national rights; and no laws shall be enacted or enforced which shall abridge the privileges, or immunities of or impose upon any persons any discrimination, disability or restriction whatsoever on account of race, nationality, or religion, or deny to any person the equal protection of the laws.

4. The principle of minority representation shall be provided for by the law.

5. The members of the various national as well as religious bodies of . . . shall be accorded autonomous management of their own communal institutions whether they be religious, educational, charitable or otherwise.

6. No law shall be enacted restricting the use of any language and all existing laws declaring such prohibition are repealed, nor shall any language test be established.

7. Those who observe any other than the first day of the week as their Sabbath shall not be prohibited from pursuing their secular affairs on any day other than that which they shall observe; nor shall they be required to perform any acts on the Sabbath or Holy Days which they shall regard as a desecration thereof.[1]

The Alliance Israélite Universelle, however, while advocating the recognition of Jews as a religious community, declined to support the demands for Jewish nationality rights. In the document entitled "On the Legal State of the Israelites in Eastern Europe," the Alliance theorizes that all religious and cultural minorities should be free to direct their own religious, educational and philanthropic institutions.[2]

This diversity of views disrupted the Jewish delegates at the Paris conference, and the divided house of Israel presented a sorry spectacle. Eventually some semblance of unity was established with the formation of the Comité des Délegations Juives ("Committee of Jewish Delegations"), comprising emissaries from Palestine, the United States, Canada, Russia, the Ukraine, Great Britain and Poland. Julian William Mack (1866–1943), was appointed Chairman and among the six vice-chairmen were Louis Marshall (1856–1929) and Nahum Sokolow (1860–1936). The Polish delegation, headed by Leon Reich, Dr. Michael Ringel (b. 1880) and Dr. Joseph Tenenbaum (1887–1961), was next in importance to the American delegation.

On May 10, 1919, the "Council of Four" received the following memorandum: "The Committee of Jewish Delegations at the Peace Conference, acting on behalf of various undersigned organizations and representing the interests of nine million Jews, respectfully submits the following proposals aimed at the protection of various religious, national or linguistic minorities . . . and requests you to integrate these proposals into the Peace Treaty."

On May 1, 1919, the Supreme Council appointed a small committee known as "The Committee on New States and for the Protection of Minorities," under the chairmanship of the Frenchman M. Ph. Berthelot, director of publicity at the French foreign ministry. The Committee was instructed to consider what obligations "Poland and other new states" were to assume; included among the obligations were "the protection of" racial and religious minorities. The Committee held sixty-four meetings between May 3 and December 9, 1919.

While rejecting those demands for national-cultural autonomy which might infringe upon the authority of the Polish State,[3] the Supreme Council agreed that conditions seemed "to justify special provisions," and formulated basic minority rights. The first reaction of the Polish delegation was belligerent opposition on the grounds that the "sovereignty of the State was being undermined and that their good intentions were being doubted and that their national unity was being jeopardised."

A Paderewski memorandum of June 15, 1919, recalled the Polish tradition of tolerance. "It was the former Polish State which outdistanced others," he wrote, "in the matters of assuring equality of political rights to all its citizens, without distinction of origin, language or creed, and had opened its doors to sects persecuted in neighbouring states, and had assured a refuge to the Jews from the West."[4] These assurances however, could hardly be heard above the cries of pogrom victims. The Allied Powers compelled Poland to sign the Minority Treaty that later became the prototype for fourteen other countries.

In terms specific and detailed, this treaty[5] accorded Polish Jews full civic equality, complete religious freedom and effective protection of their cultural interests. Former nationals of Germany, Russia and Austria-Hungary "habitually resident on Polish territory at the date of the coming into force of the present treaty and all those born in the territory, even if not habitually resident," were to be recognised as Polish nationals.

A special article dealt with the Jewish Sabbath.

Jews shall not be compelled to perform any act which constitutes a violation of their Sabbath, nor shall they be placed under any disability by reason of their refusal to attend courts of law or to perform any legal business on their Sabbath. This provision, however, shall not exempt Jews from such obligations as shall be imposed upon all other Polish citizens of the necessary purposes of military survice, national defense or the preservation of public order. Poland declares her intention from ordering or permitting elections, whether general or local, to be held on a Saturday, nor will registration for electoral or other purposes be compelled to be performed on a Saturday.

Article nine obliged the Polish government to provide that in

towns and districts where there is a considerable proportion of Polish nationals belonging to racial, religious, or linguistic minorities, these minorities shall be assured an equitable share in the enjoyment and application of the sums which may be provided out of public funds under the state, municipal, or other budgets, for educational, religious or charitable purposes.

In a lengthy letter to Paderewski the French premier Georges Eugene Clemenceau (1841–1929) set out the reasoning behind the treaty's provisions.

The information at the disposal of the Principal Allied and Associate Powers as to the existing relations between the Jews and the other Polish citizens had led them to the conclusion that in view of the historical development of the Jewish question and the great animosity aroused by it, special protection is necessary for the Jews of Poland. These clauses have been limited to the minimum. They do not constitute any recognition of the Jews as a separate political community . . . There is nothing inconsistent with the sovereignty of the State in recognising and supporting schools in which children shall be brought up in the religious influence to which they are accustomed in their homes.

Had Poland accepted the treaty in good faith, the emancipation of Polish Jews would have been assured. But good faith was conspicuously lacking.

In Poland reactions were highly unfavourable. "An attempt to create artificially a Jewish nation in spite of the natural laws of the historical evolution of the Israelites," protested the assimilated Union of Israelites in Poland. "Alien despotism," editorialized the *Illustrowany Kurier Codzienny*. Nevertheless the treaty was ratified by the Polish Diet by 286 votes to 11.

The League of Nations eventually evolved a machinery for enforcing the Minority Treaties. The Tittoni Report of October 22, 1920 provided that, in principle at least, every minority was free to petition the League. Each petition was considered by a Council of Three, the president and two members appointed by him. Aggrieved parties in Poland continually presented such petitions and the Council of Three devoted more time to Poland than any other country. The Jewish minority however, had grown so defeatist that it brought neither test cases nor complaints before the arbiters.

On November 11, 1921, Poland officially proclaimed that the Minority Rights clauses were part of the law of the land, but this *de jure* recognition never received *de facto* acceptance.[6] In innumerable memoranda, Poland stated that the protection of minorities could not be attained by means which were prejudicial to the consolidation of the state. Matters reached a climax on September 8, 1934, when Russia became a member of the League of Nations with a permanent seat on the Council of the League. To prevent Russia from using the League as a pretext for interference in Polish domestic affairs, Poland renounced the Minority Treaty on September 13, 1934.

Jozef Beck, the Polish Foreign Minister, declared:

The existence of such a system of minority protection has proved to be a complete failure. The Minorities themselves gain nothing from it, whilst the system is only too often misused in a manner which is quite incompatible with the spirit of the Treaty and has in a great measure become the tool of a slanderous propaganda directed against the States bound by it . . . The interests of the Minorities have been, and will continue to be, defended by the Constitution of the Polish Republic which assures the lingual, racial and confessional minorities freedom of development and equality of rights.[7]

Sir John Simon, of Great Britain, M. Louis Barthou, of France, and Baron Aloisi, of Italy, remonstrated in vain that Poland could not evade her obligations by such totalitarian action.

As far as Polish Jewry was concerned, the disputations were purely academic. From their first formulation, the minority clauses had been merely worthless words, producing nothing but controversy. Deprivation of this almost non-existent international protection hardly

worsened the rapidly deteriorating plight of the Jews, the
second largest minority in Poland. They were helpless,
unable to help themselves, and almost beyond help.

FOREIGN MISSIONS

The ink on the Versailles Treaty was hardly dry when
Jewish blood began to flow. Pogroms became an every-day
occurrence, and Jewish life was the cheapest commodity
in the peasant's market place. The much vaunted tolerance of mediaeval Poland vanished beyond recall as every
class of Polish society embraced that convenient old-new
creed—anti-Semitism. During the month of November,
1918, alone, there were pogroms of varying severity and
gravity in 110 different towns and villages. The Lwow
pogrom on November 21–23 was tragically reminiscent
of Kishinev. Homes were raided by armed gangs, soldiers
and civilians, robbing, ravaging. Innocent householders
were killed or crippled, their women violated. The Central Synagogue was sacked and the scrolls of the Law
were torn from the Ark.[8] Material damage was calculated
at 100,000 kroner (over £400,000). More than 500 families
were made homeless, and over 2,000 families rendered
destitute. Fifty-two Jews were killed and 463 wounded.[9]

With the dawn of 1919, the terror mounted in catastrophic crescendo. In Lida on April 18, 39 Jews were
killed.[10] Two days later, 55 Jews were killed in Vilna
where over 2,000 Jewish houses and stores were ransacked.
Losses amounted to over 20,000,000 rubles (about £10,-
000,000).[11] In Kolbuszowa on May 7, 1919, 8 Jews, including a doctor, were beaten to death. On August 8 in
Minsk, deaths totalled 31.[12] The Jews lived precariously
on the very brink of a simmering volcano, never knowing
when the lava would engulf them.

The flimsiest pretext served to incite the mob. A riot in Przemysl began on November 11, 1919, with the absurd fiction that the Jews had machine-gunned Poles. Promptly the authorities disbanded the Jewish militia and uniformed legionaries took the lead in the sacking of shops, the destruction of houses and the profanation of synagogues.[13] Under guise of military necessity, Jews were seized (but rarely Poles) for forced labour,[14] compelled to perform "fatigue" duties in the barracks without pay.[15] Jews ventured on the streets at their peril.[16] In 1919, there were over 107 cases of Jews attacked on the railways.[17]

The world watched, aghast. In London, the Under Secretary of State for Foreign Affairs, Cecil B. Harmsworth, informed the House of Commons on June 5, 1919, that "anti-Semitic disturbances have recently occurred in Poland and in the territories under Polish occupation, and that Polish troops have taken part in them." Addressing a large gathering in the Royal Albert Hall, London, Labor leader George Lansbury (1859–1940) demanded that national independence be withheld from the Poles until their Jewish citizens were granted equal rights. A day of mourning was observed and Chief Rabbi Dr. J. H. Hertz spoke for the whole community when he lamented that "the promise of brotherhood and liberty to the Jews of Poland on its birth and freedom had so far proved a bitter mockery."[18]

Outraged, the Jews of the United States voiced vehement protest and 15,000 forgathered in an anti-Polish demonstration in Madison Square Garden on May 21, 1919. To allay suspicion, Paderewski requested President Wilson to appoint an American Commission to investigate the facts. The Commission consisted of Henry M. Morgenthau (1856–1946), formerly U.S. Ambassador to Turkey (1913–16), Brigadier General Edgar Jadwin, Director of

Construction in the American army in France, and Californian lawyer Homer H. Johnson. Arthur L. Goodhart (later Master of University College, Oxford) acted as counsel. These three men were deputed to make careful inquiry into all matters affecting "not only . . . the various massacres, pogroms, and other excesses alleged to have taken place, the economic boycott, and other methods of discrimination against the Jewish race," but also the discovery of "the reason lying behind such excesses and discriminations with a view to finding a possible remedy." They were further required to "evolve some constructive measures to improve the situation which gives concern to all friends of Poland."[19]

Arriving on July 13, 1919, the Commission settled in the Raczyńskj Palace and remained in Poland until September 13, 1919. The Polish press expressed unbridled hostility. *Prawda Robotnika* branded Morgenthau as "Wilson's Jewish servant."[20] A. Niemojewski, deputy of the Seym and editor of the *Mysl Niepodlegla* had this to say:

Mr. Wilson ought at least to know that such a delegation takes the part of the *Shulchan Aruch* people against the people of Koscioszko and Mickiewicz. We have stated that we are on the eve of a civil war with the Jews. In sending such a provocative commission to Poland, President Wilson is throwing a blazing torch into the accumulated powder.

The investigators visited the scenes of the most notorious excesses and studied the socio-economic background. Morgenthau conferred with the Rabbi of Ger, visited the Warsaw Synagogue and took 1,500 "protocols of cases of looting, assault and murder."[21] The report of Mr. Morgenthau dated 3rd Oct. 1919 was published in full in the

New York Times of January 19, 1920. Morgenthau listed only "eight principal excesses" between November 11, 1918, and August 8, 1919. "Just as the Jews would resist," writes Morgenthau, "being condemned as a race for the action of a few of their undesirable coreligionists, so it would be correspondingly unfair to condemn the Polish nation as a whole for the violence committed by uncontrolled troops or local mobs. These excesses were apparently not premeditated for if they had been part of a preconceived plan, the number of victims would have run into the thousands instead of mounting to 280. . . . a house divided against itself cannot stand. There must be one class of citizens in Poland, all members of which enjoy equal rights and render equal duties."[22]

In a speech before the Judeans in New York (December 14, 1919), he stated:

If American Jewry wants to cure the evils of Poland, they must get at the root of it. Sending one or two million Jews to Palestine will do little good. The evil consists of allowing the Jews in towns to follow one or two pursuits . . . They must be given schools of instruction . . . They must change their mode of life.[23]

Since Morgenthau's whitewashing document was based on his desire for Jewish assimilation rather than on actual facts, it was completely at variance with the report of June 2, 1919, of the American envoy Gibson, who stated that "the present anti-Semitic campaign abroad is largely based on agitation fomented outside Poland."[24]

Five days after the American Mission's departure, the British Mission arrived. It consisted of Sir Stuart Montagu Samuel (1856–1926), President of the Board of Deputies of British Jews, and Captain Peter Wright. They came to Warsaw on September 18, 1919, and remained in Poland until December 6. The cost of the Commission, approximately £830, was borne by the British Government.[25] M. Paderewski arranged a *kosher* dinner in honour of the two Englishmen, and Dr. Samuel Poznanski held a farewell banquet in which the Rabbi of Radzimin participated.[26]

With clarity and compassion Sir Stuart reviewed the scene:

"A severe, private, social and commercial boycott of Jews however, exists amongst the people generally, largely fostered by the Polish press. . . . It is for the Poles to choose whether they will follow the example of Great Britain, the United States of America, France, Holland, Italy and the other liberal-minded States which have treated the Jew equitably, or link their fate with ancient Egypt, mediaeval Spain and modern Russia. It must further be considered that when the Jew is driven out, his capital is driven out with him. In fact in most cases it precedes him, for the poor and helpless Jew is not the first to leave in face of economic persecution such as a boycott or the fear of personal safety, but rather he who possesses the means to seek happier conditions of livelihood elsewhere. Thus, at the very time when it is vital to the interest of Poland to import capital, were the suggested policy carried into action, it would have for its result the export of capital. In addition, there is the danger that the better minds amongst non-Jews would not be willing to remain in a country wherein truth and justice are absent. . . . It is a fair retort that the Government policy is making potential revolutionaries of these people. If the Polish Government would grant the Jews a genuine, and not a masked, equality, they would secure the support of the most conservative law-abiding and loyal section of the population. All the Jews ask is to be allowed to live in peace and safety. By grinding them down by economic differentiation a certain number of these people may be induced to emigrate, but the danger will always remain that a certain residuum will be forced into the ranks of the disaffected and disloyal. The Jew may be robbed, plundered, have his beard cut and be otherwise insulted for a time, but who can be surprised if a point be reached when men will not tolerate such treatment longer and will be prepared to make the utmost sacrifice to achieve the honour of their manhood?"[27]

He refuted the allegation that the Jews were Bolsheviks, stating, "The highest estimate which I encountered was ten per cent."[28] He registered forcefully the "pain and horror with which I listened to the eye witnesses of these callous and bloodthirsty crimes." He made twelve perceptive recommendations:

1. That the Polish Government be urged to carry out the clauses of the Minority Treaty of June 28, 1919, in a spirit of sympathy with its Jewish subjects. A State can only be strong when all sections of its inhabitants are working unitedly and in mutual confidence for its welfare.

2. That a genuine and not a "masked" equality be accorded to the Jewish population of Poland.

3. That all outrages against the person or property of the subject, irrespective of religion or race, should be promptly punished and the names of the delinquents published. This latter action is especially necessary, inasmuch as the State does not punish out of revenge but as a deterrent to others.

4. That Jews in East Galicia be restored to their official positions in the same manner as non-Jews have been.

5. That Jewish railway officials and employees be restored to their posts in the same manner as non-Jews have been.

6. That no restrictions should be placed upon the number of Jews admitted to the Universities.

7. That a decree be published declaring boycotts illegal, and ordering all publications advocating boycott to be suspended.

8. That all prisoners in internment camps be brought to immediate trial, and that humane treatment be assured to all interned prisoners.

9. That facilities be afforded for the introduction of new industries into Poland with a view to converting a larger proportion of the Jewish population into producers.

10. That the British Government should assist Jews wishing to emigrate from Poland by providing facilities to proceed to countries such as Palestine, Canada, South Africa, Algeria and South America, or any other country desiring to receive them.

11. That banks be established possessing the confidence of the Jewish public, so that money might be deposited therein instead of being carried on the person or concealed in dwellings.

12. That the desirability of a secretary who understands and speaks Yiddish being added to the staff of His Majesty's Legation at Warsaw be considered.[29]

Sir Stuart's report was sandwiched between a letter from Sir Horace Rumbold, British Minister in Poland and the observations of Captain Peter Wright. Although prejudiced against the Jews and uninformed about Jewish affairs, the Captain conceded that "every independent Polish institution is as determined to oust the Jews, the national enemy, as in England, we, during the war, were to oust the Germans."[30]

The position of the Jews was in no way improved by these Anglo-American missions, but at least the emissaries proved that the conscience of the civilized world was troubled.

3

Between Life and Death

"The earth totters beneath an intolerable burden," declared King Solomon, "when a servant becomes a king."[1] This aphorism applies most aptly to Poland. Enslaved for 120 years before its emancipation by the Allied Powers, Poland was suddenly smitten with megalomania. Inflated nationalism swept aside reason and moderation. Not satisfied with her newly acquired independence, she dreamed of becoming the mistress of Central Europe, a buffer state between Sovietism and Teutonism.

While the western frontier was defined by the Treaty of Versailles and ratified by the Silesian plebiscite, the eastern frontier was not so clearly determined. The armistice of November 11, 1918, brought no peace to Poland. The end of World War I ushered in years of confusion and once more it was the Jews who bore the brunt of the tumult and turmoil as boundaries fluctuated in Eastern Europe.

Of all the minorities, none was as loyal and as dedicated as the Jews. "Do not thrust us aside," pleaded Zionist Isaac Gruenbaum. "Create living conditions that will make every Jew proud to proclaim, 'I am a Polish citizen and nothing Polish is alien to me.' " "Utilize all the creative forces of the three million Jewish citizens," entreated Dr. Thon of Galicia on February 7, 1919, "for the service of the State, we offer all our devotion."[2] These offerings were rejected.

The Russo-Polish War (1920–21) affected the lives of nearly two million Jews. The Poles accused them of sympathizing with the Russians and the Russians accused them of sympathizing with the Poles. Two secret circulars issued by the Minister of War on November 7, and December 17, 1919, ordered the removal from all military offices of "Jews and Germans since both were using their intelligence against the Polish interests." Jewish soldiers were interned in the camp of Jablonna, and on August 18, 1920, Rabbi Shapira, the *zaddik* of Plotzk, was executed on the ludicrous charge that he was signalling to the Bolshevik forces.

Paderewski, "the genius who happened to play the piano," made little attempt to stay these forces of savagery. He made pro-Jewish pronouncements abroad but at home avoided any pro-Jewish gestures that might serve to stem the flood of persecution. Josef Pilsudski, too, without any personal animosity towards the Jews, remained aloof; defence of the Jews meant political ruin for the defender. As leader of the Polish Socialist Party (Polska Partja Socjalistyczna), he urged the Jews "to join the Polish Socialists in common battles against the oppressor the Czar." In September, 1894, he commented: "The Jews must go arm in arm with the Socialists."[3] Among his intimates were Herman Diamand and Feliks Perl (1871–1927), one of the founders of the Polish Socialist Party. Yet Pilsudski did nothing to curb the anti-Jewish campaign that was the vicious offshoot of the Russo-Polish War. In his desire to liberate the Ukraine, he even associated himself with Simon Petlura (1886–1926), infamous for the inauguration of over a thousand pogroms between December 18, 1920, and April, 1921. In 998 major Petlura pogroms and 349 "minor" Petlura pogroms, 60,000 Jews were killed and 70,000 wounded.

The Constitution of March 17, 1921, modeled on the French Constitution of 1875, was one of the most democratic institutions of post-war Europe. All citizens were equal in the eyes of the law and all were eligible for public office. The Seym and the Senate were elected by universal representation on a direct proportional basis. It gave minorities the right to form, control and administer, at their own expense, institutions of a religious or social character. Theoretically, the Jews were no longer allotted inferior civil status. Theoretically, they were full citizens with the right to vote, the right to engage in any and all occupations, the right to own property, the right to move freely and to breathe freely, free men among free men.

Coalition governments became a standard feature. The constituent Seym had thirteen political parties. In 1924, there were as many as twenty-six parties. The resignation of Paderewski (November, 1919) was followed by a succession of quickly changing cabinets. Fourteen governments clutched the unruly reins between 1918 and 1926. Altogether, in the twenty-one years between 1918 and 1939, 27 governments came and went in struggling succession. Their single consistent feature was an avowed belief in the principles of equality—wedded to a chronic reluctance to put principles into practice. On January 9, 1921, the Seym passed the Sunday Closing Bill, a measure calculated to damage Jewish trade. Seven hundred rabbis petitioned Pilsudski, but restrictive measures against the Jews, like the laws of the Medes and Persians, were rarely abrogated or even amended. Even the antiquated anti-Jewish edicts of the Czarist regime were not repealed until March 14, 1931.

In the first twenty-one years of independence, Poland held six parliamentary elections. Of the 444 deputies in Poland's first Seym in 1919, 13 were Jews,[4] who fought a brave but ineffective fight.

Between 1919 and 1923, the Jewish deputies dealt with over 10,000 outrages, ranging from bloody pogroms in Katowice (August 21, 1922) and Siedlice (May 19, 1922) to minor assaults and from ritual murder accusations to window breaking. But they failed to obtain permission for the Jews to work on Sundays and Christian holidays, just as they failed to find support for the concept of a permanent department for Jewish affairs under a chairman of cabinet rank.

An election law adopted on July 28, 1922, deprived minorities of due representation. In counteraction, the Jews led by Isaac Gruenbaum formed a bloc of minority nationalities consisting of Jews, Ukrainians, White Russians, Russians and Germans. At the general election held on November 5, 1922, 67 deputies, including 22 Jews, were elected on behalf of the National Minorities Bloc. Counting 13 from Eastern Galicia, Jews totalled 35 deputies and 12 senators, the largest Parliamentary Jewish representation of the inter-war years.[5]

Attempts were made to ease the growing discord between the Jews and the Poles. Such distinguished outsiders as Alfred Nossig (1864–1943) and Lucien Wolf essayed this delicate diplomacy but were frustrated by complex factors beyond their control. Reform of the monetary system was urgently required. Poland needed the good will of the United States, and a Polish-Jewish rapprochement became a matter of expediency. Gruenbaum could see no purpose in another declaration. Yet the view of the moderate Dr. Reich prevailed, and Foreign Minister Skrzynski together with Minister of Education Stanislaw Grabski began negotiations with the Jewish deputies. Early in June, 1925 an agreement known as the *Ugoda* was signed by the Jewish deputies and the government.

Twenty-five demands had been submitted by the Jewish representatives. They required that market days and trade fairs should not be fixed for Saturdays and Jewish festivals, that tax-assessment should be equal for Jews and for non-Jews, that Jews should be eligible for loans from state credit institutions on the same terms as non-Jews, that recognition should be given to Hebrew and Yiddish school systems, that the *numerus clausus* at the Polish High Schools and Universities should be abolished, and that the Jewish community should be empowered to maintain religious and charitable institutions.

Although the official summary referred to only twelve points,[6] it sounded like the proclamation of a positively Utopian era.

The Polish Government is ready to annul the ordinance imposing the Polish language as the language of discussion in Councils of the Jewish community. It agrees to widen the sphere of activity and function of the legalised Jewish communal organizations. The right will be granted to Jewish private schools to instruct in Polish, Yiddish or Hebrew. Jewish merchants will secure credit on an equal footing with non-Jewish merchants. Jewish representatives will be included on the Board of the Polish Bank. Officials of Jewish

faith who served in State offices in Galicia will be reinstated.
A Department for Jewish Affairs will be created in the
Ministry of Education. All those who have resided in Poland
since 1910 will not be considered foreigners, but eligible for
Polish citizenship. Jewish merchants and tradesmen will be
allowed to open their stores for two hours on Sundays.

Unfortunately the vision evaporated before it could
become a reality. Pilsudski's *coup d'etat* in May, 1926
marked the beginning of "strong-arm" rule. Pilsudski
regarded the Seym as a "sterile, jabbering, howling thing
that engendered so much boredom as to kill the very flies
with sheer disgust." Restricting the scope of the Seym,
strengthening the power of the executive, and founding
a "non-party bloc of cooperation with the government"
(Bezpartyjny Blok Wspolpracy z Rzadem), he instituted
his own farcical form of democracy. With "moral hygiene"
(*Sanacja*) as his motto Pilsudski aimed at cleansing public
life, stabilizing the currency and balancing the budget.

The Jewish deputies voted for Moscicki, known as
"Ignace the Obedient," Pilsudski's nominee for President
of the Republic. Moscicki, who had studied in England
for five years, opposed the *numerus clausus* but Pilsudski's
Government virtually nullified the *Ugoda*. "The government will conclude no secret agreements with the Jewish
population," declared Professor Kazimierz Bartel, head of
the new government, on July 19, 1926.[7]

Despite the ambivalence of its key men, the Pilsudski
regime saw a slight slackening in organized anti-Semitism.
There was a slackening, too, in the Jewish fight for
equality since it seemed a hopeless battle, even to the
most optimistic of the Jewish leaders. Tacitly, they conceded defeat and set out to salvage as much as possible of
their wrecked hopes. It soon became apparent that the

Pilsudski regime would grant no protection to the Jews and in a brave, though futile gesture of defiance, the Jewish deputies voted against the government. "The Polish government," declared Ladislas Grabski, "will not change its attitude with regard to the realization of the Jewish demands because the Club of Jewish Deputies has gone over to the opposition."

The elections of March 4 and 11, 1928 were fought on the slogan "for or against Pilsudski." The government-supporting non-party bloc won 122 of the 444 Seym seats.[8] The Jewish deputies and senators decreased in number from 47 to 22. Six Jewish groups opposed each other and disunity prevailed in the Jewish Club itself. The Leon Reich group believed in co-operating with the government, while the Gruenbaum group refused to compromise.

On August 30, 1930, the Seym was dissolved. By ruthless methods the government assured itself a clear majority. Many deputies of the former Seym were imprisoned at Brzesc. Opposition newspapers were closed down and election meetings were dispersed. Consequently it was no surprise when the elections of November 16 and 23, 1930 resulted in a parliamentary majority for Pilsudski and his party. The Bloc of Cooperation obtained 247 seats and the National Minorities 33. The eleven Jewish deputies and senators presented a picture of dismal disharmony.[9] They represented three separate groups. The six Zionists sat on the right behind the Ukrainian Minority deputies. The three Jewish deputies in the government Bloc were scattered among the non-Jewish deputies, while the Agudist deputy, Aron Lewin, sat in stately isolation.

While the non-party group dominated the Seym, anti-Jewish excesses abounded. In the six days from November 26 to December 2, 1932, 361 Jews were injured as riots broke out in Warsaw, Vilna, Cracow and Czestochowa. The Nazi rise to power in January, 1933 launched a twelve-year reign of terror for German Jewry, and this resulted initially in a strange anomaly. Anti-Semitic Poland protested to the German Foreign Office about thirty-two instances of persecution of Polish Jews in Germany. The firm stand taken by Polish diplomats and consular representatives mitigated to some extent the suffering endured by Polish residents in Germany.[10] Meanwhile impoverished Polish Jewry collected vast sums, in aid of their German co-religionists. Over 500 mass meetings were held, and an emergency conference of 850 delegates from 435 towns was convened in Warsaw.

The German-Polish Ten Years Non-Aggression Pact of January 26, 1934, inaugurated a nightmare of "make believe." Forgotten were the words of General von Seeckt in 1922 that "Poland's existence is intolerable and incompatible with the essential conditions of Germany's life. Poland must go and will go—as a result of her own internal weakness and of action by Russia with our aid. The obliteration of Poland must be one of the fundamental drives of German policy."[11] Criticism of Germany was stringently suppressed while the Jewish Anti-Hitler Boycott Committee was declared illegal and members liable to ten years' imprisonment. Few restrictions were imposed on Nazi propaganda, for which purpose twenty million marks were expended in Poland in one year.[12] Over 90 per cent of all the German newspapers and libraries, as well as cultural institutions in Poland, were subsidized by the Reich. Poland's five million Ukrainians were thoroughly indoctrinated with the Nazi gospel of hate.

"Wherever there are three Poles there are four political

parties." The old saying was still very true in the twentieth century. But though they differed on almost every subject, the Poles were unanimous in their antipathy towards the Jews.

The most blatant anti-Semites were the National Democrats (Stronnictwo Nardowe), the "Endeks." This party was founded in 1897 by Roman Dmowski, Jan Poplawski and Sigismund Balicki, fathers of Polish anti-Semitism, who vowed to make their country "a national State and not a State of nationalities." They planned to achieve this simply by depriving the Jews of citizenship and deporting them. As the first step in this direction, Premier Ladislas Grabski crushed tens of thousands of prosperous Jewish businessmen in 1925 through swollen, disproportionate taxation. The Endeks represented the middle class. Five powerful daily newspapers and fifteen other periodicals disseminated the Endek gospel. Although their political power waned in the 1930's, they could still mould public opinion at will. "The Jews take away our bread," "The Jew is your enemy," "The towns must be completely Polonized"—these were the seeds they sowed. And malevolent acts followed fast upon the slogans, with wide-scale boycotting of Jewish stores.

In 1934, the young National Democrats formed a fascist group under the name *Nara*. On February 7, 1937, the Nara chief Boleslaw Piasecki called for a revolution to set up a totalitarian regime on the Nazi model and the total expulsion of the Jews from Poland.[13] "Germany's success," wrote the *Gazeta Warszawska* (April 19, 1935), "teaches us in Poland to adopt the same policy, which will force the Jews to organize their own mass emigration. We can do that only by making the Jews realise once and for all that there will be no stopping until not a single Jew is left in Poland."[14]

It would be unfair to attribute all anti-Semitic activity to the Endeks, although they were certainly the pace setters. Even Paderewski's Conservative Party (Stronnictwo Pracy) had a special place in its program for this specific purpose. Clause eight specified: "This party will fight for the complete elimination of Jews from industry, trade and business,"[15] a theme which pervaded both Conservative organs, *Nowa Prawda* and *Nowa Rzeczpospolita*. The party, established in 1922, guided by Counts Tarnowski and Sobanski, represented the nobility and the landowners. Unwilling to introduce the agrarian reforms which would revive Polish agriculture, they encouraged the peasantry to oust the Jews from the towns. For the Jews were "a destructive force whose object and desire it is to injure Aryan societies."[16]

Piast, the Peasant Party, spoke in the name of universal brotherhood. According to article fourteen of its charter, Piast based its relationship with minorities on principles of justice and harmonious co-operation solemnly guaranteed by the constitution. Piast leader Stanislas Thugutt tried to impress this precept on his followers. "Poland must and can be strong not through the mere love of Poles alone," he declared, "but through the love of all her citizens."[17] Again the promise proved illusory.

In 1935 the Populist Party (Stronnictwo Ludowe), an offshoot of the Peasant Party, adopted a clause with a contradictory qualification:

All citizens in Poland, irrespective of creed and nationality, must enjoy equal rights. The Jews, however, as has been proved, cannot be assimilated and are a consciously alien segment within Poland. As a middle class they occupy a far more important position in Poland than in other countries, so that the Poles have no middle class of their own. It is, therefore, most vital for the Polish state that these middle class functions shall more and more pass into the hands of the Poles. We must realise this objective not through fruitless acts of violence, which only brutalize the nation, but above all through the development of the co-operative movement in the country.[18]

The Polish Socialist Party (P.P.S.), a Marxist party, affiliated to the Socialist International, owed much to Jewish idealism. Herman Diamand, Herman Lieberman (1869–1941) and Adolf Gross (1864–1936) were among the founders. It upheld the resolution of the Seventeenth Party Congress of 1917 that "all citizens must be guaranteed full rights regardless of sex, religion and nationality." It protested against pogroms and many socialist students literally took up the cudgels on behalf of Jewish students when ghetto benches were introduced in the Universities. Yet even the P.P.S. was not free from anti-Jewish bias. In 1937, the Socialist J. M. Borski stated: "Only those Jews who are thoroughly integrated into Polish culture and political life will be able to remain and live freely in Poland."[19]

It is an understatement to say that the government was not disposed to help the Jews. But such was the ugly mood of the masses that even attempts to help proved disastrous. When Bronislaw Pieracki, Minister of the Interior, outlawed Endek activity, closing its clubs and suspending its daily newspaper, he was assassinated, and the Endek assassin was proclaimed a national hero.

The death of Pilsudski on May 12, 1935, removed a stabilizer from the unsteady ship of state. Although Pilsudski had carefully refrained from taking a positive stand

on the Jewish question, he enjoyed higher esteem among
the Jews than any other statesman. Rabbis walked in the
procession which escorted his remains from Belvedere
Palace to St. John's Cathedral where he lay in state. One
hundred Jewish delegations from all over the country
participated in the funeral, constituting the largest representation of all the minorities living in Poland. General
Bernard Mond, a distant relative of Lord Melchett and
the only Jewish general in the Polish Army, was responsible for the funeral arrangements and the task of examining Pilsudski's brain was given to a Jewish physician,
Dr. Maksymilian Rose of Vilna.

The amended Polish constitution of April 23, 1935,
declared that the "Polish State is the commonweal of all
its citizens. . . . Resurrected by the efforts and sacrifices
of its worthiest sons it is to be a bequest—an historic
heritage from generation to generation. It is the duty of
each generation to increase the power and authority of
the State by its own efforts."[20] The power of the legis-
lature was strictly limited, and the number of its members
reduced to 208 in the lower house and 96 in the upper
house, one-third of the latter being nominated by the
president. The new electoral law reserved the right to
nominate candidates for the Seym and Senate to a limited
body of members designated by social groups supporting
the new regime.

The elections to the fifth Polish Seym on September 8
and 15, 1935, accentuated the divisions in the Jewish community. Jewish parties, with the exception of the Aguda,
boycotted the polls. Only 46.5 per cent of all Jews entitled to vote actually voted. However, the General Zionists, the Mizrachi in Central Poland and the Zionists in
Galicia participated. The boycott was effective. In all the

Jews elected only four deputies and two senators. The Minorities Bloc obtained 51 seats.

Under the new government the work of the Endeks went on unabated. Attacks took place in many towns, among them Grodno, Otwock, Parczew. Many factors combined to create a permissive atmosphere for pogroms: the half-hearted and perfunctory efforts of the local authorities to quell riots, the token punishments imposed on non-Jewish offenders and the severe retribution exacted from Jews who dared to defend themselves. However, unlike Czarist Russia where pogroms were actually organized by the state as a diversion for the masses, the Polish government merely paved the way. In 1935, outbreaks occurred in Lwow, Poznan, and Lodz. In 1936, 348 anti-Jewish excesses took place in the Bialystok area. Only in 40 cases was any action taken by the authorities. Endek agitation was leaving its bloodstained mark.

Fairly typical was the ordeal endured by Przytyk, a little town of 3,000 inhabitants of which 90 per cent were Jews. In the evening of March 9, 1936, another 3,000 peasants arrived in the town for the annual Spring Market Day. The following afternoon the police arrested a young man for attempting to prevent a peasant from buying from the Jews. This was the signal. The peasants rose in fury and fell upon the defenceless Jews.[21] Three were killed and over sixty injured.

At Mińsk Mazowiecki, thirty miles from the capital, the outbreak was so serious that 5,000 Jewish inhabitants fled panic-stricken to Warsaw, while the remaining 2,000 were besieged for four whole days. Over 1,000 Jews were injured and 56 killed during 1936, a year of unenlightened gloom. Officially the Government condemned violence and condoned only economic harassment. Prime Minister

General Skladkowski maintained on June 4, 1936: "My Government considers that nobody in Poland should be injured. An honest host does not allow anybody to be harmed in his house. Economic fight? That is in order (*Owszem*)."[22]

The Catholic Church in Poland supported the reactionary anti-Semitic groups. In 1936, in a pastoral letter, Cardinal Hlond, Primate of Poland declared:

A Jewish question exists, and there will be one so long as the Jews remain Jews. It is an actual fact that the Jews fight against the Catholic Church, they are free-thinkers, and constitute the vanguard of atheism, bolshevism and revolution. The Jewish influence upon morals is fatal, and their publishers spread pornographic literature. It is also true that the Jews are committing frauds, practising usury, and dealing in white slavery. It is true that in the schools, the Jewish youth is having an evil influence, from an ethical and religious point of view, upon the Catholic youth . . . Not all the Jews are, however, like that. One does well to prefer one's own kind in commercial dealings and to avoid Jewish stores and Jewish stalls in the markets, but it is not permissible to demolish Jewish businesses.[23]

Life in Poland came to a dramatic standstill on March 18, 1936, when millions of Jews joined by thousands of Polish workers, came out on strike in protest against government sponsorship of anti-Jewish terror. It was a most impressive manifestation of a Polish Jewry united by despair. Although organised by the Jewish Labour Union, all classes of the Jewish population observed it faithfully and not a single Jewish newspaper appeared. Positive results were, of course, negligible.

Yet the "honest host"—an appealingly inaccurate description—made no attempt to protect his "guests." The year 1937 saw the continued incitement of the populace by press and politicians against the Jew. In the first three months of 1937, 11 Jews were killed and 467 wounded, 14 bombs were exploded and countless incidents were reported in 57 towns.

A new Government Bloc, known as the Camp of National Unity (*Obóz Zjednoczenia Narodwego*) or *Ozon*, was launched on February 21, 1937. It was sponsored by Moscicki, President of the Republic, by Marshal Smigly-Rydz, "the second personage in the Republic," and by practically all the members of the Cabinet. Uncompromisingly nationalistic, anti-Communist and anti-Semitic, the Bloc demanded that Jewish participation in the economic life of Poland should be drastically reduced and that Jewish influence should be eliminated from the cultural and social scene.[24] Jews were not eligible for membership, not even ex-Servicemen who had fought for Polish independence. Chief-of-Staff Colonel Kowalewski stated on April 21, 1937:

We admire the Jews who made the effort in the fight for Poland, but they cannot be members of our party. No more than Poles could belong to Zionist Organizations. The Jews are a nationality, and therefore will not be admitted to the Camp, which is a national Polish organization. Even those Jews who consider themselves of the Polish nationality, who think of Judaism only as a religion, are excluded from the Camp. The simple acknowledgment of Polish nationality cannot suffice for admission. Not even those who have given unmistakable proof of their Polish patriotism will be accepted as members.[25]

On May 13, 1937, Brest-Litovsk was the scene of fearful devastation. The peasants aimed primarily at destroying Jewish sources of livelihood, so ridding themselves of competition. They wrecked shops, broke up sewing machines, smashed the mirrors of Jewish barbers, stole the tools of Jewish cobblers and cabinet-makers. Vandalism started at nine in the morning and continued for sixteen terror-stricken hours until well after midnight. The authorities disregarded the appeals of the frantic victims and took no measures to deal with the disorders. In this planned orgy no fewer than 50 Jews were injured, 1,200 Jewish houses and shops demolished, buildings gutted, synagogues violated. Damage was estimated at 487,735 zlotys.[26]

On May 25, 1937, another demonstration was organized by Polish Jewry. For two hours, starting at noon, all Jewish shops, cafes, restaurants, workshops and factories were closed. Protests poured in from all over the world. Philosopher Henri Bergson warned: "Anti-Semitism is the first step towards barbarism."[27] "The present anti-Semitism agitation in the country makes me regret that I am not a Jew," were the poignant words of the French author Romain Rolland, "for I am ashamed of my brethren the Christians."

But Poland was deaf. On June 19, it was Czestochowa's turn for three days of organized destruction amounting to half a million zlotys (£200,000) of material damage. "Long live the Police!" yelled the mob in appreciation of the militia's non-intervention. Two hundred and thirty Jewish families were ruined, one Jew was slain and 75 were wounded.[28] In England, October 5 was proclaimed by the Jews as a day of mourning and David Lloyd George observed: "It cannot be a matter of indifference if the Jewish minority in that country suffer degradation of status through the failure of the government to fulfill its trust obligations."

In the sixth Polish Seym (elected on November 6, 1938) there were 5 Jewish deputies and 2 senators.[29] Only the 900,000 Jews of Galicia participated in the elections. Refusing to accept the undemocratic electoral law the Zionists, the Bundists, the Socialists and the Peasants abstained. The election manifesto of "the Camp of National Unity" stated: "The solution of the Jewish problem will not be achieved by street disorders and by smashing windows but by economic fight and regulated mass emigration of the Jews from Poland."

The Austrian *Anschluss* gave Poland the opportunity to legislate for the de-nationalization of persons who had lived outside the country for more than five years. On October 28, 1938, over 15,000 Polish Jews, some of whom had spent practically all their lives in Germany, were aroused from their beds by the Nazis and driven without money or possessions of any kind across the frontiers of Poland. Among them were old people, invalids and infants. The train stopped four miles from the Polish frontier and the passengers were ordered to leave the carriages.[30] Five thousand were kept virtual prisoners in a camp at Zbaszyn, a small Polish township, where they lived under the most pitiful, fever-fostering conditions. Within twenty-four hours of the expulsion, officials of the American Joint Distribution Committee in Warsaw had organised relief measures. Polish Jewry rose heroically to the occasion and raised 2,000,000 zlotys out of their depleted resources. A General Relief Committee for Jewish Refugees from Germany in Poland was formed under Professor Schorr. At a special conference in Warsaw held on March 20, 1939, it was reported that 16,000 zlotys was being spent daily and more than 500,000 zlotys monthly for the refugees.[31] But in spite of all guarantees offered for their maintenance, Poland refused to admit the Zbaszyn refugees into the interior.

In 1939 Hitler put forward territorial claims with regard to Poland. He demanded Gdansk and Pomerania. Poland rejected these demands and in April signed a pact of mutual assistance with Great Britain. The alliance of Poland with the democratic powers did not blunt the edge of its anti-Semitism. While the fate of Poland swayed in the balance, the Jewish question occupied a prominent place in Colonel Josef Beck's discussions in London.[32] But despite its maltreatment during the twenty-one years of Poland's independence, Polish Jewry as one man endorsed Colonel Beck's declaration on May 8, 1939, that "Peace is a valuable and desirable thing. But peace, like almost everything in this world, has its price, high but definable. We in Poland do not recognize the conception of peace at any price. There is only one thing in the life of men, nations, and states which is without price, and that is honour."[33]

The Jewish deputies called upon the community to help defeat the "intentions of Hitler to make Poland a country of slaves." The Warsaw Rabbinate urged Jews to support the Air Defence Loan. "No Jew," they wrote, "must fail to subscribe to the loan." Rabbi Chayyim Ozer Grodzenski of Vilna and the Chassidic rabbis of Suchaczew, Alexander and Ger all endorsed this appeal.[34] "The fate of Jewry," wrote the Gerer *rebbe*, "is bound up with the fate of the State." The response was typically generous and when the National Air Defence Loan was concluded on May 6, it was disclosed that the Jews had subscribed fully 35 per cent of the total. General Berbecki termed it a "touching manifestation."[35]

Physically as well as financially Jews played an active

role in defence measures. Old and young, some of them with dangling *payot* (earlocks) and long *kapotes,* dug trenches. Many even worked on the sabbath, holding that the war danger absolved them. No discordant note was heard. "This must not be a second Munich," underlined an editorial of the Zionist *Haint*.[36] "We are ready to make the supreme sacrifice," echoed the Bund.[37] But only when Hitler was literally on the march did the Polish authorities at last liquidate the camp at Zbaszyn. The ten thousand Jewish refugees were distributed through the country and seventy children left for London.

At four o'clock on September 1, 1939, German military forces, without a declaration of war, crossed the Polish frontier into Silesia, Poznan and Pomorze. The Jewish deputies in the Seym pledged Jewish support for Poland, a declaration warmly applauded.[38] During the next four years, ten centuries of Polish Jewish history were to come to a bitter end. This was the valley of the shadow of death.

4

Economic Warfare

Regaining her freedom, Poland was confronted with a complex of massive problems. Under alien rule, Polish economy had been orientated towards the occupying powers. Before World War I, almost 85 per cent of Poland's trade had been with Germany, Austria and Russia. These Partitioning Powers had deliberately hindered the process of capitalization and investment. The Germans exploited only the agricultural potentials of Poznan and Pomorze as a granary for the Reich. The Russians encouraged industrial development in regions under their control, but naturally these industries were geared to the requirements of the Russian market.

Next to Belgium, Poland suffered the greatest devastation during World War I. Half the bridges were destroyed, and many of the factories ruined. Two hundred towns and 900 villages suffered material damage amounting to over a billion rubles ($5,000,000,000). Nearly 11,000,000 acres of agricultural land were rendered unusable. Losses of livestock totalled 2 million head of cattle and 1 million horses.[1] A hundred thousand Jewish homes were demolished and 500,000 Jews were impoverished.[2]

On every side the new Poland was beset with difficulties. Her elongated frontier with Russia and Germany had no natural defences. Yet each of her neighbours was vastly superior in military power and each had territorial claims upon her. One-third of the state's budget was allotted to national defence. Whereas before the war Russia had absorbed 90 per cent of Poland's exports, her post-war share of Polish foreign trade amounted to a trifling average of 1 per cent per annum. High tariffs similarly served to reduce Germany's demand for Polish products. Only 159 of Poland's 459 factories were operating in 1921 and the textile industry was working at about 30 per cent of its pre-war capacity. To add to the confusion, five kinds of coinage were circulating simultaneously: Austrian crowns, Czarist rubles, German marks, Ost rubles and the new Polish marks. But the liquidation of these assorted currencies was a minor matter compared to the task of uniting a nation that had so long been subject to three different economic and social systems.

Inflation was uncontrolled. On January 31, 1922, a dollar could buy but 3,442 marks. On January 31, 1923, it could buy 35,000 marks. On 30th September 1923, it could buy 350,000. On December 31, 1923, it could buy no less than 6,400,000 marks.[3]

Poland's rate of population increase for the years 1920 to 1929 was 29.9 per cent, the highest in Europe. The average density of population in 1939 was 89 to the square kilometre (228 to the square mile). With two-thirds of the population settled in rural areas, "Poland had the population of an industrial country and the economic structure and degree of industrialization of an agricultural country."[4] Half of the industrial workers in the country earned from 10 to 30 zlotys a week.[5] Unemployment soared from 185,000 in 1929, to 456,000 in 1938.[6] The influx of foreign capital was inadequate and population growth far outstripped economic development.

It was at this critical stage that Poland could have exploited creatively and commercially the vast potential of its Jewish community. A financial expert, the Right Honorable E. Hilton Young reported:

Polish territory is rich in all the resources of nature. She has a matchless system of natural waterways. She has coalfields which are some of the most important in Europe. . . . She has a soil of remarkable fertility, cultivated by a peasantry of unsurpassed industry. Large areas are specially suitable for the cultivation of sugar, commonly the most lucrative of crops, and there is a good equipment of sugar factories. She has forests which in proportion to their extent are second to none in value.[7]

The Jews were able and eager to help develop Polish economy and commerce. Yet, even though it crippled the industrial life of the country, the state adopted administrative measures specifically calculated to incapacitate the Jews, a policy diligently practiced by every Polish government in the inter-war years. It was not a very difficult assignment. An easy victim of the Russo-Polish War, Jewry was already deeply scarred by these embattled years.

Industrious and resourceful, the Jews of Poland had played many vital roles. There were 3 times as many Jews as Gentiles in commerce and industry, 8 times as many in trade. Out of every 100 Jews in 1931, 42 were workers and craftsmen, 37 were businessmen and clerks, 4 were farmers, 4 were in transportation and insurance. Two out of very 5 Jews gainfully employed were artisans.

The proportion of Jews engaged in trade fell from 62.2 per cent in 1921 to 42.3 per cent in 1931. The proportion of Jews in manufacturing increased from 38.9 to 45.4 per cent, while among the non-Jews the percentage rose from 46.4 to 49.1 per cent. Those engaged in trade declined from 39 to 38.2 per cent. Poland was the only country in which the industrial and craft section of the Jewish population increased. Low domestic consumption, immoderately high fiscal charges, growing competition of the co-operative movement in marketing food and agricultural products, are some of the causes for the decline.

There were 74,000 Jewish shops as against 123,000 non-Jewish shops and 20 Jewish merchants to each non-Jewish one. Some trades, such as grain and timber, were almost exclusively developed by Jews.

Jews supplied 40 per cent of all shoemakers, 35 per cent of all bakers, more than 33 per cent of all glaziers and 75 per cent of all barbers. They controlled 95.6 per cent of all the leather and fur industries,[8] 25 per cent of the metallurgical and chemical works, and 40 per cent of the printing industry.[9] Almost every second Jew (46.7 per cent) worked in the cloth industry and every third Jew in the food industry.

In 1931, industry and commerce provided a livelihood for 80.2 per cent of the Jews of Warsaw and for only 55 per cent of the non-Jews.[10] Jews were *treggers*, porters, in the streets of Warsaw, Lodz and Bialystok, carrying their heavy loads like beasts of burden. Only 3.3 per cent of Jewish wage earners worked in large-scale industry. Almost half of them were employed working in medium-sized establishments. According to the 1931 census, the unemployment among Jewish workers was 28.2 per cent while among non-Jewish workers it was 21.2 per cent.

The following table demonstrates the industrial distribution of the Jews and non-Jews in Poland in 1921 and 1931.[11]

Industry	Total Population		Jews	
	1921	*1931*	*1921*	*1931*
Agriculture	66.7%	61.4%	5.8%	4.3%
Manufacturing	15.8	19.4	36.7	42.2
Trade	6.4	6.1	41.3	36.6
Transportation & Communication	3.3	3.6	3.4	4.5
Free professions	3.0	4.1	4.2	6.3
Service	1.1	1.4	1.4	0.8
Others	3.7	4.0	7.2	5.3

The textile industry in Lodz was mainly built by the Jews. Of the 40,035 Jews employed in Lodz industries, 4 per cent were employed in large undertakings and 77 per cent in small enterprises. The zinc industry at Bedzin were directed by Szymon Furstenberg and the steam mill at Lwow by D. Axelbrad.

These key factors enabled the Jews to place awkward obstacles in the joint efforts of the Polish and German governments to increase their trade with each other. Jews effectively boycotted German goods, while the Lodz textile industry halted credit aid to Danzig firms in protest against Nazi anti-Semitic agitation.[12]

One hundred thirty-five thousand Polish Jews worked on the land. Of the 22,103 Jewish farms in Poland more than half were in Galicia, chiefly eastern Galicia. There were 5,000 Jewish farms in the eastern provinces of Poland and 4,000 in the central areas. About three-quarters of these farms were small, averaging some 12 acres each; only 3.5 per cent of the farms covered an area of 50 or more hectares.[13] Throughout Poland, 19.6 per cent (4,335 of 22,103) of all Jewish holdings employed hired labour.[14] Of the 8,233 smaller farms, however, only 7.7 per cent did so. Every one of the 770 estates of over 50 hectares used hired labour. These Jewish agriculturists received neither aid nor encouragement from the state. On the contrary, they were actively obstructed. "The Government does not view with favour the Jewish agricultural colonist movement in Poland," admitted M. Miesabitowski, Minister of Agriculture. "There is a great scarcity of land."

Poland was an agrarian country. In 1931, 61.4 per cent of its total population was engaged in agriculture, and monopolist landlords controlled half the land. As a result, the Polish agricultural worker enjoyed the lowest standard of living in Europe with the exception of Estonia. He could hardly afford bread. Land reform was a pressingly urgent issue; for a modest redistribution, as in Czechoslovakia, would have satisfied millions of hungry Poles. Yet instead of resolving this chaotic situation by instituting long-overdue land reforms, the government took the line of least resistance and encouraged the superfluous population to resettle in the cities. From 1919 to 1936, only 2,422,000 hectares were parceled out to the needy.[15]

Suddenly turned humanitarian, Poland readily subscribed to the Washington forty-eight-hour-week convention, adopting on December 18, 1919, the compulsory Sunday Rest Law which gave workers thirty-six-hours of uninterrupted rest. Sabbath-observing Jews were thus compelled to refrain from work for two days each week, while in the winter (when the Sabbath commences early) they lost another half-day. With the workless days resulting from Jewish and Christian festivals, observant Jews now faced 137 wageless days a year,[16] although they were forced to pay taxes for a full working week. Many

Jews grappled with a painful dilemma: economic ruin or desecration of the Sabbath. Leading Polish rabbis presented a petition to the Seym protesting against this law and a second petition was handed to Pilsudski, but the Government remained adamant. In 1923, compulsory Sunday observance was instituted in Volhynia, Bialystok and Vilna. It was only after more than a decade of struggle that the Jews were grudgingly permitted to work on Saturday evenings.[17]

STATE MONOPOLIES

Anti-communist Poland suddenly changed her coat, abandoning the *laissez-faire* policy of a liberal economy for *étatisme*, national Bolshevism. The state became the leading employer, taking over major enterprises and establishing monopolies in salt, tobacco, alcohol, matches and lotteries. Inevitably the Jews, constituting 74 per cent of those engaged in trade and commerce, suffered most from these totalitarian take-overs.

The tobacco monopoly controlled the purchase of raw materials. With a net revenue of 349 million zlotys in the fiscal year 1938–39 it operated 14 plants employing over 8,000 workers.[18] Jews had worked for more than fifty years in this industry and already in 1885 there were 1,000 Jewish tobacco workers in Warsaw.[19] In 1918, 90 per cent of the tobacco trade, wholesale and retail, was directed by Jews. When the Polish government took over, it reorganized this trade four times without any increase in government revenue. But at least one major task was accomplished: 30,000 Jews, including many war-veterans, were ousted.[20]

In Bialystok, Grodno, Vilna and Warsaw, where originally 95 per cent of the tobacco trade was in Jewish hands, Jews were gradually dismissed from all government-owned factories.[21] In 1933, the number of Jews granted licences for wholesale trading was greatly reduced. By 1938, Jews received only 1,523 out of a total of 4,889 licences. In Pinsk 10 out of 26 concessions were given to the Jews. Only in Grodno did an enclave of 300 Jewish workers remain at Szereszewski's tobacco factory.[22]

More than 100 Jews were dismissed from the Warsaw distilleries when the government took control. The management of one large distillery admitted that it had received verbal instructions not to employ Jews.[23] Whenever an industry became nationalised, it automatically became *judenrein*.

Another characteristic of the new Polish economy was the cartel system. In 1930, 56 cartels with a capital of more than 18 billion zlotys (between 15 and 25 per cent of the total national wealth) controlled 37 per cent of the total industrial production of the country.[24] Here, too, repercussions on the Jewish community were disastrous.

Since the tax potential of urban areas was greater than the tax potential of the rural regions, taxation in the townships was disproportionately heavy and the Jews bore the brunt of it. A merchant paid over 500 zlotys a year while a peasant paid only 2 zlotys or the value of ten eggs.[25] Of more than 3.5 billion zlotys of state and municipal taxes paid by the entire population of Poland in an average year, 40 per cent (amounting to more than 1.5 billion zlotys) was paid by the Jews who formed less than 10 per cent of the population. On the whole the Jewish businessman paid more than four times as much tax as his non-Jewish counterpart.

POLONIZATION

The pernicious "Polonization" policy was rigorously applied to minorities, which constituted less than 31 per cent of the population. But whilst most of these minorities were peasants, rooted to the soil, it was a known fact that 86 per cent of all Polish Jews lived in towns and here every conceivable measure was taken to snatch the last morsel of bread from a Jewish populace already struggling for survival.

"Market stalls for peasants," and "markets without Jews," were the slogans of the day. Of 75,000 market stalls, 35,000 to 40,000 were owned by Jews, a situation which was rapidly remedied. Jewish traders were denied permits and municipalities rented all available market space to non-Jewish institutions or to agents deputed to deny Jews admission. By-laws, long in abeyance, were revived, such as a regulation permitting the sale of only locally produced goods. Under this pretext, Jews arriving from distant districts were turned away at the gate whilst non-Jewish traders, often arriving on the same cart or train, were welcomed. Of the 311 market days in Western Poland, Jews were admitted to only 136, and often these days were deliberately set for Sabbaths or Jewish Festivals. Special courses even were held for non-Jewish stall-holders to help them compete with the Jews.

From priest to peasant few would enter a Jewish shop, and diversified forms of persecution were employed. Jewish peddlers were assaulted. Jewish houses were pelted with stones, even bullets. Cornfields were laid waste, orchards uprooted, cattle maimed or poisoned. Thousands lived in fear lest their concessions be canceled or renewal denied. By 1933, some 27,136 traders had been reduced to such poverty that they could not even raise enough money for license fees.[26]

Strategems for debarring the Jews were ingenious indeed. The Guild Law, passed in 1927, required master craftsmen who wished to take an apprentice to pass a stiff examination. On January 1, 1937, the law for the mechanization of the bakeries took effect, and since most of the Jewish bakers were too poor to modernize their bakeries, many of them (50 in Warsaw alone) were forced to close down and many families were literally without bread.[27] Jewish participation in the import trade was cut to a minimum. The Council of Foreign Trade introduced a sub-division on importing forms to determine the faith of applicants. Converted Jews were classified as Jews.

BOYCOTT

By early 1919, the anti-Jewish boycott had assumed formidable proportions. "I have found," wrote British Zionist writer Israel Cohen (1879–1961), "the economic boycott of the Jews maintained with unabated vigor and that the Poles who sold a house or property to Jews were branded as traitors."[28] Pamphlets distributed throughout Warsaw warned the populace against permitting the city to become "a greater *Nalewki* [a Jewish street]." Under the auspices of first the anti-Jewish "Green Ribbon League,"[29] and later the Endeks, Boycott Weeks were organised. Tens of thousands of leaflets were distributed and posters proclaiming "Do not buy from Jews" were displayed everywhere. Pickets, including schoolboys and students, drove would-be customers from Jewish to non-Jewish stores.[30] A man who braved the pickets and actually shopped in a Jewish store would pay a high price for such foolhardiness: hoodlums would seize him and attach to his coat a placard proclaiming: "This person is a traitor: he bought in a Jewish shop." The Warsaw High Court ruled that such picketing was not a punishable offence, and the Prime Minister Skladkowski lent benevolent support. "If it was illegal," he stated in extraordinary vindication of mob rule, "the authorities would have to arrest 200 people in every small township." In the few places where these "peaceful" pickets were not completely effective, more violent measures were adoptd, including the burning or the bombing of Jewish property.

Under pretext of reducing the differential between market prices and urban consumer goods, the government fostered the development of the co-operative shops which carried supplies direct from purchaser to consumer. Co-operatives known as Centrojuz & Maslosojuz were established with branches throughout Western Galicia. This rendered the Jewish shopkeeper obsolete and by 1933, 10,000 village shopkeepers had been ruined. Proclaimed Boguslaw Miedzinski, Vice-Marshal of the Seym and editor of the semi-official *Gazeta Polska*:

The development of the co-operative movement is a healthy and satisfying phenomenon and we should support it notwithstanding the fact that it spells disaster to Jewish trade. I like the Danes very much but if there were three million of them in Poland I would pray to God to take them away. Maybe we should like the Jews very much if there were only 50,000 of them in Poland.[31]

THE ILLIBERAL PROFESSIONS

The Constitution of 1921 declared all citizens equal and forbade discrimination of any kind. Like so many other Polish declarations, it was utterly unrealized. The 1921 census listed 40,520 Jews in the liberal professions. A decade later the number had risen to 83,740, i.e., 6.3 per cent of the population, an increase attributable not to a more liberal outlook but to the fact that even barbers and laundrymen were listed as "employees for health facilities."[32]

Few Jews had infiltrated the sacred ranks of the civil services. They were not represented among the clerical or administrative staffs of either the president, the Seym or the Senate. Only 2 Jews were employed by the ministry of the interior and only 40 Jews, i.e., 1.1 per cent, were employed by the whole central government. In the finance ministry in Warsaw, there was only one solitary Jew. In the Government Bank there were 21 Jews, i.e., 0.66 per cent of the total employees.[33] Ten thousand post office savings banks derived 60 per cent of their deposits from Jews, but there was not a single Jewish official among them.

In the second century B.C.E. Ben Sira counselled: "Honour the physician with the honour due unto him."[34] Jews have always shown a predilection for the healing arts. In 1931, 4,488 or 55.5 per cent of Poland's 7,950 physicians were Jews.[35] In 1938 Jews still comprised 35.8 per cent of the total profession. In Lwow alone there were 1,170 doctors (51.7 per cent), in Lodz 466 (48.8 per cent) and in Cracow 720 (38.8 per cent).[36]

Yet at a time when the number of physicians in Poland was 3.7 per 10,000 of the population (as compared with 12.4 in the United States and 7.3 in Germany) recognition was denied to holders of medical diplomas from foreign universities and medicine was made a "restricted" profession for Jews.[37] Although there were many Jewish doctors of considerable distinction, among them Dr. Samuel Goldflamm and Dr. Henryk Flatau, yet it was almost impossible for a Jew to be appointed to a university faculty. A rare exception was Dr. Marian Eger, the only Jewish professor of medicine at Vilna. On May 9, 1937, the Union of Polish Physicians adopted the "Aryan Paragraph" by 140 to 103 votes, and in the following year, at a conference at Katowice on May 29, 1938, it was resolved that no Jews were to be admitted to medical school until the percentage of Jewish physicians conformed to the ratio of Jews to the total population.

Although Poland was now a land of almost unequalled inequality, many Jews practiced law. In 1931, 3,187 (39.7 per cent) of the 8,022 advocates were Jews. They formed 52 per cent of the total number of barristers, constituting 44, 67, and 72 per cent in Warsaw, Cracow and Lwow respectively. Claiming that the profession was overcrowded, Minister of Justice Grabowski, on June 4, 1938, exercized his right to close the candidate list for lawyers and law clerks, for a definite period of time in any district or locality.[38] The Polish news agency was at least forthright. "The object of the law," it admitted, "is to reduce the disproportionate number of lawyers belonging to minority nationalities. The present situation, where the Jews constitute 53 per cent of the lawyers, and in some judicial districts even 73 per cent, can no longer be tolerated."[39]

This arbitrary governmental intervention was welcomed by the Polish lawyers. In the autumn of 1937, the Supreme Council of Barristers failed to include a single Jew in the list of sixty-three candidates submitted to the Minister of Justice.[40] Every loophole was hermetically sealed. Under threat of disciplinary action, legal bodies in Warsaw and Cracow required members to display on their letter-headings the exact form of their names as registered on their birth certificates.[41] Here the motivation was the noble necessity of "protecting the legal profession and Polish society against Jewish influence."

These examples set a pattern that other sections of the so-called liberal professions were quick to follow. Jewish teachers were generally restricted to Jewish schools. In 1935–36 some 5,625 of the 98,384 teachers were Jews, a representation reflected in the high schools with only 125 Jewish teachers (*i.e.*, 2.8 per cent) and in the Universities where Jewish teachers formed 2.9 per cent. There too, "the children of Israel are too many and too mighty for us."[42] At a conference in Cracow on March 20–21, 1938, the Association of High School Teachers requested its executive committee to exclude persons of Semitic descent.[43]

Bitter paradoxes prevailed. Polish authorities loudly lamented the lack of qualified engineers, while some 2,000 Jewish engineers were unemployed.[44] Of the 40 per cent who were employed, only half worked in their own trade: the rest were employed as book-keepers and clerks.[45] It was more important to enforce the "Aryan Paragraph" than to foster national interests.

Even in those municipalities where Jews lived in large numbers they were denied the right to work. In Warsaw, where the Jewish population was 32.5 per cent, the municipality employed only 3 per cent of Jewish workers. In Lublin, where the Jewish community constituted 34 per cent, the percentage was 2.6 per cent, and in Chelmo, where half the population was Jewish, they were a mere 12 per cent. There were just 2 Jews among the 4,392 people employed on the municipal transport in Warsaw in 1928. Of the 67,000 employed by municipal under-takings, only 700 were Jews.

"Will you murder us?" the Jews asked the Poles in the Middle Ages. "Polish gentlemen do not murder," (*Polska szlachta nie morduje*) was the reply. "Will you rob us?" persisted the Jews and again they were reassured: "Polish gentlemen do not rob." (*Polska szlachta nie rabuje*).[46] Polish gentlemen were not so gentlemanly in the twentieth century. Robbery and murder were condoned, although more subtle methods were preferred as the ruling class pursued with maniacal passion their openly avowed aim of dislodging the Jews from the economic life of Poland.

5

From Cheder to Yeshiva

"Polish nationals who belong to racial, religious, or linguistic minorities shall enjoy in law and in fact the same treatment and security as the Polish nationals," declared a key clause in the Minority Rights Treaty.

In particular, they shall have an equal right to establish, manage, and control at their own expense, charitable, religious and social institutions, schools, and other educational establishments, with the right to use their own language and to exercise their religion freely therein. . . . In towns and districts where there is a considerable proportion of Polish nationals belonging to racial, religious, or linguistic minorities, these minorities shall be assured an equitable share in the enjoyment and application of the sums which may be provided out of public funds under the state, municipal or other budgets for educational, religious or charitable purposes.[1]

This idyllic state of affairs existed only on paper. No "equitable share" of funds was made available to the Jewish community. In fact, hardly any funds were allotted to Jewish education. The state maintained over a thou-

sand schools for Ukrainians and several hundred schools
for Germans, but there was not a single state school in
which Yiddish or Hebrew were part of the curriculum.
In 1924, the ludicrous sum of £100 was allocated for the
entire Jewish educational system. Whilst the budget for
the Ministry of Religion and Public Enlightenment (i.e.,
ministry of education) reached 300 million zlotys in 1935,
Jewry received just 183,000 zlotys.[2] A similar pattern was
followed by local authorities. The subsidy of 60,000 zlotys
for the Jewish schools in Warsaw was reduced to 17,000
zlotys in 1934–5 and even this was subsequently withdrawn.[3]

In 1921, a network of thirty state-owned Polish elementary schools known as *Sabatowka*, which closed on
Saturdays and opened on Sundays, served the needs of
many Jewish children. Gradually the authorities either
closed the Sabatowka or appointed non-Jewish masters.[4]
In Warsaw, 12 per cent of the Jewish children did not
attend schools because no schools were provided for them.[5]
Education became compulsory in 1919, yet in 1931 23
per cent of all Poles over ten years of age were illiterate.[6]
Jewish school enrollment was high. Whilst 343,671 Jewish
children attended municipal schools in 1935, 180,181
Jewish children attended the 1,465 Jewish educational
institutions. Overtaxed, overburdened, unemployed, afflicted, Polish Jewry spent 20 million zlotys annually on
education and developed a carefully layered structure of
educational establishments. The percentage of persons
able to read and write was higher for Jews than for the
rest of the population. Among Jews 86.8 per cent of males
and 79.3 per cent of females were literate.

"Studies," says Francis Bacon, "serve for delight, for
ornament and for ability." For the Jew, learning was more

than a means to an end. It was a way of life, and the torch of scholarship was kindled in the *cheder*. This cheder has often been the target of criticism and the object of derision. Its setting was unsavoury, often unsanitary. Its methods were at variance with accepted pedagogic principles. Conditions had not changed since philosopher Solomon Maimon described them in 1761. Graphically he depicted the small, smoke-filled hut in which the pupils sat on benches or on the floor. The teacher wore a dirty blouse and held between his knees a bowl in which he ground tobacco into snuff. His assistant was invariably the *kantschik* (the whip). So it probably was in twentieth century Poland.

Thirty to 40 children from the ages of 3 to 12 were compelled to sit for hours in the cramped dingy area which often served as class-room, living-room, bedroom and kitchen combined. These private *chedarim* depended entirely on the parents who made many sacrifices to scrape together the meager fees. Yet despite their physical limitations, these schools laid the firm foundations of a Torah-oriented life.

Under Aguda influence, many *chedarim* and Talmud-Torah centers were combined into the Chorev schools which devoted ten to twelve hours per week to secular studies. In 1937, there were a 107 such institutions with 15,106 pupils and 745 teachers. One hundred and five Chorev chedarim and Talmud-Torah centers were devoted exclusively to Jewish religious studies with a student enrollment of 17,120 and a staff of 500.[7] To obtain government recognition as "equivalent to state schools," Polish was the language of instruction for mathematics, natural science and Polish history, traditions and cultural achievements. Jewish subjects were liturgy, Bible, Mishnah,

Gemara, Jewish laws and Jewish history. A convention of Polish rabbis resolved that "Hebrew shall not be the language of instruction in the chedarim, although Hebrew must be included in the syllabus."[8]

By 1937 Chorev operated a total of 208 *yeshivot*, with a budget of 111,795 zlotys serving 18,000 students. Also under Chorev auspices were a teachers' training school, the Chofetz Chayyim Library in Warsaw, with 5,000 religious books, and a children's home in Dlugosiodlo.

Graduating from the cheder, the student entered the *yeshiva ketana*, the junior yeshiva which prepared him for the yeshiva proper.

> In the Yeshiva reigns a sacred silence
> Which he, the youth, is first to break;
> For there, in the dark corner, wait for him—
> Faithful companions since the day he came—
> Three friends: his stand, his candle and his Talmud.
> As if the moments could not move too swiftly
> That lie between him and his trusted friends,
> He hastens to his place and takes his stand,
> And like a pillar stands from morn' till night.
> Granite is yielding clay compared with him—
> A Jewish boy unto the Torah vowed.

So in his poem the "Matmid" ("The Diligent Student") does Chayyim Nahman Bialik paint the youthful scholar.

In the inter-war years Poland was the home of great yeshivot, usually situated in tiny towns which became the Cambridges, the Oxfords, the Harvards and the Yales of the entire Jewish world. As Javneh to the Holy Land and Sura to Babylon, so was Mir to the Diaspora. "The Jews believed," wrote Professor Heschel "that the existence of the world is conditioned not upon museums and libraries but upon Yeshivas and Houses of Study. To them, the

House of Study was not important because the House of
Study existed in it. To them life without the law and the
precepts was chaos."[9]

The renowned academy of Mir established in 1817 by
Rabbi Samuel Tiktinski (d. 1833) was the foremost Torah
college of new Poland. Among its 500 students were 30
from the United States, 40 from Germany and 18 from
England, as well as young men from Lithuania, Latvia,
Belgium, Hungary and Switzerland. Under the guidance
of Rabbis Yerucham Levovitch (d. 1936) and Eliezer
Yehuda Finkel, students were instructed in Musar (moral
theology) as well as in Talmudic and Rabbinic studies.
In the Kamieniec Yeshiva under the guidance of Rabbi
Baruch Dov Leibovitch (1866–1939), however, the entire
day (from 9 A.M. to 2 P.M., and 4 P.M. to 10.30 P.M.) was
dedicated to the study of the Talmud and only half an
hour was devoted to *Musar*.

Three hundred youths attended the yeshiva at Radin,
home town of the "Chofetz Chayyim," Israel Meir ha-
Kohen, the greatest *gaon* of his time. The "Chofetz
Chayyim" himself delivered two weekly lectures, on Friday
nights and on Saturday nights, which were the pinnacles
of Radin's academic program. Himself a *kohen* (priest),
he deplored the neglect of *kodashim*, the Fifth Order of
the Mishnah dealing with the minutiae of ritual slaughter,
sacrifices and temple rites. In Radin, careful attention was
given to these "neglected" subjects and other yeshivot
followed suit.

Lomza, established in 1863 by Rabbi Eliezer Schulwitz,
disciple of Rabbi Israel Salanter, developed different
characteristics. Although of *Mitnaggdic* tradition, it welcomed youngsters from Chassidic backgrounds and even
encouraged them to wear their black *kapotes* (top coats)

and their lengthy *payot* (earlocks). The yeshiva at Kleck, headed by Rabbi Nathan Zevi Finkel, was the home of 260 youngsters. In response to an urgent appeal from Rabbi Jacob Ridbaz (1845–1913), the Slutzker *Rav*, Finkel, sent fourteen distinguished disciples to establish a yeshiva in Slutzk, naming these forerunners *yad hachazka* (an allusion to the fourteen-section work of Maimonides, *yad hachazaka*; numerically, *yad* equals 14).

Rabbi Elchanan Wassermann (1875–1941) was the principal of the yeshiva at Baronowicze, near the Russian border. When the voice of the Torah was suppressed throughout the Soviet Union, Baronowicze became a haven for students escaping the Yevsektzia (the Jewish branch of the Communist party). A disciple of Rabbi Eliezer Gordon (d. 1910), of Telshe, and Rabbi Shimon Yehuda ha-Cohen Shkop (1859–1940), author of *Shaare Yosher*, Wassermann excelled both as instructor and as organizer. His yeshiva was divided into six grades, with thirty students in each grade.

In addition to the celebrated yeshivot at Bialystok, Kamieniec, Kobryn, Vilna, Brest-Litovsk, Otwock, Pinsk, Rowne, Slonim, Grodno, a Chassidic yeshiva flourished at Swietojerska 18 in Warsaw. This was the Mesivta established in 1919 under Rabbi Meir Don Plotzki, rabbi of Ostrowiec. Chassidic youth, reluctant to travel to far-off institutions, converged upon this local fount of scholarship. No candidate was admitted under the age of thirteen, and no one was accepted unless he was able to master unaided one page of Talmud and *Tosaphot* (Talmudic commentaries compiled in the twelfth and thirteenth centuries).

During the first year, the student studied 245 pages of the Talmud. This was progressively increased so that the number of pages rose to 305, 345, 404 and 430 in the second, third, fourth and fifth years respectively. In all, a student mastered 1,735 pages of the Talmud in the course of his studies.[10] Unlike other yeshivot, which concentrated wholly on Talmudical studies, the Mesivta devoted two hours each day to Polish language, mathematics and history. This "revolutionary" departure, which did not go unchallenged, was condemned as "heresy" by Rabbi Chayyim Eliezer Shapiro of Muncasz.

"Nowadays, yeshiva students should not live in shacks and eat like beggars," declared Rabbi Meir Shapiro. "I will build a palace for them." At Lublin, one-time seat of the medieval Council of the Four Lands, and home of Rabbi Solomon ben Jechiel Luria, the "Maharshal," Shapiro erected his "palace" under heavy verbal fire. "Wasteful" and "untimely" were terms used by the rabbi of Titkin, opinions which many critics echoed. Yet the dynamic Lubliner rabbi crushed the opposition and overcame every obstacle.

The foundation stone was laid on *Lag B'Omer* (18th of *Iyar*), 1924, in the presence of fifty thousand people including the rabbis of Ger and Czortkow, and the new yeshiva was consecrated on the 28th of *Sivan*, 1930. On the entrance was inscribed this verse from the Psalms: "Come ye, children hearken unto me: I will teach you the fear of the Lord."[11] The Lubliner Yeshiva was one of the finest pre-war buildings in Poland, six storeys high with 120 rooms, a huge auditorium, stately lecture halls, a library of some forty thousand books, and even a model temple, designed by Henoch Weintrip, to aid the studies of *kodashim*. Only the most promising candidates were admitted and they were required to know by heart two hundred pages of the Talmud.

Among state concessions granted to *Yeshivat Chachmei Lublin* students, was that of buying railway tickets at half price, like regular university students.[12] When Shapiro died at the age of forty-six, such men as Rabbis Shalom Eiger, Joseph Koningsberg, Moses of Boyan and Zevi Frumer maintained the high level of scholarship set by the founder.

An interesting development was the Navardiker movement propounded by devotees of practical Cabbala, the mystical interpretation of Judaism which laid the stress upon asceticism. It originated at Navardok, a small town near Minsk, Russia, where a yeshiva had been established in 1896 by Rabbi Joseph Hurwitz (1850–1920). In 1915, in response to a call from Baranowicze, Hurwitz sent his son-in-law, Rabbi Abraham Jaffe, with several hand-picked disciples to create a new Torah institute in Poland. The venture was successful. At Navardok every student was trained not only "to learn" but also "to teach." He was expected to turn Torah commando for three months a year, spreading the Law throughout the land. These missionaries set up over a hundred new Torah centers during the inter-war years. At a conference of "Navardiker Yeshivot" graduates on 15–21 *Shevat*, 1933, it was decided that a regular course of *musar* should be introduced in the curriculum. A quarterly journal *Or ha-Musar* ("The Light of Musar") was launched and sixteen issues appeared.

Whilst these yeshivot enriched the intellectual life of Polish Jewry, they were a severe strain on the community's exhausted finances. Yeshiva principals became fund-raisers, periodically touring Western Europe and the United States. And the *meshilach* ("messenger") became a familiar sight. But benefactors came to the rescue. Work-

ing at the Pasteur Institute in Paris, Russian-born bac-
teriologist Waldemar Mordecai Wolff Haffkine (1860–
1930) discovered a serum against cholera and bubonic
plague. In 1888, he was appointed Assistant Professor of
Physiology at the Geneva Medical School, and the following year he became assistant to Pasteur in Paris. Here his
researches led to the discovery of a method of inoculation
with attenuated virus, against cholera. Having successfully
tried the vaccine on himself, Lord Dufferin, then British
Ambassador to Paris, persuaded Haffkine to work under
the auspices of the Indian government. In 1896, the
young researcher became Director-in-Chief of the Government Plague Research Laboratory, now known as the
Haffkine Institute, in Bombay. He bequeathed an annual
subsidy of £2,750 sterling (the income from £45,225 deposited in the Banque Cantonale Vandoise in Lausanne)
for yeshivot in Eastern Europe—Poland, Galicia, Lithuania, Rumania, Hungary. This fund was administered by
the Hilfsverein der Deutschen Juden (German Jews' Aid
Society) and during the period 1931–38 £6,835 was allocated to Polish yeshivot.[13]

While the yeshivot in Congress Poland and Galicia
were under the wings of the Chorev movement, those of
the eastern Provinces were linked by the *Vaad Hayeshivot*.
This was established at a three-day conference in Vilna in
1925 (2–5 *Tamuz*) with the participation of the Chofetz
Chayyim. Particularly active in the *Vaad* were Rabbis
Chayyim Ozer Grodzenski and Joseph Shuv of Vilna
(1897–1943).

The yeshivot struggled for survival and so did the students. The financial plight of the average yeshiva student
was pitiful. Rabbi Meir's *Baraita*, written in the second
century of the common era, relates to a situation some two

thousand years later with an almost uncanny accuracy: "This is the way that is becoming for the study of the Torah: a morsel of bread with salt thou must eat, and water by measure thou must drink; thou must sleep upon the ground, and live a life of trouble the while thou toilest in the Torah."[14]

Food hardly figured in the schedule. Students ate according to a unique rota system whereby generous householders would invite them to share the family meal on a certain specified day. Many of them could not afford to pay for lodgings and in Warsaw it was not uncommon for students to act as night-watchmen in shops and factories. Despite hunger and hardship, the voice of the Torah was heard by day and by night. Bialik describes it well:

> "Oi, Omar Rabba tonu rabonon,
> Thus Rabba speaks, and thus our teachers taught,"
> (Backward and forward swaying he repeats,
> With ceaseless singsong the undying words);
> The dawn, the garden, the enchanted fields,
> Are gone, are vanished like a driven cloud,
> And earth and all her fullness are forgotten.

So the yeshivot tended the flickering but inextinguishable flames of Torah and the torch was handed from father to son in a tradition as old and undying as the Jewish people itself. Danger and death lurked at each corner. They were hated. They were hounded. They were undernourished, emaciated, ill-clad, penniless. Yet within the "four cubits" of the Torah, its students, young and old, found refuge and release. At a time when it was hazardous for the Jew to walk the streets of Warsaw, he let his cabined spirit roam the flowered metaphysical meadows of Midrash and Gemara where all men were free and equal.

THE DAUGHTERS OF ISRAEL

"Honour thy father and thy mother," enjoins the Law of Moses. Yet although Judaism places the mother on a par with the father, there was no place for the daughter in Poland's educational system. "He who teaches his daughter the Law instructs her in what is unseemly for her," warned a Talmudic dictum.[15] "Let the words of the Torah be burned rather than be handed over to women," declared another.[16] "The boys were dedicated to God," it was said, "but the girls were dedicated to *Azzazel*" (Leviticus XVII:5), a reference to the steep mountain from which sacrificial animals were hurled to destruction. These statements were taken quite literally by East European Jews and religious instruction was denied to its womenfolk.

However, while secular studies were forbidden for boys it was not unusual, even in Chassidic circles, to bestow a sound secular education upon girls. Private tutors were in great demand and many girls attended public schools. Women were often the breadwinners, and a knowledge of the Polish language stood them in good stead in their dealings with peasant and *poritz* (squire). The reasoning of parents was materialistic and myopic. They failed to foresee the intellectual impact of secular knowledge. New horizons opened. Educated young women discarded the *Zeenu Urennu* ("Go Forth and see, ye daughters of Jerusalem," a yiddish amalgam of rabbinical commentaries and legends) by sixteenth century Rabbi Jacob Ashkenazi in favour of *Pan Tadeusz* by Adam Mickiewicz. They began to examine analytically the traditions of their fathers. As a result, many rebelled and refused to follow in the footsteps of their meek pious mothers.

Sarah Schenierer, dressmaker turned educationalist, provided a new approach. A school for girls, the first *Bet Jacob* Institute, was founded in Cracow in 1917, and a year later the founder recorded in her diary: "The school is going from strength to strength. My dreams are being realised. Already forty pupils are studying there." Schenierer was a great propagandist as well as a born pedagogue. By 1924, there were 19 schools with 2,000 students. "The Bet Jacob Schools," acknowledged the *knessiya Gedola* of the Aguda, "are the best solution for the education of girls." The Keren Hatorah gave financial support.

By 1937, there were 250 *Bet Jacob* schools with a student population of 38,000. Courses covered Pentateuch, Prophets, Psalms, Jewish liturgy, law and customs, Hebrew language and literature, Polish language and literature, history and geography. Each student was obliged to learn fifty psalms by heart. In some towns children would attend municipal schools for secular studies and Bet Jacob for daily sessions in Jewish studies. In other areas Jewish and secular studies were taught under one roof.[17]

To supply the teachers for this mushrooming movement, the Bet Jacob Teachers' Seminary was built in Cracow in 1925 at a cost of 60,000 dollars. Ten thousand pounds and $25,000 were raised for this purpose in England and in the United States respectively. One hundred and twenty young women began their training in 1925 and 50 students graduated each year. "The Seminary is a sunny isle that sends its rays out to the whole Bet Jacob movement," a journalist, A. M. Ragawy, wrote in lyrical praise. "It is a forge of Jewish thought, Jewish outlooks . . . and beliefs. . . . There is no distance between theory and practice. . . . What is taught is practiced and observed.

The Torah ideals are not talked about but lived."[18] Bet
Jacob graduates formed themselves into an association
known as *Batia* and many became the backbone of the
Aguda Women's Movement known as Benot Agudat
Yisrael, which numbered 20,000 in 1937.

Sarah Schenierer was fortunate in her associates. One
of them was Juda Leib Orlean (1900–43), Chassid of Ger,
friend of Hillel Zeitlin and disciple of Nathan Birnbaum
(1864–1937). As principal of the Bet Jacob School at
Twarda 37, Warsaw, and later head of the Seminary at
Cracow, Leib Orlean proved himself an excellent ad-
ministrator as well as a fine educator. "Your tests have
shown," he told his graduates, "that you know how to
learn and how to teach. The problem which troubles us
is whether you will also understand how to train Jewish
souls."[19]

Another of Schenierer's supporters was Dr. Leo Deutsch-
lander, Director of the Agudat Yisrael Fund and the
Keren Hatorah, one-time director of Jewish educational
affairs for the Lithuanian Government (1919–1920). He
represented the Aguda at the Seventh International Congress for the Suppression of Traffic in Women and Children, held in London in June, 1927. He spent two or
three months a year in the Seminary and prepared the
ground for a network of schools throughout the country.
The movement issued two papers: *Gan Yeladim* ("Garden
of Children") and *Frishinke Boymerlech* ("Fresh Young
Trees") and published many valuable textbooks.

MIZRACHI SCHOOLS

"The nationalism of the Mizrachi is religious," declared Rabbi Isaac Nissenbaum (1868–1943) "and its
religiousness is national." A Torah-centered Palestine was

the Mizrachi ideal. By 1938, under the auspices of Yavne (educational branch of the Mizrachi) there were 229 institutions with 15,923 students. These included nurseries, elementary schools, secondary schools, courses for boys and courses for girls. Secular studies were part of the curriculum, not as a concession to government pressure or to elicit governmental recognition, but because Yavne aimed at producing a balanced education which would prepare young people for life both in the Holy Land and in the Diaspora. Under Rabbi Rife, the agricultural department at Yeshiva Bet Shmuel students spent time on *Hachshara*, preparation for pioneering in the Holy Land.

At a Mizrachi conference in 1919, it was resolved to set up the Tachkemoni Rabbinical Seminary of Warsaw at Grzybowska 19, for graduates of the Yavne schools. With a staff of twenty-one, the Seminary devoted some two-thirds of the syllabus to secular subjects. In addition to Bible, Talmud and modern Hebrew, students were taught the humanities. The Tachkemoni opened in 1920 with forty-eight pupils and quadrupled its enrollment in the next decade. Secular subjects were supervised by Meir Balaban and Dr. Moses Alter. Rabbi Moses Soloveitchik (son of Rabbi Chayyim, 1853–1918) and Rabbi Yechiel Blumenfeld, Joshua Shreibman were the lecturers for Talmud and Rabbinics. Of the forty-eight hours of instruction, twenty hours were devoted to secular subjects. By 1937, 177 young men had been awarded the rabbinical diploma by Rabbi Solomon David Kahana of the Warsaw Rabbinate. Among Tachkemoni publications were *The Truth of Judaism* (a quarterly in Polish), *Bet Shmuel* (in Hebrew), *Torah and Work* (a monthly publication in Hebrew) and *The Jewish Voice* (in Yiddish).

THE TARBUT SCHOOLS

Before the outbreak of World War I, Warsaw had a number of Hebrew kindergartens. The hebraic pioneer Samuel Lob Gordon, known as *Sheleg* (1867–1933), publisher of Hebrew poems, translator and Biblical commentator, was one of the first to introduce Hebrew as a living language into Jewish schools.

At the Fifth Conference of Polish Zionists in Lodz in 1919, it was resolved that "the magnitude of the Hebrew educational and cultural task necessitates the creation of a special autonomous organisation for that task—an organisation that is under the auspices of the Zionist organisation." The problem of Jewish education was closely interwoven with the national revival in Palestine and it was essential to use Hebrew as the medium of instruction in Tarbut schools.

At first the Hebrew schools were under private direction. Then Tarbut, the Zionist educational and cultural organization, was set up in 1921. By 1937–38, Tarbut was directing 269 institutions with 47,372 pupils. These included a Teachers' Seminary, Hebrew *Gymnasia* (grammar schools), elementary, kindergarten, and evening schools, educational and dramatic forums for adults, pedagogical courses, secondary and agricultural schools. In addition to Hebrew, Bible, Mishnah, *Aggada* and Jewish history, due importance was attached to Polish, German, Latin, arts and sciences. Students were conversant with the works of Ovid, Cicero and Virgil; Mickiewicz, Schiller, and Goethe, as well as with Smolenskin, Bialik, Saul Tschernikhovski (1875–1943) and Achad Ha-Am ("One of the people," a pen name of Asher Ginzberg 1856–1927). To maintain a regular flow of teachers,

Tarbut established Teachers' Seminaries in Vilna (1921), Lwow (1922) and Grodno (1926).

Tarbut received subsidies from the American Jewish Joint Distribution Committee (American Jewry's overseas relief and rehabilitation agency). The remainder of the 1937/38 budget was derived 70 per cent from fees, 2 per cent from municipal grants, 3 per cent from Jewish communities. The government viewed Tarbut schools with disfavor and denied them the recognition that would have enabled students to enter universities. An exception was made for the Gymnasia of Pinsk and Bialystok. Tarbut graduates were avid readers of the Hebrew newspapers, *Hatzphira* ("The Dawn") and *Hashiloah* ("Siloam"), and of the numerous Hebrew publications that rolled off the presses of the publishing houses Achiosoph and Tushiya. Sixty per cent of the Polish Jewish immigrants to Palestine were Tarbut disciples.

There were also close ties between Tarbut schools and Zionist youth organizations Hechalutz Hatzair ("The Young Pioneer"), Hashomer Hatzair ("The Young Guard") and Hashomer Haleumi ("The National Guard"). To a high degree Tarbut realized the aims outlined by Bialik: "The Hebrew School of the Diaspora must equip the young with a Hebrew, as well as a general education, so that, upon leaving it, the students will be not merely Hebrew speaking people but Hebrew speaking scholars."[20] Tarbut activities were not confined to youth. Libraries and institutes were set up for adults in 203 cities.[21]

THE CYSHO SCHOOLS

Yiddishist Isaac Leib Peretz (1852–1915) was instrumental in establishing, in Warsaw in 1915, a Yiddish school for little refugees from the war zones. "The Jews constitute one nation whose language is Yiddish," declared Peretz. "In this language we shall accrue our national treasure, create our culture, awaken our spirit, and culturally unite ourselves in all lands and at all times."[22] In 1919, 3,500 children were attending Yiddish schools in Vilna, and 2,500 of Warsaw's children received instruction in Yiddish.

The Cysho (Central Yiddish School Organization) was set up at a conference of 400 Yiddish teachers, held in Warsaw in 1921, as a secular socialist school which would fight "the remnants of stubborn Jewish conservatism."[23]

The school must prepare, not only for life in the present transitional period, but for life in the near future, for life in a socialist society. . . . The principle of labour is to be the nucleus around which the whole content of the school develops. It is the basis for preparation for a future life of devotion and productive creativity that are the foundations of the new society.[24]

The language of instruction was Yiddish and the curriculum included Yiddish and modern Hebrew literature, Bible criticism, Polish language and literature. Periods were allocated to physical training, Yiddish folk music (instrumental and vocal), and natural sciences. *Cysho* administered children's homes, elementary schools, high schools, evening schools and teachers' seminaries. In 1934–35, over 15,000 students attended 169 Cysho establishments. Cysho also published excellent organs, *Nayer Shul* ("The New School"), *Shul Leben* ("School and Life"), *Shul Vegen* ("School Ways").

The average student's fee was to 2–4 zlotys (40–80 cents) a month. Regarding these Bundist schools as "fighters for freedom" and potential insurrectionists, the government denied them subsidies, and, between 1921 and 1933, closed down 33 of them under a variety of pretexts. Cysho survived on grants from the American Joint Distribution Committee, the Canadian Aid Committee and the London Workers' Aid Committee.[25]

THE BILINGUAL SCHOOLS

A Hebrew-Yiddish School "where the Jewish child will be educated as a perfect Jew and where he will not be cut off from the rich heritage of Jewish history," this was the aim of the Poale Zionists who, in June, 1928, established "The Federation for Schools and Culture" (*Shul un Kultur Farband*) commonly known as Shul-Kult. It was warmly supported by Sholem Asch, Dr. I. Schipper and Abraham Goldberg, editor of the Yiddish paper *Haint*. By 1935–36, it operated 35 institutions catering to 2,800 pupils. Midway between Cysho and Tarbut, Shul-Kult satisfied government specifications with regard to secular studies whilst imparting a sound knowledge of Yiddish and Hebrew.

BRAUDE SCHOOLS

In 1912, Dr. M. Braude established in Lodz a Gymnasium for boys which became the model for many post-war schools. The latest techniques of educational methodology current in the United States and Germany were used, and Dewey's ideas, as expounded in his book, *Creative Intelligence*, were carried into effect. Students were imbued with a sense of responsibility, and discipline was achieved by means of "self-government." These innovations brought excellent academic results and a high percentage of these students graduated with the *Matura* (General Certificate of Education) which enabled them to enter university. In 1934–35, there were 41 establishments with a faculty of 230 and catering for 4,785 students.[26] General subjects were taught in Polish, and Jewish studies in Hebrew. Its objectives were to equip the young both with a general education, in the style of the state Gymnasium, and a Jewish education embracing a knowledge of modern Hebraic culture.

The Institute for the Science of Judaism (Instytut Nauk Judaistycznych) was opened on February 19, 1928. It included departments for Biblical studies and Semitic languages, Jewish history, Hellenistic studies, philosophy of religion, Talmud, sociology, homiletics and Hebrew literature. Among departmental heads were Moses Schorr, Meir Balaban, Abraham Weiss (now at Yeshiva University), Dr. Abraham Joshua Heschel (now at the Jewish Theological Seminary of America), Dr. Samuel Atlas (now at the Hebrew Union College, Cincinnati), and Dr. Arye Tartakower (now in Jerusalem). In the school year 1929, the Institute transferred to its own quarters at Nowolipia 3, and the state contributed 23,000 zlotys, i.e., 43 per cent of all its budget. The Institute published important scientific works and also issued a periodical *Miesiecznik Zydowski* and the *Young Historian*.

There was also a School for Teachers of Judaic studies, (Panstwowe Seminarium dla Nauczycieli Religii Mojżeszowej), established in 1917 by Marcus Zeev Braude and Dr. Osias Thon. The institute at Gesia 9 produced 15 to 25 graduates annually. Among its faculty were Dr. Aaronson, M. Balaban, Abraham Weiss, Janus Korczak and

Yerachmiel Weingarten. With the death of Poznanski in
1921, Dr. Meir Tauber became principal.

"Where there is Torah there is wisdom," runs a popular
Yiddish adage and side by side with the great Torah
academies in Poland, there flourished the sturdy seedlings
of Jüdische Wissenschaft (The Science of Judaism).

6

The Battle of the Ghetto Benches

"A University should be a place of light, of liberty and of learning,"[1] envisaged Disraeli. This utopian state of affairs existed in medieval Poland. The University of Cracow, then the country's capital, was founded in 1364. One of the oldest universities in Central Europe, it numbered among its illustrious alumni the astronomer Nicholas Copernicus who "stopped the sun and moved the earth." The University of Cracow became a focal centre for European scholars, sunning in the proud Polish tradition of liberality.

By 1937, Poland had state-recognized universities in Cracow, Warsaw, Lwow, Vilna and Poznan. There were also fifteen other major educational institutions. In the academic year 1921–22, 8,426 of the 34,266 students enrolled in the universities were Jews.[2] By 1938–39, only 4,113 out of 49,967 students were Jews.[3] This represents a decline from 24.6, to 8.2 per cent.

Most of the Jewish students were enrolled in the faculties of law and philosophy. In 1938–39, Jewish student distribution in medicine was 9.3 per cent, in pharmaceutics, 5.7 per cent, in dentistry 13.3 per cent, in philosophy 14.8 per cent, in agriculture 5 per cent and in technical sciences 8.1 per cent.[4] There were twenty Jews among the professors, for as Captain Peter Wright of the British Mission reported in 1919: "Jewish professors, however able, have been turned out of the universities; Jewish doctors, however famous, of the hospitals."[5] In certain educational fields, Jews were debarred from the onset; among these were the University of Poznan and the University of Lublin.

The Minister of Education K. W. Kumaniecki condemned the *numerus clausus* as a violation of the Constitution,[6] a condemnation that was meaningless since his Ministry openly conspired with colleges that limited Jewish enrollment under assorted pretexts. Lack of classroom space was a legally permissible ground for denying admission to candidates and this was often used as camouflage. In the case of the Lwow Law School both the *numerus clausus* and lack of class-room space were devices employed to limit Jewish enrollment.

As if this were not enough, a bill was drafted on June 19, 1923, by the Education Commission of the Seym, its terms clear and specific. "In the admission of students, candidates who belong to a racial, religious and linguistic minority which possesses academic schools of its own, shall be admitted to their respective faculties in the proportion of the quantitative ratio of each minority to the general population."

The Polish authorities underestimated the outraged reaction of the world for cries of violent disapproval were heard from far and near. The *Ligue des Droits d'Homme* directed the attention of Premier Poincaré to this contravention of the Minority Treaty of June, 1919, whilst the Board of Deputies of British Jews brought the bill to the notice of the League of Nations.[7] Still sensitive to public opinion, the Polish government recanted and informed the Committee of Three (the Executive Committee of the League of Nations) that the infamous bill had been withdrawn. "No danger of infraction," reported the League with unjustified optimism.

Under cover of this tactical retreat, Glabinski, Minister of Education, dispatched a confidential circular to every university in the country to the effect that "the Ministry of Education permits the University to limit the number of entering Jewish students as it sees fit."[8] It was only after the Club of Jewish Deputies proposed a vote of non-confidence in the government that A. Sujkowski issued an official communique annulling the Glabinski secret circular. Annulling the annulment was the fact that it came after the registration period for the scholastic year, and the Jewish deputies persisted with their protest.

Whilst the government officially denounced and unofficially endorsed the *numerus clausus*, a number of Polish scholars raised reproving voices. Particularly outspoken was Ryszard Ganzyniec, classical philosopher and professor at the University of Lwow.

As an exceptional law applied to a certain class of Polish citizen, the *Numerus Clausus* is in contradiction to the Polish constitution. It gives occasion for the introduction of more politics and unrest to the Polish Universities: the *Numerus Clausus* has a demoralizing effect on Polish scholarship and the education of youth, by maintaining protectionism, and developing among Polish youth the sense of a privileged class; it has a demoralizing effect also because it creates a precedent for other spheres of life, for other classes of the population. Therefore I oppose the present *Numerus Clausus Iudaeorum* as a man and an educator, as a scholar and as a Pole.[9]

In the autumn of 1925, there were four hundred Jewish candidates for the medical faculty in Cracow.

Only thirteen were admitted. To rejected students who sought to pursue their studies abroad, Professor Leon Pawel Marchlewski issued the following certificates: "The Dean of the Medical Faculty of the University of Cracow testifies that——has not been admitted to the University owing to the *Numerus Clausus*."[10] In 1929, there were eight thousand Jewish students enrolled at foreign universities, mostly in France and Czechoslovakia. By 1933, there were as many as ten thousand dispersed through Europe. Graduates of foreign universities had to wait five years for licences to practice their professions.

Yet even those few Jews who actually penetrated the closely guarded portals of learning were not left in peace. It had long been the policy of fascist elements in Eastern Europe to turn students into propaganda instruments; for the traditional autonomy of the university gave great scope to unruly elements.

Many students succumbed to Endek influence. Warsaw's anti-Jewish "Green Ribbon" League developed rapidly. The nationalists proclaimed "A week without Jews," and the "Aryan Paragraph" figured in the new statute of the Warsaw Polytechnic. It placed the Jews outside the student code of honor as persons with whom non-Jews were to have no dealings, and who could not even be challenged to duels. Studies were hampered too, for Jews were debarred from laboratory work involving the dissection of non-Jewish corpses. As if these measures were not vicious enough, violence followed. Students were attacked with sticks, knives, iron bars and razors. Between November, 1935, and April, 1936, 100 Jewish students were wounded and 10 permanently disabled.[11] At the Lwow Polytechnic, 60 Jews were seriously injured. A National Democratic student, Stanislaw Waclawek, was

killed in a Vilna riot and another student, Marcus Landes-
berg of Lwow Technical High School, suffered a fractured
skull.[12]

Endek propaganda, savage and unsubtle, fell upon eager
ears. "Students, do not hesitate to be brutal, do not be
shamed," exhorted a pamphlet distributed to all Warsaw
High Schools, "The words progress, science and democracy may sound very well but behind them is concealed
the disgusting Jewish spirit. Remember, if you have a
Jew or a Communist in a lonely spot, hit him with an
iron bar in his teeth. Do not be afraid and do not feel
sorry for him."

Successive Polish ministers of education condemned
the riots as "zoological patriotism."[13] The prime minister
opposed the substitution of brawls for academic life. Not
surprisingly, these protestations carried no conviction.
They neither protected the Jew nor inhibited the Endeks.

In Warsaw a campaign was launched to enforce separate
seating for Jews and by order of the Dean's Council,
"ghetto benches" were introduced in two departments of
the Lwow Polytechnic in 1935. Under threat of expulsion,
Jews were prevented from occupying seats assigned to
non-Jews and non-Jews were not permitted to mix with
Jews. But in face of determined opposition inside and outside the Seym, the Endek victory was short-lived and the
ghetto benches were not maintained.

Soon the reactionaries regained the upper hand. In vain
did the minister of education affirm that "Student ghettos
would not be introduced at the Polish universities." Disturbances at the universities assumed alarming proportions
as the campaign for the segregation of the Jewish students
received official sanction on October 5, 1937, when the
rector of the Polytechnic Institute of Warsaw ordered the

institution of ghetto benches.[14] The rector took his au-
thorization from a ministry decision empowering such
measures "for the maintenance of peace." In the Warsaw
Polytechnic the benches assigned to Jews and to non-Jews
were marked "W" and "B" respectively, the initials of
Jewish and non-Jewish student organizations.[15] Tri-
umphantly the paper *Dziennik Narodowy* announced,
"We are advancing along the entire line."[16]

This final humiliation was just too much for the long
suffering Jews and they staged a standing protest. Forced
to occupy the section of the classroom reserved for them,
they remained on their feet throughout the lectures, some-
times for as long as six hours a day. They leaned against
the wall or sat upon the floor, but they resisted attempts
made by university authorities to force them to sit in their
assigned places. Jews were tried by the Warsaw academy
court for the crime of standing.

Polish Jewry rose in protest. "A Week for Jewish Students" was observed from October 20 to 27, 1937, in
which Jews refrained from all unnecessary expenditure,
boycotting theatres and places of entertainment. An impressive six-hour demonstration took place on Tuesday,
October 19, from 8 A.M. to 2 P.M. in the Jewish quarter
of Warsaw. All Jewish shops, workshops, factories, banks,
offices, schools, cafes and restaurants were closed. No
Jewish newspaper appeared and work was suspended in
every Jewish institution.[17]

The Wawelberg Technical High School in Warsaw became one of the principal battle grounds. Although there
were only 55 Jewish students out of a total of 940, the
rector not only introduced ghetto benches but also refused to allow the victims to stand during the lectures.
By an ironic twist of fate, this was the school that had been

founded in 1901 by two Jewish industrialists, Hypolit
Wawelberg (1843–1910) and Henryk Rotwand. It was
given over to the state on May 24, 1919, on the understanding that there would be no anti-Jewish discrimination.
Yet the Wawelberg High School was the first college to
expel a student for refusing to occupy the ghetto bench.

The Jews were not completely alone in their struggle.
A few Polish intellectuals condemned this retrogressive
step and over fifty noted professors signed a protest.[18]
"Why do you do this?" reprimanded Professor Mikolaj
Rudnicki "Why do you attack the Jews, your fellow-
students?" "Because we are Christians," chanted the Endek
ruffians in his class. "If Christ had been alive today," the
Professor replied, "he would have taken his seat with the
Jews on the left side of the lecture room."[19]

Leading figure in the struggle against ghetto benches
was the famous Polish physician, Professor Mieczylaw
Michalowicz, who refused to obey his rector's edict. As a
result the Children's Clinic in the Pilsudski University of
Warsaw housed the only faculty in Poland where ghetto
benches were not introduced. "As a senator of the Polish
Republic," declared the professor, "I have taken an oath
to abide by our constitution. I refuse to violate it. As long
as the Polish Constitution has not been abolished I shall
not violate it."

There were other outstanding instances of men of
courage and conviction. Professor Tadeusz Kotarbinski
became known as the "standing professor" for he insisted
on lecturing standing up as a mark of sympathy for his
Jewish students.

"As a scientist and as a Pole," protested Professor Adam
Czyczewicz, "I consider the introduction of the ghetto
benches a return to mediaevalism and a shame to Polish

culture."[20] Manfred Kridl, professor of Polish literature in Vilna, ordered the edict instituting ghetto benches to be removed from the notice board. Stanislaw Kulczynski of the John Casimir University wrote in an open letter on January 11, 1938:

I have resigned from the office of rector because I did not want to put my signature to an act which in name is called "decree of the rectorial authority," but which in essence is a cheque exacted under terrorist pressure to be cashed by a political party and paid for by the University at the expense of its prestige and its vital interests. . . . Learning cannot develop under conditions of compulsion, not because such is the whim of the professors, but because learning is free thought and thought that is not free is not scientific thought.[21]

The executive committee of the Socialist Trade Union and the Council of the Faculty of Humanities registered vigorous opposition and occasionally Socialist students demonstrated their solidarity by joining the Jews in their "stand-up" strike. The academic world watched with dismay. Over three hundred British professors signed an anti-ghetto-bench manifesto. Signatories included Sir Arthur Eddington of Cambridge; Dr. H. D. Lindsey, the Master of Balliol; and Sir Charles Grant, the Vice-Chancellor of Birmingham University. "To seek peace at the price of intolerance," they wrote, "appears to us to violate the very basis upon which University life must rest."

Students followed this professorial example. The National Students Organization in London declared: "We condemn this action as being contrary to the spirit of University life." The New World joined the Old World in protest. In December, 1937, the Committee on International Relations of the American Association of University Professors, including 5 Nobel Prize winners, 59 college presidents, and 107 deans, condemned the ghetto benches as "absolutely destructive of gains in human progress."[22]

Poland hovered on the verge of disintegration. The voices of conscience at home and abroad were ignored with impunity. The victory of the dark forces was complete. The ghetto benches survived but the university spirit suffered, academic standards deteriorated and one-third of the school year was frittered away destructively. Again and again universities were forced to close their doors and acts of terror disrupted the campuses. Professor Kazimierz Bartel himself confessed that anti-Semitic excesses prevented him from delivering 36 per cent of his lectures at the Lwow Technical High School.

"With the measure wherewith a man measures, shall he be measured," say the rabbis.[23] Those who resort to violence became victims of violence. Six months before the outbreak of World War II, Danzig Nazis tried to force Polish students to occupy "ghetto benches" at the Polytechnic.[24] The writing on the wall was not read. Poland was weighed in the scales and found wanting.

7

A House Divided—Parties and Politics

"Two Poles and a sofa make a political party," mocked an old Polish saying, for an intricate party system complicated the political life of the country. In no other land were Jews so conscious of politics and so involved in politics. In addition to electioneering each Jewish party maintained its own press, its own schools and its own institutions.

Under such men as Isaac Gruenbaum, Dr. Thon and Leon Reich, the Zionists became the most influential of the Jewish parties. Dual loyalty was never an issue. "We are focusing our attention both on the local and the Palestinian scenes," insisted Gruenbaum, and the two were closely linked. "The battle for the rights of the Jewish nationality in the Diaspora necessarily implies an anticipation of a future life in Palestine. The struggle for the Palestine of tomorrow, in turn, must be preceded by today's fight against any kind of oppression and prejudice—a fight for the full rights of the Jewish nationality."[1]

The Zionists were well organized. Regular conventions, seminars and banquets were held locally, regionally and nationally. Poland was the stronghold of the World Zionist Organization, providing some of its most eminent leaders. It also accounted for two-thirds of the pre-1939 immigration to Palestine. In 1921, the Zionist Organization (organizacja Zjonistyczna) numbered five hundred separate societies under Dr. Meir Kalomell.[2]

By 1925, there were four Zionist Federations (in Congress Poland, Vilna, West Galicia and East Galicia), each operating independently and sparked by regular visitations from Zionist leaders of all shades, Nahum Sokolow (1860–1936), Selig Brodetsky (1888–1954), Yitzchak Ben-Zvi (1884–1963) and Yoseph Sprinzak (1885–1959). These Zionist Federations succeeded in obtaining legal recognition from the Polish government.

In 1923, forty thousand Polish Jews, the largest number of *maaser* (dues) payers in Europe, were making regular contributions to their chosen Zionist federation, a remarkable achievement in view of the community's ebbing finances. The Jewish National Fund in 1937–38 collected 706,805 zlotys and the Palestine Foundation Fund amassed 1,119,559 zlotys.[3] In East Galicia alone, 42,886 *shekalim* were bought in 1936 by 22.2 per cent of the Jewish population.[4] In 1938, 205,681 Jews voted in the Zionist Congress elections which took place in 579 towns.[5]

Diversified ideologies splintered the Zionists even further. Al Hamishmar ("On the Watch") led by Gruenbaum, opposed the enlargement of the Jewish Agency (the representation of the Jewish people in matters relating to the upbuilding of the Jewish National Home in Palestine) and campaigned for Jewish rights within the confines of the Polish State. In direct opposition the Et Livnot ("A time to build") group broke away from the Zionist Federation after the Fortieth Annual Conference in 1937.

It advocated the expansion of the Jewish Agency and co-operation with the Polish government.

Despite the dissensions and divisions among themselves, the Zionists presented a united front to the world. The 1936 disturbances in Palestine served to strengthen the bond of unity among all parties, and a General Co-ordination Committee for Poland was set up to co-ordinate Zionist activities. The "Palestine Week" in July, 1936, was attended by David Ben Gurion, Chairman of the Executive of the Jewish Agency. On August 27, 1936, Zionists observed a "Day of Protest" against Arab terrorism. On May 22, 1939, they observed a two hour general strike and fasted in demonstration against the British White Paper.

In 1937, the Zionists put out 42 publications: 23 in Yiddish, 13 in Polish and 6 in Hebrew.[6] They also operated *Gemilat Chesed* (loan centers) in seventy-five towns.[7] Zionist youth movements sprang up, lively and productive, with hundreds of branches and thousands of members. Hanoar Hazioni ("Zionist Youth"), five thousand strong with 120 branches, organized summer camps and central rallies.

The Galician Scout Organization Akiva (Agudat Han-noar Haivri) developed, by 1935, 147 local divisions with 12,000 members. It published a weekly *Divrei Akiva* ("Words of Akiva") for adults and a bi-weekly *Zeirim* ("Youth") for the youngsters. Akiva was strongest in Eastern and Western Galicia, and served to link youth with Jewish tradition.

Hechalutz ("Jewish Pioneers"), was founded in 1917, and provided over 100,000 young people with *Hachshara* training at 554 farms at Grochow, Klessaw, Verba and other towns. Its Galician counterpart Hechalutz Haklal

Zioni ran 44 such training farms. From April, 1929, to October, 1935, 4,505 *Chalutzim* left for the Holy Land.

Women too, flocked to the Zionist banners and in West Galicia, *Wizo* alone listed ten thousand members.

"Zionism must fuse with Socialism," declared Dr. Nahman Syrkin (1886–1924), a leader of the Poale Zion ("Workers of Zion"), "in order to become the ideal of the entire people. . . . The Jewish State must adopt as its ideal, justice, righteousness, social planning and social solidarity."[8] Poale Zion called for the abolition of capitalism, the complete socialization of the means of production, and the territorial solution of the Jewish problem through mass settlement in Palestine. They rejected the anti-Zionist philosophy of the Bund and demanded the recognition of the Jews as a national group.

At the Fifth Convention in Vienna (July 27–August 8, 1920) the party was split into Left Wing and Right Wing. The Poale Zion, right, had a controlling influence in the Hechalutz and Haoved ("Union of Artisans") organizations, with twenty-three thousand members. It founded the Freiheit ("Freedom") and Hechalutz Hatzair ("The Young Pioneer") youth organizations.

The Poale Zion, left, favoured affiliation to the Comintern and Yiddish as the language of Palestinian Jewry. The strongest party next to the Bund, it totalled fifteen thousand members in over three hundred localities in Congress Poland. It took an active part in municipal and parliamentary elections and participated in the Cysho school movement. Among its leaders were Melech Neustadt-Neu and Jacob Zerubavel.

Another small group was the Zionist Socialist party (known as "Z.S."). Britain's offer in 1903 of a Jewish home in Uganda struck a sympathetic chord with many of

these Zionist Socialists who believed that territory outside
Palestine could provide a suitable haven for Jewish workers. They were in close touch with Polish Socialists.

The last year of World War I saw the birth of Hashomer
Hatzair ("The Young Watchmen"), a movement devoted
solely to preparation for pioneering in Palestine. It numbered twenty-seven thousand, its adult members being
obliged to undergo a period of vocational training and
published two regular periodicals, *Hamadrich* ("The
Leader") and *Nowa Mlodziez* ("New Youth").

The Zeire Zion ("Youths of Zion") was a radical group
which had flournshed in Eastern Europe since 1906. These
were ardent potential pioneers, mainly from the lower
middle class. At the First World Conference of the Zeire
Zion in Prague in 1920, the majority of Zeire Zion and
Hapoel Hatzair amalgamated with Hapoel Hatzair under
the name of Hitachdut (The Union of Jewish Socialist
Workers).[9] A census in 1938 showed that Hitachdut had
three thousand members, a youth organization Gordonia
and a weekly paper *Erd un Arbeit* ("Land and Work").
In the 1922 Seym elections, the combined list of Poale
Zion and Hitachdut secured six deputies. In the third
Seym (1928–30), they were represented by one deputy.
Among their prominent leaders were Dr. Isaac Schipper,
Dr. Zevi Heller, Adolf Silberstein and Abraham Levinson.

In 1932, the Poale Zion World Confederation united
with Hitachdut. The amalgamation, however, was not
implemented in Poland where Hitachdut carried on its
activities independently.

"The aim of Zionism is the establishment of a Jewish
State on both sides of the Jordan under the auspices of a
Jewish majority." This doctrine was proclaimed at the
foundation conference of the Revisionist Party held in

Paris in April, 1925, when Vladimir (Zeev) Jabotinsky (1880–1940) was elected president. The progress of the new party was rapid. At the 1925 Zionist Congress, they were represented by five delegates, but, by 1933, Revisionists had become the third strongest party, numbering fifty-two.

In 1935, the Zionist Actions Committee prohibited further "independent political activity by Zionist groups." Jabotinsky seceded from the World Zionist Organization and established the New Zionist Organization. His Berit Trumpeldor or Betar (initials of Hebrew *Berit Yoseph Trumpeldor*, i.e. "Yoseph Trumpeldor League") combined *chalutziut* with defence training and attracted over ten thousand youngsters. Other important Revisionist groups were Brit Hachayil (for ex-soldiers), Yavne Veyodefet (for undergraduates), Masada (for high school students), an orthodox group (Achdut Yisrael) and a religious youth section (Brit Hashmoneans).

The Revisionists, however, were no longer united. A minority broke away and established the Jewish State Party under the leadership of Meir Grossman (1888–1964). But, it remained within the Zionist movement and was represented by eight delegates at the Twenty-first Congress.

"The Land of Israel for the people of Israel on the basis of the Torah," this was the motto of the Mizrachi organization which was founded in 1902 at a Vilna Conference of Russian Zionists by Rabbi Isaac Jacob Reines (1839–1915) of Lida. By 1937, the Mizrachi had branches in 900 towns and the Union of Mizrachi rabbis numbered 270.[10] Under Mizrachi's auspices were a network of schools, a rabbinical college (Tachkemoni), youth organisations Hashomer hadati ("The Religious Watchmen"), Torah

V'Avodah ("Torah and Labour"), Bnei Akiva ("Children of Akiva"), Hechalutz Hamizrachi ("Pioneers of Mizrachi"), a Yeshiva Bet Shmuel ("House of Samuel"); a women's organization Bnot Mizrachi ("Daughters of Mizrachi") and two newspapers: *Undzer Shtime* ("Our Voice") and *Di Yidishe Shtime* ("The Jewish Voice").

Yet a considerable number of pietists remained who had no nationalistic aspirations. They were simply concerned with Torah here and now. It was the urgent need to find "the solution of contemporary problems in the spirit of the Torah" that led to the Katowice conference and the birth of the Agudat Israel ("Union of Israel") in 1912. In the gathering at Katowice, Upper Silesia, on May 27, 1912, were three hundred communal leaders, laymen and rabbis, *mitnaggdim* and *Chassidim*. Among them were scholars from many lands, luminaries of international repute.

Many and differing reasons brought the delegates to Katowice. Jacob Rosenheim, Vice-President of the Free Union of the Interests of Orthodox Judaism (founded by Rabbi Samson Raphael Hirsch in 1883) yearned to integrate the unorganized Orthodox masses of Eastern Europe. The Mizrachists had been driven to seek new pastures by the adoption by the Tenth Zionist Congress of the Syrkin Cultural Committee Report urging them "to intensify cultural work in Palestine and the East." Others felt that only a strong Torah-entrenched citadel could hold back the tidal waves of heresy, the militant anti-religious ideology of the secularists and the arid nationalism of the Zionists.

No discordant voices were heard at Katowice. Dr. Francks of Altona, leader of the German Mizrachi, welcomed the assembly and the main German Zionist organ

Die Welt greeted the foundation of the Aguda in most cordial terms as "an event whose importance in the development of contemporary Judaism must not be underrated." Although Rosenheim, the movement's founder and lifelong guide, maintained that they were not establishing "an organisation at the side of other organisations," the Aguda ultimately adopted the whole familiar complex of organizational accoutrements: constitution, general council, executive committee, acting committee plus a Moetzet Gedole Hatorah (Rabbinical Council), with an executive of eleven members, a Torah fund and even a Press Bureau.

There were soon sizable Aguda groups in Budapest, Amsterdam and Vienna. Nominally its headquarters remained in Frankfurt until 1935, but its heart and soul were lodged in Poland. During the inter-war years nearly a third of Polish Jewry was associated with the Aguda, by then an intricately organized and widespread structure. The Aguda maintained its own schools, published a daily newspaper (*Yiddishe Togblat*), set up its own publishing house (*Yeshurun*), youth organizations (Tzeire Aguda and Pirche Aguda), and even a women's division (Benot Aguda), which had by 1939 some three thousand branches with twenty-five thousand members. For the first time in the history of Polish Jewry, religious women and girls assembled in 1931 to discuss their problems at an all-woman conference. The Aguda held four conventions with 780 delegates and 2,000 rabbis participating in the Fourth Convention at Kaminska's Theatre in 1934.

The Aguda formed its Workers' Branch, the *Poale Aguda*, and the Bund was no longer the sole protector of the working class. It established a fund for sick workers and a kitchen for the unemployed. In 1933 it started to publish *Der Yiddisher Arbeiter* ("The Jewish worker"). Fighting against internal prejudice, the Poale Aguda campaigned against Jewish manufacturers in Lodz who refused to employ religious Jews.

Economically, the Aguda wielded tremendous power. In 1936, it controlled 115 co-operatives with a membership of 15,825.[11] Striving to achieve a dominant role for Torah in the life of each Jew as well as in the life of the *Kehilla*, the Aguda wrested communal leadership from the Assimilationists and participated in municipal and Parliamentary elections. Between 1927 and 1937, the Aguda virtually dominated Polish Jewry, and 242 delegates represented Poland at the Knessiya (Aguda world conference) in 1923.

The Agudist ideal was the revival of "the traditional concept of *klal Yisrael*," a reunion of the scattered splintered Jewish people. They did not succeed in fulfilling this missionary and messianic concept even though they included the greatest scholars and rabbis of the day. By its very nature, the Aguda was handicapped from the start. It could not reconcile its world wide aims with its strictly sectarian principles. Article Four of the Constitution specifically laid down that "members of organisations whose principles are in contradiction to those of the Aguda are not eligible for membership in the central organs." This automatically excluded all other factions of Jewry, even the Mizrachi.

Moreover, in an intricate and often devious manner, the Aguda did play party politics. Isaac Breuer (1883–1946), one of the founders, believed that

"political Zionism seeks to exchange the *Galut* of Israel for the *Galut* of the nations . . . Political Zionism, blind to the significance of history, regards God's kindly law as nothing but religion, nothing but the private concern of the individual. It proves itself the true child of the deadly pair, anti-Semitism and assimilation. Political Zionism fails in the greatest opportunity for service to the Jewish State, namely, making God's law a part of the actuality of the State through the divine law."

These beliefs coloured the Aguda attitude. Consequently it collaborated with the Assimilationists rather than the Zionists. It rarely co-operated with the Club of Jewish Deputies in Poland and never with the Jewish Agency. It supported the Polish Pro-Government Bloc and its Parliamentary representatives were thereby forced to accept the discipline of a government whose avowed object was the economic strangulation of the Jews. The Polish government preferred to grant the minor religious requests of the Aguda rather than the wider demands of other parties.

Admittedly, the Aguda was anti-Zionist. Yet, in a poignant paradox, it was also passionately pro-Zion. In 1923, resolving to support "the Jewish people spiritually and physically in the Holy Land and abroad," it established a Palestine Office and a settlement fund to provide training camps in Poland and to acquire land in Palestine. The Gerer Rabbi visited Palestine six times and urged his followers to support the *Yishuv*. But for most Agudists, love of Zion remained a spiritual passion, and only a few translated the ancient yearning into practical terms.

"Alas a worker!" (*nebbich, ein arbeiter*) was a contemporary catch-phrase which aroused the ire of the Bundist. The Bund (Allgemeiner Yiddisher Arbeiterbund in Lite, Poilen un Russland), ("General Federation of Jewish Workers in Lithuania, Poland, and Russia"), was founded in 1897, as the first official attempt to mould the Jewish proletariat into a class with status and culture of its own. The Bund believed that the "final solution to the

Jewish problem could be achieved only when the capitalist system of production gives way to a socialist society."
Its Jewishness was linguistic and non-religious and it
helped to stimulate the development of Yiddish language
and Yiddish literature.

The Bund's objective was to further socialist principles
among the Jewish masses. It linked the fate of the Jewish
people inextricably with that of the country it inhabited.
But while the Bundist had no sympathy for Zionism and
no time for religion, he also despised assimilationists as
the product of Jewish bourgeoisie. A Bundist was before
anything else "a man of will, a man of deeds and a sober
man."[12] The Bund flourished. In 1921, it numbered fifty
thousand: by 1937, there were over a hundred thousand.
In 1927, 50 per cent of Jewish workers were allied with
the Bund, and they had 378 representatives on the Polish
municipal councils. Skiff and Zukunft ("Future") were
the Bund's youth organizations.

Contact with fellow socialists was, for the most part,
neither as close nor as cordial as one might expect of a
creed that preached the brotherhood of man. A highlight
in the history of the Bund was the Protest Day on March
17, 1936, a demonstration against legalized anti-Semitism
in which non-Jewish workers demonstrated side by side
with Jewish workers.

The Bund received international acclaim on its fortieth
anniversary, November 13, 1938. The anniversary conference was attended by 960 delegates representing 280
local organizations in different parts of Poland. Greetings
were received from, *inter alia*, Major (now Earl) Attlee
and Herbert (now Lord) Morrison, in the name of the
British Labour Party.[13]

The Jewish People's party, the Folkisten (Folkspartay),
was established in July, 1916, by Noah Prylucki (1882–

1944). It demanded Jewish national and cultural autonomy and equal rights for Jews both as individuals and as an ethnic group. The Folkisten were particularly powerful during the early post-war years. In 1918, they even had two members in the Seym. In 1926, however, the Vilna section of the movement seceded from the party and the Folkisten gradually receded from the scene. They did not join the Minority Bloc, an abstention that was censured even by Dubnow, their spiritual father. "The National Minority Bloc," wrote Simon Dubnow, "was essential in the circumstances."[14]

Certain religious Jews were reluctant to participate in orthodox Jewish parties with political programs. Supported by Belzer Chassidim, they set up their own groups, Machzike Hadat (1931), in Eastern Galicia.

Only a handful of Jews belonged to the Communist Party (CWPP), established in 1918, but of the five members elected to the executive committee, three were Jews. Prominent fellow travelers were Adolf Warsawski (Warski), Marx Horowitz (Walecki), Aleksander Minc and Abe Flug.

Abortive attempts were made from time to time to create a united Jewish representative body. A temporary committee including all parties with the exception of the Bund, right wing Poale Zion, the People's Party and the Aguda was created in June, 1937.[15] On December 5 of that year the presidium announced that elections would be held on January 30, 1938. The elections were never held and the project was pigeonholed.

THE JEWISH PARLIAMENT

Jewish communities (*Kultusgemeinden*) in the whole of Central and Eastern Poland were governed by a decree of the chief of state, Pilsudski, dated February 7, 1919.

This decree provided, among other things, that the *Kehilla* be empowered to maintain its rabbinate and establish religious institutions. In January, 1921, a ministerial commission was set up by Premier Witos to legislate for the administration of Jewish organizations. Little progress was made, although the Polish Jewish Agreement (*Ugoda*) of 1925 records, "the Cabinet instructs the Minister of Public Worship and Education to prepare a draft of the law regarding the organisation of the Jewish religious communities throughout the country."

The last act of the Grabski government before its resignation was the promulgation of a decree on October 14, 1927, whereby the Jewish communities of Poland were combined into a single "Religious Union." This comprised 17 rabbis and 34 lay members elected by the community, with another 8 laymen nominated by the government. Minimum age for candidates was thirty. The *Kehilla* was to be administered by an executive board (in towns of less than five thousand Jewish inhabitants) and by both a council and an executive board in larger towns. Voting for the executive board and council was to be by secret ballot according to proportional representation and every Jew over 25 was entitled to vote. Yet the Jewish Committee was permitted to exclude from the voter's list anyone who openly defied Jewish religious law. Elections were to take place every four years and the government reserved the right to confirm election results and to approve budgets.

Protests against this projected Jewish Council were made by a conference of eight hundred leading rabbis whose vehement opposition was based on the ground that the Torah was the sole authority for the Jews.[16] The council was never convened. There were 599 organised

Jewish communities in Congress Poland and Galicia.[17] Grzybowska 26, headquarters of the Jewish Community in Warsaw, passed through many stormy periods in the first five years of its existence. The very first meeting of the council broke up in disorder, a protest against governmental insistence that proceedings be conducted in Polish. No meeting was held for nineteen months until February, 1926, when the government issued a decree giving the *Kehilla* the right to conduct its proceedings in either Polish, Yiddish or Hebrew.

Duties of the *Kehilla* covered the maintenance of the rabbinate, the synagogues, the ritual baths, the cemeteries, religious education, provision of kosher meat, control over community funds, philanthropic institutions and general welfare. Expenditure was met by a tax which the *Kehilla* assessed and exacted by distraint if necessary. The executive board determined the tax capacity of each individual. In Lodz, 21,774 taxpayers contributed 1,192,970 zlotys.[18] Forty-seven per cent paid less than 10 zlotys each and only 0.6 per cent (253) paid over 1,000 zlotys.[19] There were even 51 people in the "super-tax" class who each paid 2,500 to 5,000 zlotys. The budget of the Warsaw *Kehilla* soared from 1,640,332 zlotys in 1926 to 3,265,528 zlotys in 1938,[20] and its income in 1930 was 3,739,972 zlotys.[21] In 1938 the total budgeted revenue of the Jewish communities amounted to 40,000,000 zlotys. In 599 *Kehillot*, religious needs accounted for over 40.3 per cent of the total expenditure.[22] Income from ritual slaughter amounted to 10,833,138 zlotys.[23]

During the period of Zionist hegemony in Warsaw, the *Kehilla* donated 2 million marks to the *Keren Hayesod*.[24] It subsidized both religious and secularist Yiddish schools and half its budget was devoted to social, philanthropic and educational purposes. The *Kehilla's* many-faceted program included: allocations of 5,000 zlotys for the Jewish Art Society, 5,700 for Jewish sports, 3,500 for Maccabi, 700 for *Bar Cochba*, 10,000 for adult evening classes and people's universities, and grants for Jewish theatre and Jewish music. At one time, 30,000 zlotys were allocated for the provision of *matzot* for Jews in the Soviet Union.

The Zionists and Bundists wanted to extend the scope of the *Kehilla* beyond purely religious matters. The Agudists, however, insisted that anti-religious bodies should not be represented on the council. Section 20 of the government edict of October 24, 1930, divided Jewry into two categories, observant and non-observant, permitting non-observant Jews to be debarred from office. In Warsaw, the ruling was not enforced. On the other hand, the community of Lodz used it to deny membership to Bundists. According to Agudist deputy Leib Mincberg, orthodox factions were satisfied with the new regulation because it excluded the political propagandists who attempted to convert Jews into "Moscow cells of irreligion."[25] In small towns, autocratic councils sought to deprive Jews of voting rights if they appeared in public bare-headed, conversed with women or shaved their beards.

Voting for the *Kehilla* took place amidst frenzied excitement, vilification and even violence. Meetings were held in public squares. Houses in Jewish quarters were pasted with party posters and the streets resounded with party slogans. In the elections of July 1, 1926, in 26 major communities, 39 per cent of the elected council members were Agudists, 54 per cent belonged to the National Bloc and 7 per cent were Folkisten. In 39 smaller communities, the ratio was 45 per cent Aguda to 55 per cent National Bloc.[26] In Warsaw, the Aguda obtained 15 seats, the Jewish National Bloc 12, the *Mizrachi* 5, the Bundists 5, the Folkisten 3, and Left Wing Poale Zion 3. The Mizrachist Szyja Heszel Farbstein was elected President (1926–1931).[27]

In the elections of May 20-27, 1931, there were no fewer than thirty different parties. Among them were Bloc for Real Work, Independent Poor Jews, Committee of the Jewish Socialist Artists, United Workers Bloc, *Poale* Zion, All who Live in the Sixth District of Warsaw, Right Wing of *Poale* Zion, Non-Party Bloc of Philanthropic Institutions, Zionist Organisation of Praga, Official Zionist Party in Warsaw, United Committee for Independent Jews, Union of Non-party Religious Jews, Aguda, Democratic Group, Small Traders, Mizrachi, Democratic Economic Bloc, Adat Yisrael, Praga Artisans, and United Religious Societies. Only 32 per cent of the voters went to the polls and altogether 69,431 votes were cast. The Aguda received 19 of the 50 seats, the Zionists 12 and the Mizrachi 4. The Aguda, the majority party headed by Elijah Mazur, devoted the major part of its budget, over 200,000 zlotys, to religious affairs.

The balance was redressed in favour of the secularists in the elections of 1936. The Bund received 10,000 votes and 15 mandates while the Aguda tied with the Zionists, each acquiring 8,000 votes with eleven mandates.[28] The success of the Bund was due directly to the failure to keep the doors of Palestine open for Jewish immigration, and the desire of the masses to strengthen the hands of the Polish Socialist Party which was closely associated with the Bund.

On January 5, 1937, the government appointed Maurice

Meisel, president of the Union of Jewish Tradesmen and director of the Palestine Foundation Fund, as head of the Warsaw *Gemina*. He was assisted by a committee of ten, representing the Aguda and the Union of Jewish Ex-Servicemen.[29]

There was no chief rabbi in Warsaw for strong differences among the various parties made it impossible to reach unanimity on this issue. Religious affairs were supervised by a *Vaad Harabbanim* of twenty rabbis, each receiving a monthly salary of 850 zlotys.

Although the Jews paid 40.5 per cent of the state taxation, they received little in return. Overtaxed, underpaid, impoverished, the Jewish masses were compelled to finance their own welfare organizations. Anti-*Shechitah* legislation severely curtailed the revenue from *Shechitah*. As a result, communal institutions were faced with grave financial difficulties and on November 29, 1938, community presidents discussed the situation at a conference in Warsaw.[30]

MUNICIPALITIES

In 1929, there were 4,650 Jewish councilors out of a total of 12,315 for all Poland. Thirty-two per cent of all urban councilors were Jews and there were 212 Jewish councilors on the rural and urban boards. In the election of March, 1934, the Jews returned 1,603 councilors or 25 per cent of the 6,405 total. In these elections the Zionist group elected 43 per cent of the councilors, Folkisten 20.6 per cent, Aguda 18 per cent and the Bund 10.2 per cent.[31] However, there was not a single Jewish mayor.

As in the *Kehilla*, the Jews had no unified party to represent them at municipal elections. Twelve separate

Jewish lists were presented in Warsaw in 1927. In 1934, the Jews lost many votes owing to internal dissensions. Although Warsaw Jewry was entitled to 40 per cent of the council seats, it won no more than 24 per cent. In Lublin, the Jews were splintered into twenty parties. Between December, 1938, and April, 1939, the Bund obtained 70 per cent of the Jewish vote. Of 89 towns, one-third elected Bund majorities. In Warsaw itself, the Bund gained 20 seats.[32]

Inevitably, the Jews did not receive their share of grants. The Warsaw municipality allotted only 10,000 zlotys (£2,900) to the two Jewish technical schools administered by the Warsaw *Kehilla*, and 15,000 zlotys to the Jewish technical school directed by Ort (the society for the promotion of trades and agriculture). In Cracow, where Jews accounted for 25 per cent of the population, 7,625 zlotys were assigned to Jewish institutions out of a total allocation of 23,660,000 zlotys.

8

The Fires of Chassidism

It was Eastern Europe which, in mid-eighteenth century, gave birth to the greatest revivalist movement in the history of the Jewish people. This was Chassidism, the cataclysmic force that wiped away the narrow intellectualism that had estranged the Jewish masses from their heritage. Chassidism focussed upon fundamental Judaism, sublimely simple principles that stressed the joy in life, love of man, sincerity in word and deed, qualities that the common people potentially possessed in full measure. Thus mystically, almost miraculously, Chassidism brought comfort, courage and a form of other-worldly ecstasy to these suffering step-children of humanity.

Like drowning men, the Jews of Eastern Europe clutched at this rejuvenated Judaism. From the Ukraine the movement spread across the border, "converting" a high portion of Polish Jewry. Later as the lights of Jewish life were extinguished in the Soviet Union, sparks began to fly and the flames began to burn with a new brilliance in the deepening Polish gloom. Captain Peter Wright, a member of Sir Stuart Samuel's Mission in 1919, estimated that the *Chassidim* constituted half Poland's Jewish population. In a changing and challenging world they upheld traditional Judaism against the onslaught of secularism, assimilation, Bundism. Forgotten were the futile feuds with the *Mitnaggdim*, their one-time bitter opponents. Even the *halachic* luminary, the Chofetz Chayyim, conceded that Chassidism was "a pillar of fire to Jewry."

During the crucial inter-war years, the power of the Chassidim increased. This was a period of political awakening. No longer confined to the *stiebel*, they began to exert their considerable influence on every phase of Jewish life. Almost every town, almost every village, had its own Chassidic Court. It is a fact that many a tiny far-flung Polish hamlet owes its immortality to the Chassidic rabbi who lived there and adopted its name as his title. So with Belz, Ger, Alexander, Bobov, Sedlice, Biala, Novominsk, Ozarow, Radzyn and countless others.

Luminous personalities arose, men of vision and vitality, who moulded and remade the lives of men. Many of the *zaddikim*, as they were called, maintained huge households, receiving and entertaining hundreds of visitors. For many-faceted was the role of the *zaddik*. He was the attorney (*melitz yosher*) who pleaded for his clients before the august assembly of the heavenly court; he was the *guter yid*, the friendly father figure to whom his children could pour out their hearts. Whether they needed spiritual strengthening or *gezunt und parnossa* ("health and sustenance"), the *rebbe*'s blessing and his assurance that the "Almighty would help" fell like manna on the parched lips of the afflicted Jews, sunk in the deep valleys of despair.

The Chassidim lived in a world of their own. They were known by the dress they wore, by the way they spoke, by the melodies they hummed. In the eyes of a gentile observer, they formed an "immense mass of squalor and helpless poverty," and this may well have been the case. But a faith immovable and immortal as the mountains enabled them to inhabit simultaneously an inner and invisible world which was an indescribable foretaste of the Golden Age to come.

A new breed of leaders emerged who guided the community with wisdom and inspiration. The power of the *rebbe* was far-reaching. His most casual utterances were invested with many layers of mystical meaning and his considered judgments were counsels beyond cavil. He wore infallibility like a silken *kapote* and his endorsement was thought to "guarantee" the success of any project.

With the exception of the followers of Belz and Alexander, most of the Chassidic rabbis were associated with the Aguda and participated in communal, municipal and parliamentary elections. But their primary role was to preserve a Torah-oriented-tradition and any breach aroused violent antagonism. The opening of a Jewish shop on the sabbath brought *tallit*-wrapped Chassidim in militant demonstration.[1] Nor were their interests confined to regional religious problems. The rabbis appealed for the provisions of *matzot* for Russian Jewry,[2] and their support was solicited for National Defence Loans.

Contrary to popular misconception, women played a major role in Chassidic life. Before the establishment of the Bet Jacob schools, many Chassidic daughters received a thorough secular education. Ladies in the latest Paris fashions were often seen walking alongside (or a few paces behind) husbands clad in eighteenth century garb. Yet these Polish "duchesses," fluent in Polish and in French, found a place in the Chassidic milieu.

The Chassidic firmament was a complex cosmos com-

The Ghetto Memorial in Warsaw.

Examining *Tzitzit* in Lwow.

A typical market scene.

Jewish children playing chess.

A Jewish street in Cracow.

The Jewish quarter in Vilna.

A street in Cracow.

A street in Tarnow.

Ulica Klacszki, a street in Vilna.

A *Cheder.*

A courtyard in Warsaw.

A newsstand, Warsaw.

Rabbi Joseph Isaac Schneersohn of Lubavitch.

Rabbi A. I. S. Perlow, *Rebbe* of Novominsk.

The *Rebbe* of Mezritz.

Mr. I. Greenbaum.

Rabbi N. D. Rabinowicz, the Biala *Rebbe*.

Rabbi Moses Mordecai Heshel.

Two leaflets regarding elections of the Community Council, one from a religious and the other from the Zionist party. (Courtesy The Jewish Historical General Archives, Jerusalem)

A Jewish workman.

Girls studying Hebrew.

Three elderly Jewish women.

A Jew reciting psalms.

posed of many planets, each set in its appointed place, each revolving around its own orbit, each contributing to the radiance that floodlit the Jewish world. There were marked differences in outlook between the rabbis of Kotzk (Kock), Sochaszew and Ger, yet all were united in fraternal fellowship. Prayer was a common, or more accurately uncommon, denominator. The *stiebel* or *claus* was the heart of Chassidism. Literally a "room," its very unpretentiousness served to underline the vital principle that its adherents preached. It was both a place of worship and a house of study, a second home for its frequenters and occasionally their only home.

The rabbis established *stieblech* in the various towns in which their followers resided. In Poland, most towns had both a Gerer *stiebel* and an Alexander *stiebel*. In Lodz, there were 35 different *stieblech* each catering for a different Chassidic sect. Only in their own *stiebel* did the Chassidim feel really at home. At five o'clock on dark cold winter mornings, young men would already be clustered round the tables. Each man studied at his own pace and in his own style, finding comfort and companionship and reward in the living pages of the Talmud.

Life centered around the *stiebel*. Here, townsfolk, too, foregathered to celebrate a *simcha* (festivity), to console each other in times of trouble and to take counsel together. It was the mystique of Chassidism to add a new dimension to the mundane, to sanctify the profane. A piece of bread broken in fellowship became a banquet. The *Seudah Shelishit* ("The Third Sabbath meal") was pregnant with other-worldly meaning. Even a *Yahrzeit* (anniversary of a kinsman's death) became an occasion for rejoicing, since in Chassidic legend it marked the ascent of the soul to higher and still higher spheres (*Madregot*).

Ger, a townlet on the Vistula, became the Jerusalem

of one of the greatest Chassidic dynasties of all time. "The sun also ariseth and the sun goeth down," says Ecclesiastes,[3] a verse which applies to Ger. Rabbi Isaac Meir Rothenburg, the *Hiddushei Harim,* founder of the Gerer dynasty, died on the 23rd of *Adar* 1866. On the seventh of *Tevet,* 1864, his grandson Abraham Mordecai was born to become virtual emperor of Polish Chassidism from the very day that he succeeded his father, Rabbi Yehuda Leib, author of *Sefat Emet* ("Lips of Truth"), on the 5th of *Shevat* 1905.

"In Kotzk we do not have a clock, we have a soul!" declared Rabbi Mendel (1783–1859). This concept of spontaneous prayer led many Chassidim to bypass the appointed hours of prayer and to pray whenever and wherever the spirit moved them. The accession of Rabbi Abraham Mordecai marked a return to rigid observance of the Shulchan Aruch. Services at 7.30 A.M. were re-established and the emphasis was on Torah study. On Friday evening, and on the sabbath between *Shacharit* (morning service) and *Musaph* (the additional Sabbath service), time was set aside for study. Following ancestral tradition, the rabbi of Ger refused to accept *pidyonot* (donations) from his followers lest he become dependent on the gifts of flesh and blood.

Like his grandfather, Abraham Mordecai had a deep sense of communal responsibility. At the Hamburg Conference in 1909, he helped prepare for the founding of the Aguda and he attended the three Agudist Conferences of 1923, 1929 and 1937. The 1937 conference at Marienbad discussed the report of the Peel Commission proposing the partition of the Holy Land into two sovereign states, one Jewish, the other Arab, with a small area under British mandate covering historic and strategic sites. In forceful opposition the Gerer *rebbe* quoted Joel IV:2, "I will gather all the nations, and I will bring them down into the valley of Jehoshaphat: and I will enter into judgment with them there for my people and my heritage Israel, whom they have scattered among the nations and divided my land." He supported the Bet Jacob movement and the Warsaw Mesivta.

Six times the Gerer *rebbe* visited the Holy Land. His fifth visit, in 1936, lasted for almost half a year and when he returned to Poland after Passover he already regarded himself as a Palestinian and did not observe in Palestine *Yomtov Sheni*, (the second day of the Festival in the Diaspora). A passionate lover of Zion, he wrote in a letter dated 7th of *Iyar*, 1921: "I am pleased to note that it is possible to conduct oneself in the Holy Land in the way of our fathers and forefathers. . . . It is possible here to observe Judaism without any hindrance."[4] Yet he discouraged his Chassidim from contributing to the Jewish National Fund because Sabbath observance was lax on J.N.F. landholdings.[5] "Having learnt that it is reported that I have moved nearer to the position of the Mizrachi," wrote this staunch Agudist, "I declare publicly that I have not changed my view in the least, that this organisation is a danger to Judaism and especially to Polish Jewry."[6]

Sixty members of the family of the rabbi of Ger perished in Nazi Europe. His son-in-law Isaac Meir Alter was shot before his very eyes. In 1940, a few days before Italy entered the war, the *rebbe*, together with his son Israel and his son-in-law Isaac Meir Lewin (chairman of the Agudat Yisrael Executive Committee) left Warsaw and escaped to Israel. He died on *Shavuot* (Pentecost) 1948. Dr. Isaac Herzog, then chief rabbi of the Holy Land, pronounced these words in fitting eulogy: "On *Shavuot* the Torah was given and on *Shavuot* the Torah was taken away."

For nearly a century, Aleksandrow, or Alexander as the Jews called it, a little town near Lodz, occupied a unique position in Chassidism. What Safed was to the Cabbalists in Palestine, Alexander was to the Chassidim in Poland. As Ger was the "fortress" guarding Warsaw, so Alexander shielded Lodz. No other Chassidic dynasty, apart from Ger, attracted so vast a multitude. Whilst Ger lured the scholars, Alexander drew the *baale batim* ("house-holders"), the merchants and the masses. Considerable rivalry existed not so much between the leaders as among their followers. Alexander, the third force in Poland, stood aloof from political parties, associating neither with Machzike Hadat of Belz, nor with the Aguda of Ger. Alexander Chassidim were free to follow their own political bent and many were closely associated with the Mizrachi.

In the inter-war years, the Alexander dynasty was headed first by Rabbi Samuel Zevi (1910–1924), author of *Tiferet Shmuel* ("The Glory of Samuel"), and then by his son, Rabbi Isaac Menachem Mendel Dancyger (1880–1942) who stood at the helm for 18 years. Father and son laid the stress on Torah, *Tephila* (prayer) and service to fellow-men. Isaac Menachem Mendel organized *Yeshivot* both at Alexander and Lodz.

WARSAW

A "pioneering" pietist was the first rabbi of Ger who first brought Chassidism to Warsaw. Soon the capital of Poland became a luminous galaxy of Chassidism, the home of over fifty *zaddikim*.

One of the most prominent rabbis was the rabbi of Novominsk, Alter Yisrael Shimon Perlow (1873–1933), scion of the dynasties of Ustilla, Koidanov, Chernobyl, Karlin and Berdychev. His father Jacob (1847–1902) was brought up in the home of Rabbi Solomon Chayyim Perlow of Koidanov and married Hava Hayye Perl, daughter of Rabbi Leibish of Proskurow. "Go to Poland, raise a family and establish a dynasty," Rabbi Isaac ben Mordecai of Neschitz (1789–1868) counseled the young rabbi and faithfully Jacob fulfilled his mission. He set up his "court" in Minsk Mazowiecki where he made many "converts" and won wide recognition. Here he built a huge yeshiva where hundreds of young men lived and learned and a great synagogue which held over a thousand worshippers. This was a showpiece *hof* (court), complete with its own gardens, orchards, stables and horses. A "tourist industry" sprang up and the municipality actually ran special trains for the tremendous traffic in Novominsker Chassidim.

Rabbi Abraham Isaac Kook (1865–1935), later Chief Rabbi of the Holy Land, described Rabbi Jacob as "unique in his generation." On his death on the 23rd of *Adar*, 1902, his eldest son, Alter Yisrael Shimon, aged 27, took over the leadership of the Chassidim of Novominsk. He married Feige Dina, daughter of Rabbi Baruch Meir Twerski of Azarnitz, Russia, the seventh direct descendant of Rabbi Israel Baal Shem Tov (1700–1760), the founder of Chassidism.

In 1917, the rabbi settled in Warsaw. His home at Franciszkanska 10 became one of the thriving centers of Chassidism; Chassidim of all "denominations" flowed to the Novominsker Court.[7] He knew the whole Mishnah by heart and to the end of his days he rehearsed nineteen chapters daily. On the sabbath he only spoke Hebrew.

Crowds thronged to listen to his famous sabbath discourses, remarkable for their length as well as their profundity, and which were said to hold his hearers spellbound from beginning to end. His eloquent addresses, his soul-stirring prayers, his melodious voice and his mature wisdom spread his fame far and wide. Hillel Zeitlin used to say, "Whenever I felt depressed and in need of repentance I visited the Novominsker." Once heard, the melodies of the Novominsker were never forgotten. They were expressions of his soaring soul, a revelation that awed and elevated his listeners. His prayers before the reader's desk on the High Holy Days, particularly at *Neila* (the concluding service on the Day of Atonement) were highlights in the lives of his Chassidim.

Faithfully, the Novominsker *rebbe* ministered to his people. Every day he set aside several hours to receive petitioners. From Warsaw and from the provinces people flocked to him for help, for guidance, for comfort, and inspiration. With infinite patience he would listen and give practical painstaking counsel. He was associated with the Agudist Rabbinical Council and yet he was on cordial terms with all the Chassidic rabbis. The rabbi of Ger was a devoted friend who rarely passed Warsaw without visiting him. "Go to the Novominsker," the Gerer *rebbe* advised many of his followers.

From his famous forefathers the Novominsker *rebbe* inherited a remarkable legacy: from Rabbi Shlomo Chayyim of Kaidanov, prayerfulness, from Rabbi Levi Isaac of Berdychev, love of humanity, from Rabbi Phineas ben Abraham of Koretz (1726–1791), love of music and from his father, diligence and a phenomenal memory. He died on the 6th of *Tevet*, 1933, leaving twelve children and ten volumes of writings on Torah and *Cabbala*.

Many of these manuscripts perished in the holocaust. *Tiferet Ish* ("The Glory of *Ish*," i.e. acrostic Alter Yisroel Shimon), a commentary on the Passover *Haggadah* was published posthumously.

His successor was his gifted son Joseph, son-in-law of Rabbi Eliezer Taub of Volomin (1870–1938), a descendent of Kuzmir. So fragile in physique that even the Nazis exampted him from forced labour, he was yet so indomitable in spirit that he regularly gave away his own meager ration of food. He died in Bergen-Belsen concentration camp on April 16, 1945, on the morning after the liberation by the British Second Army under General Sir Miles Dempsey. He was twenty-eight years old.

Rabbi Alter Yisroel Shimon's brother Solomon Chayyim Perlow (1860–1943) married the daughter of Rabbi Joshua Hershel of Bolechow. He was the author of a commentary on the *Siddur Kehillat Shlomo* (1907) and a 1,781-page Chassidic anthology on Psalms entitled *Mikdash Shlomo*, published in Bilgoraj, in 1937. A second brother, Yehuda Arye Perlow (1877–1961), one of the forerunners of Chassidism in the United States, authored *Lev Arye* ("The Heart of a Lion"), published in 1939, and *Kol Yehudah* ("The Voice of Judah"), published in 1946. The tradition is continued today by Rabbi Alter Yisroel Shimon's eldest son Rabbi Nahum Perlow, Novominsker rabbi in New York. The Novominsker's twin sister Rifka Reizel married Rabbi Moses Mordecai Heshel (1866–1918), the Pelcovizna Rabbi, son of the Rabbi of Miedzyborz, Abraham Joshua Heshel, a descendant of Rabbi Israel of Rhyzin (1798–1851), and Abraham Joshua Heshel of Apt (Opatow).

Most illustrious of the Novominsker progeny was his son-in-law Nathan David Rabinowicz, the Biala rabbi

(1900–1947). When little Nathan David was barely six years old, he knew the Five Books of Moses by heart, and his uncle and guardian, the rabbi of Radzymin, prophesied a brilliant future for him as a *Gadol B'Yisroel* ("a great man in Israel"). At the age of seventeen, he married Szaindla Brachah, the first and favourite daughter of the rabbi of Novominsk and for ten decisive years he lived under the influence of his father-in-law. In 1928, Rabbi Nathan David sailed for England to kindle the flame of Chassidism in London's arid East End. This was a new-era rabbi, equally at home with contemporary scholarship and ancient Cabbala, equally at ease with old time Chassidism and their semi-alienated children. His personality, his perception, his humanity and his humour set him apart from the Chassidic rabbis of his day.

Nathan David died at the age of forty-seven. Shortly before his death he wrote a moving message to his family and his followers. This document later published as "The Will and Testament of the Biala Rabbi,"[8] is a resounding declaration of faith. Comfortingly, the Biala *rebbe* writes of death as a transition, the changing of one garment for another. With loving fatherly words, he implores his people to live in brotherly harmony and keep faith with God and man. With fathomless faith, he voices his acceptance of his fate and his trust in the Master of the Universe. For he was in many ways the noblest of the sons of Biala.

The founder of the Biala dynasty, Rabbi Jacob Isaac Rabinowicz (1847–1905),[9] son of Rabbi Nathan David of Sydlowiec (1814–1866), was a direct descendant of Rabbi Jacob Isaac, "the Holy Jew" of Przysucha (1766–1814). Significantly the rabbi of Biala (Podolska) was born on the Sabbath on the 15th of *Tevet*, the day on which mediaeval scholar-poet Abraham Ibn Ezra (1098–1164) composed his famous epistle on the Sabbath. For the Sabbath, more than any other *mitzvah*, absorbed the heart and soul of the Biala *rebbe*. There is hardly a discourse in which he does not touch upon some aspect of the Sabbath, and it runs like a luminous thread throughout his writings. He married Rachel Levia, daughter of Rabbi Joshua ben Shloma Leib of Ostrow (d. 28th of Sivan, 1873), and his father-in-law became a second father to him. In reverential tribute, Rabbi Isaac Jacob called his first book *Yishre Lev* ("Upright of Heart"), an acrostic of his father-in-law's name, "for most of my wisdom I derived from him." It is revealing that this book, too, deals with the significance of the Sabbath.

The *rebbe* of Biala followed the doctrine of Przysucha. Protestations of piety were discouraged. Action and service, charity and loving-kindness were encouraged as the true measure of a man's sincerity. The *rebbe* was known far and wide for his warm heart and open house. A special kitchen at his "court" provided meals for visiting Chassidim and poor townsfolk. In his deep concern that standards of preparation should be high and that the poor should be treated as members of his own household, the rabbi himself regularly "tasted" the dishes.

In the true tradition of Biala, Rabbi Jacob Isaac left a will of high spiritual import, which yet underlines the essential humility of the man. He implores his Chassidim to "notify" his saintly ancestors, his father, his father-in-law and the "Holy Jew," of his death that they might intercede on his behalf. "I pray that you publicize by means of placards and through the newspapers the fact that I beseech forgiveness of those people who brought me gifts while I was alive. They gave me money because they regarded me as a *zaddik*. But verily I am unworthy."

The four sons of the Biala rabbi branched out further

and established their own dynasties. The eldest, Nathan David of Parczew (1866–1930), married Lea Reizel, daughter of Rabbi Yechiel Jacob of Kozienice. The second son, Meir Shlomo Yehudah (1868–1933), settled first in Miedzyrzec and subsequently in Warsaw where he attracted the scholars and intellectuals. The third son, Abraham Joshua Heshel (1875–1933), devoted his life to the publication of his father's many works. It was he who edited *Yishre Lev* ("Upright of Heart") and *Divre Binah* ("Words of Understanding"), on the Pentateuch. Most gifted of the sons was Yerachmiel Zevi (1890–1906) who wed Hava, daughter of Yehuda Arie Leib of Ozarow (d. 1903), author of *Birchat Tov* ("The Good Blessing"), a commentary on the Pentateuch.

Yerachmiel Zevi was one of the most remarkable of all the Chassidic rabbis. A great Talmudist, he was also an accomplished violinist and a painter of rare promise. His sketches reveal extraordinary insight and his voice could stir the soul, awakening sinners to new consciousness. He died at the age of twenty-six, after being rabbi for barely six months, leaving six small children. The eldest and most illustrious of these children was Rabbi Nathan David Rabinowicz, Biala *rebbe* in London, mentioned earlier in this chapter.

Rabbi Mordecai Joseph Lainer (1800–1854), author of *Mei Ha-shiloah* ("Waters of Siloam"), was the founder of the Radzyn-Izbice dynasty which produced five outstanding teachers in the course of just one century. For thirteen years, Rabbi Mordecai Joseph was a disciple of Mendel of Kotzk (Kock). Then he rebelled against his great master and established himself in Izbice. His son Rabbi Jacob (1828–1878) was the author of *Bet Jacob* ("House of Jacob"), a commentary on the Torah and on the Passover

Haggadah. It was Rabbi Joseph's son, Rabbi Gershon Chanoch (1839–1891), who brought Radzyn into the limelight. In the format of a Talmudic tractate, he wrote a classical work called *Sidre Taharot* (the sixth and last order of the *Mishnah* dealing with the laws of purity), a tractate which was the wonder of the scholarly world.

In 1887, he published a dissertation *Maamar Sefunei Temunie Chol* dealing with the problem of the *psil techelet* (the strand of blue in the ritual fringes prescribed in Numbers XV:38). According to Jewish Law the *tzizit* should have seven strands of white and one strand of blue. Somehow the process for obtaining the blue was forgotten and the Jews for more than a thousand years did not wear *psil techelet* ("the chord of blue").

Accompanied by his beadle, Israel Kotzker, the rabbi travelled to Italy. He became an expert on marine life. He published a second book on the subject *Maamar Psil Techelet* ("Discourse on the Strand of blue"). He claimed to have discovered the sea fish *(sepia officinalis)* known in Talmudic literature as *Chalozon*, from which he extracted blue dye. On the 1st day of Chanukah, 1889, he attached a blue thread to his fringes and his Chassidim followed suit. It was also adopted by the Umaner Chassidim, followers of Rabbi Nachman of Braclaw (1772–1812), known after his death as the *Toite* Chassidim ("Dead Chassidim"), as well as by the great Halachic authority Rabbi Shalom Mordecai Cohen Shvardon of Brezany.

A workshop for the manufacture of ritual fringes was established at the rabbi's court in Radzyn. Among scholars who opposed him were Rabbi Joshua of Kutno and Isaac Elchanan Spector (1817–1896). Gershon Chanoch studied medicine by himself and actually wrote prescriptions in faultless Latin. He was a fine musician and adept in many arts. He died on the 4th of *Tevet*, 1891.

Gershon Chanoch's son Rabbi Mordecai Joseph Eliezer (1865–1929) settled in Warsaw in 1914 and dedicated himself to the publications of his father's writings. In all, nine texts were published while fifteen remained in manuscript. Among the published works were *Teferet Achanochi* ("The Glory of Chanoch"), a commentary on the Zohar and *Dalsot Shaare Ha'ir* ("The Doors of the Gates of the City"), 1892 on Tractate *Erubin* and *Sidre Taharot* (1903). To pacify critics who condemned a work published in the form of a Talmudical tractate, he inscribed on every page *Sepher Seder Taharot*, i.e., the book of the section of *Taharot*. He was active in communal life too, conferring with Pilsudski and Socialist leader Herman Diamand.

The son of the Radzyner, Rabbi Samuel Solomon (1908–1942) married Mirel, daughter of Rabbi Joseph ben Menachem of Amszynow (1878–1937). In 1928, he left Warsaw and returned to Radzyn. With fatherly solicitude, he cared for the young students in his charge and opposed the humiliating system of rota eating days in different homes. In his yeshiva, Sod Yesharim, over two hundred students lived in comparative comfort. During the Nazi occupation, the rabbi's courage enflamed his Chassidim and he urged them to fight back. He denounced the collaborators: "Whoever treads the lintels of the *Judenrat* [the Jewish council appointed by the Nazis]," he warned, "will forfeit both worlds, for they are aiding the Nazis in the extermination of the Jews." Poet Isaac Katznelson (1886–1944) wrote in tribute "The Song Concerning the Radzyner."

The dynasty of Radzymin, founded by the "Miracle

Worker" Jacob Arye Guterman (1792–1877), played a leading role in Poland. Guterman's grandson Rabbi Aaron Menachem Mendel (1842–1934) was very wealthy and owned twenty-one houses. Educator, organizer, social worker, he founded the Shomer Sabbath Society (Sabbath Observance Society) and *Tomchei Assurim* (Prisoners' Aid Committee) and was president of Rabbi Meir Baal Haness (the Diaspora charity funds for poor Jews in the Holy Land). In 1928, Rabbi Aaron Menachem Mendel himself journeyed to the Holy Land to settle a dispute over the distribution of philanthropic monies collected abroad.[10] It was he who insisted upon segregating the sexes at the Wailing Wall, placing a partition between the men and women worshippers.

A beloved figure was the Sokolower *rebbe*, Isaac Zelig Morgenstern (1867–1939), a great-grandson of Rabbi Mendel of Kotzk and the son of Rabbi Chayyim Israel of Pilev, the great religious Zionist. At the age of 18, Isaac Zelig married Chayya, daughter of a Gerer Chassid, Mordecai Schonfeld of Pinczow, and soon after he was appointed rabbi at Sokolow. Dr. Zygmunt Bichowski had instructed him in medicine and like the Radziner *rebbe*, Isaac Zelig wrote prescriptions in Latin.

"Give me two hundred Jews who have not bowed to Baal," cried Rabbi Mendel of Kotzk who tended to pessimism. Isaac Zelig was more charitable in his judgment of fellow Jews. In 1910, he was a delegate at the Conference of Communal Leaders in St. Petersburg (Leningrad) and there came into contact with Rabbi Chayyim Soloveichik (1852–1918) and Rabbi Joseph Isaac Schneersohn of Lubavitch. He joined the Aguda in 1919 and also became Vice-President of the Agudat Harabbanim. He delivered stirring orations at the Aguda conferences and his discourse appeared in the Rabbinical journals *Degel Hatorah* ("Flag of the Torah") and *Be'er* ("Well").

Like his father, author of *Shalom Yerushalayim* ("Peace, O Jerusalem"), in 1886 the Sokolower *rebbe* urged his followers to support the *Yishuv* and he visited the Holy Land in 1924. Mendel, rabbi of Wegrow, son of the Sokolower *rebbe*, was murdered by the Nazis on *Yom Kippur*, 1939. The aged father, celebrating *Succot* (the Feast of Tabernacles) sensed the bitter news. The cup of wine fell from his hands. "They have killed my son!" the broken-hearted father cried. The Sokolower *rebbe* died on the 3rd of *Heshvon*, 1940.

Rabbi Meir Yechiel Halevy Halstock (1851–1928), son of Abraham Isaac, a *bagel* (rolls) baker, was born at Sabin near Warsaw in 1851, the year when Yechiel Meir, the Mogielnicer *rebbe*, died. He was adopted at the age of ten by Rabbi Elimelech of Grodzisk and was widely regarded as an "Illui" (a prodigy).

He was ordained by Rabbi Joshua Trunk of Kutno, Rabbi Elijah Chayyim of Lodz and Rabbi Chayyim Eliezer Waks of Kalisz, who exclaimed with rhapsodic rhetoric, "How can a fly with broken wings testify against an eagle who flies in the skies." At the age of 27, Meir Yechiel became rabbi at Skierniewice, where he spent ten peaceful years. In 1888 he moved to Ostrowiec. An assiduous student, he would go over the entire Talmud in the brief four-week period between *Purim* and Passover.

For forty years he fasted every day, eating only a frugal meal at night. He was proud of his father and of his humble origin. "My father of blessed memory," he would frequently remind his distinguished visitors, "used to say that the best thing is a freshly baked bread." When he died on the 19th of *Adar*, 1928, at the age of seventy-seven, fifty rabbis and ten thousand people attended his funeral. The grateful community granted a pension of 400 zlotys a year for life to the widow.[11] His son Ezekiel, author of *Kodshei Yichezkel* ("The holiness of Ezekiel") and *Meir Eine Chachamim* ("He Who Enlightens the Eyes of the Wise"), succeeded him. He established a yeshiva, Bet Meir, in memory of his father. Ezekiel together with his seven sons died a martyr's death at the hands of the Nazis, exclaiming to the very end: "Hear, O Israel, the Lord our God the Lord is One."

Kuzmir (Kazimiersz) and Modzyz occupy a high place in the history of Chassidic musicology. The family tradition of Rabbi Ezekiel of Kuzmir (1806–1856) was upheld by Rabbi Saul Yedidia Eliezer Taub who was born in 1886 at Ozarow, Radom. From 1918 to 1922, he was rabbi in Rakow and, in 1929, he settled in Otwock near Warsaw. He was the product of neither conservatoire nor musical academy. No professor instructed him in the rudiments of musical theory, yet music surged through his veins. Not only Chassidim but famous composers, Jewish and Gentile as well as cantors from Poland and abroad, and even *maskilim*, flocked to Otwock to listen to the compositions of this untutored genius. He is said to have been the composer of more than seven hundred melodies. More than a thousand Chassidim sat at his table every sabbath at the third meal (*shalosh seudot*) to hear his Torah discourses and his melodies. What other rabbis achieved through scholarship, Rabbi Taub accomplished through music and he won many adherents to Chassidism.

At the outbreak of the Second World War, he lived in Vilna. Narrowly, he escaped the Nazi holocaust and he died in the Holy Land on the 16th of *Kislev* (November

29), 1947, on the very day of the United Nations decision to partition Palestine. He was the last person to be buried on the Mount of Olives in Jerusalem.

The tradition of music remained with the Chassidim even to the end, even along the dark despairing paths that led to the crematoria where multitudes perished. It was at that anguished moment that Rabbi Azriel Pastag composed a heartsoaring melody, a triumphant affirmation of belief in God and man. "I believe, with perfect faith," sang Rabbi Azriel and hundreds of thousands sang with him, "in the coming of the Messiah, and though He tarry, I will wait daily for His coming." This was the faith for which the Chassidim lived, and this was the faith for which they gave their lives in Sanctification of the Holy Name.

From Lublin, too, came famous Chassidic rabbis. Rabbi Solomon Eiger, and Rabbi Moses Mordecai Twersky, son of Rabbi Leib of Trisk (d. 1943), who married a daughter of Rabbi Jacob of Novominsk. His home at Lubertowska 40 was a throbbing center of Chassidism.

What Ger was to Poland, Belz (Belza) was to Galicia. "The whole world," as Chassidim of Belz were wont to say, "journeys to Belz." The rabbis of Belz underlined sincerity and simplicity as the fundamentals of the good life. Rabbi Isachar Dov (1854–1927), second son of Rabbi Joshua Rokeach, was a militant upholder of tradition. In October, 1922, Count Galecki, Governor of Lwow, backed by several orthodox supporters of the assimilationist camp, urged the Belzer *rebbe* to direct the Jews to vote against the Minority Bloc. Unequivocally, the rabbi of Belz refused.

In 1927, Rabbi Aaron (b. 1880), named after Rabbi Aaron of Karlin, succeeded to his father's throne. His seven children were killed by the Nazis. Miraculously he escaped the Hitlerian terror and finally reached the Holy Land. Far removed from earthly matters he dedicated himself to the service of God and study of the Torah. Yet, during the Sinai campaign (Israel-Egyptian tussle October 29–November 5, 1956) he neither ate, nor drank, nor spoke for forty-eight hours while praying for a Jewish victory. "My sons," he said, "we have won with the help of the Almighty." He died on the 24th of *Heshvon*, 1957.

Next in importance to Belz was the dynasty of Bobov. In the tradition of his father Solomon, Rabbi Benzion Halberstamm (1874–1941), a noted composer, created many melodies for his Chassidim. His Friday night *nigun* (melody) *Yo Ribbon* ("God of the World") was renowned through the country. He was one of the two hundred rabbis at the Lwow conference in 1927 which adopted a resolution calling upon Jews to vote only for lists which were loyal to the State, a move against the Jewish Minority Bloc.[12] Like the rabbi of Ger he was actively engaged in the education of Jewish youth. He established a yeshiva, Etz Chayyim ("The Tree of Life"), which eventually developed forty-six branches throughout Galicia. A special society, Tomchei Tmimim ("Upholders of the Perfect") looked after the physical needs of the students.

Strangely enough Poland, the home of Torah, was not at first the home of great yeshivot. During the 19th century, *mitnaggdic* Lithuania had the monopoly, and the "voice of the Torah went out from Mir, and the word of the Lord from Slabodka." Chassidic *bachurim* ("young men") studied in the *stieblech* and the *bate midrashim* ("Houses of Study") of the *rebbes*. The trend towards Chassidic yeshivot developed in the inter-war years when the *rebbes* began to establish their own religious academies. The young followers were spared the difficult choice between inadequate study in the home atmosphere of the *stiebel* and a thorough Talmudic grounding in the alien setting of a Lithuanian or *mitnaggdic* yeshiva, such as Mir, Baranowicze, Radin and Ponovez.

During his residence in Otwock (1927–1939), Rabbi Joseph Isaac Schneersohn of Lubavitch founded a number of Tomchei Tmimim ("Supporters of the perfect") yeshivot. Rabbi Menachem Mendel Alter Kalisch of Pabianice (near Lodz) established yeshivat *Darke Noam* ("Ways of Pleasantness").

Equally successful was Rabbi Shlomoh Henoch ha-Kohen Rabinowicz (b. 1882) of Radomsko, son of Rabbi Ezekiel, author of *Knesset Yichezkel* ("Gathering of Ezekiel"). His yeshiva, Keter Torah ("Crown of the Torah"), opened thirty-six branches in Poland and Galicia. In Cracow, there were more Radomsker *stieblech* than Gerer *stieblech*. Although many rabbis followed the Radomsker, he regarded himself as a Chassid of Czortkov. The rabbi of Radomsk was a man of substance who owned a glass factory as well as houses in Sosnowiec, Berlin and Warsaw. He had one of the finest libraries in Poland and was the author of *Tiferet Shlomo* ("Glory of Solomon"), homilies on the Pentateuch and Festivals.

The Radomsker's successor-designate was his first cousin and son-in-law Moses David ha-Kohen Rabinowicz (b. 1906), a disciple of Rabbi Dov Berish Weidenfeld of Chebin and the author of *Zivchei Kohen* ("Sacrifices of a Priest"). Three times a day he lectured the hundred and fifty students in the *Kibbutz Gavoa* (Higher Study Academy) in Sosnowiec. Under his guidance, the yeshivot of Radomsk achieved high standards of learning, particularly in the famous Keter Torah ("Crown of the Torah") colleges at Lodz, Sosnowiec, Bendin, Radomsk, Kielce,

Katowice, Auschwitz, Piotrkow and Czestochowa. The rabbi himself supplied half the budget of the yeshivot and the remainder was subscribed by his Chassidim. No provision was made for the Rabbinical Diploma. Emphasis was on study for the sake of study and not for certification. Gemara (Talmud) and Tosaphot (critical and explanatory notes on the Talmud by French and German scholars) were the main subjects of this concentrated curriculum. Under the influence of the *Chofetz Chayyim,* much time was devoted to the study of *Kodashim* (Fifth Order of the Mishnah). Students and teachers were not necessarily Radomsker Chassidim. In Sosnowiec the principal of the Radomsk Yeshiva was Joseph Lask, a Chassid of Ger. Together with his son-in-law the Radomsker was slain on Sabbath 18th of *Av,* 1942, at Novolipie 30. Both were buried in the sepulchre of the Rabbi of Novominsk in Warsaw.

As the holocaust raged, the lights of Chassidism were dimmed and a deathly pall descended. Sages by the score perished with the Holy Scrolls in their hands and holy words on their lips. The Jewish quarters of Warsaw, Lodz, Lublin, Otwock, once citadels of piety and learning, became piles of rubble, physical symbol of the almost total destruction of Chassidism in Poland.

Yet, the story is not ended. For out of the ashes, phoenix-like, a new Chassidism has arisen. Pietists in long silken *kapotes* and streaming side curls add their unquenchable spiritual fervour for Jewish community life of New York, Jerusalem, London. Proudly they proclaim their identity as Chassidim of Lubavitch, Ger, Belz, Novominsk, Biala and Bobov; and these euphonious names linger lovingly upon their lips. These are the contemporary Defenders of the Faith who have rejuvenated the traditions of their fathers in the lands of freedom.

9

Life and Literature

"Lo, it is a people that shall dwell alone and shall not be reckoned among the nations,"[1] prophesied Balaam thousands of years ago; and the prophecy was fulfilled to the letter in Poland. Despite a continuous history of nearly ten centuries, the Jews were isolated from their fellow-citizens by religion, by culture, by language, even by dress. The Polish Jew had his own educational system, his own communal organization, his own youth movements, his press, theater, his party politics.

Nowhere else in the world were there such great concentrations of Jews. In a number of towns and villages, Jews even formed a clear majority. Only a smattering of assimilationists broke away from the closely-knit community and settled among their gentile neighbours. Not only were there invisible walls between Jew and Pole, but there were even barriers between Jew and Jew. On the one side were the ultra-orthodox Chassidim; on the other side were the Bundists who substituted *Das Kapital* of Karl Marx for the Torah of Moses.

"The Yiddish language has no future," said the Polish

Minister of Education. It was a debatable prognosis and certainly Yiddish had a lively present. In the 1931 census, 79 per cent of Poland's 3,113,993 Jews gave Yiddish as their mother tongue; 12.2 per cent named Polish and 7.9 per cent Hebrew. Poland was the center of Yiddish printing. Yiddishist Boris Klatzkin established a great printing house to awaken interest in modern Yiddish literature. He published the works of Peretz, Sholem Aleichem (pseudonym of the Yiddish humourist Sholom Rabinovitch (1859–1916), Joseph Opatoshu (1886–1934), Oizer Warshawsky, and a literary weekly *Literarishe bleter*. He edited the first modern Yiddish philological journal, "Green Trees." In 1925, he transferred his business from Vilna to Warsaw where it became the largest publishing plant in Poland.

Another prolific publishing house was Central, which issued the works of Mendele Mocher Sepharim (1836–1917). Established in April, 1921, the Jewish *Kultur* League published between two hundred and three hundred books a year. Its first venture was the dramatic works of a young writer Beimish Steinmann (1879–1919), *Beim Toyer* ("At the Gate") and *Messiah ben Joseph*. The League published the works of Sholom Aleichem, Sholem Asch (1880–1957), Simon Dubnow (1860–1941), Moses Nadir (1885–1943), Max Arik, Shimen Horonczyk and a monthly entitled *Bicher Welt* ("In the World of books").

Although the new Poland produced neither a second Sholem Asch nor another Isaac Leib Peretz, it brought forth a rich measure of notable Yiddish novelists, dramatists and poets. Asch was actually the father of *Shtetl* literature, for it was he who first realized its vast literary potentialities. To him, the *Shtetl* was a miniature Jerusalem set on Polish soil. Yiddish was its language and

Torah its lifeblood. The *Shtetl* continued to be the theme of many novels written in this period. Their vista was narrow and parochial. They utilized the idiom whose theme was religious and purpose secular.

Outstanding among the writers was Z. Segalowicz (1884–1954), one of the most popular Yiddish novelists of his generation. Whilst Asch portrayed the "sabbath" of the *Shtetl* in a vision spiritual and almost unearthly, Oizer Warshawsky focused on the seamier side. His novel *Shmuglares* ("Smugglers") traces the relationship between Mendel the Smuggler and Natasha the courtesan. Love is the catharsis redeeming them both. He gives a vivid picture of the Jewish underworld in a naturalistic setting.[2]

As in every society, the novel reflected the crises and clashes of the day. In *Roish fun Mashinen* ("The Roar of Machines"), Shimen Horonczyk (Horontchik) describes the impact of the industrial revolution on the rural community. The city, souless, sterile, was the magnet which lured the people from the unspoilt ways of the village Eden. This was a stark school of writing in which people were either good or evil, the heroes poor and pious, the villains invariably capitalist.

Moses Kulbak (1896–1937) was the novelist of the common man. He preached that the poor would not only inherit the world to come but were also the creators of the messianic ideal on earth. According to Kulbak, it was the ordinary Jew not the sophist or the scholar who was the eternal messenger of the eternal God.

Where Kulbak discerned the *Shechina* on the brow of every humble Israelite, Israel Raban (1898–1941) saw the devil incarnate. His novel *Balut* took for its setting the working quarter of Lodz where all was toil and squalor, a jungle in which only brute force flourished and man fought tooth and nail for sheer survival. Raban stripped the protective covering off society in a style as raw as the strata of life he described. But although he had little respect for Man, he fought for the betterment of the worker.

In his poem "Prayer for Rest," he writes:

> God, You have seen the sun go down in me.
> You have seen the blood asleep in me.
> You have seen my heart weep in me.
> You have seen the world lament in me.
> You have seen how my joy dies in me.
> You have seen how someone is laughing in me,
> An empty laughter that someone is laughing in me.
> You have seen the reckless wind in me
> Go rushing over an autumn field in me.
> You have seen how every limb in me
> Wants rest, wants sleep, wants everlasting sleep in me.
> God, I have prepared nothing for You.
> My heart is ready like a slaughtered dove.
> Take my heart; let rest in me
> Rock my soul to silent death in me.[3]

With greater subtlety yet equal strength, Joshua Perl (1883–1943) surveyed the passing scene with the warm humanity of a Peretz, and the robust realism of a Sholem Aleichem. *Yidn fun a Ganz Yur* ("Jews all the Year Round") is a picture gallery of a vanishing world, rich with material for the sociologist of today.

Aaron Zeitlin (b. 1889), son of Hillel Zeitlin, inherited many of his father's qualities. His famous novel *Brenidige Ert* ("Burning Earth") transports the reader from America to England, to Turkey, to Palestine. The scene where Amrom and Dardanski are hanged in the prison of Damascus is one of the most memorable in the whole realm of Yiddish literature.

Writing in Yiddish, yet Polish in mood and manner,

M. Bursztyn (Burshtin) breathed a lilting love of the Polish landscape. Leib Raskin returned to the *Shtetl* for inspiration. In *Di Menshen fun Gadlibashitz* (pseudonym for Kazimierz) he compared the virtues of the *Shtetl* with the vices of the town where the intellectuals were corrupt, the pious insincere, the peasants uncultivated. Even the sabbath was no longer the sabbath in evil suburbia. Ah, but in the *Shtetl*, sabbath was painted in rhapsodic colors as a foretaste of heaven itself.

Capturing the essence of Jewish farm life, Rachel Corn wrote of the countryside she knew and loved so well. Her novels depicted the Jewish peasantry with an abundance of realistic detail. Mordecai, hero of *Erd* ("Earth"), was as real as the earth on which he walked.

A writer who lived forty-one years in Poland before settling in the United States, Israel Joshua Singer (1893–1944), delved in *Yoshe Kalb* (entitled "The Sinners" in the English version), behind the scenes of the *rebbe's* court. *Di Brider Ashkenazi* ("The Brothers Ashkenazi") sketched the industrial conditions in Lodz a city in transition, caught between the old handicraft way of life and the new conveyor belt machine age. It is a fascinating socio-historical record. Singer writes:

It was a bitter miserable struggle. The officials of the new regime were as hostile and contemptuous as the Germans had been. A furious wave of anti-Semitism was passing through Poland, and the Lemberg pogrom had been the signal for a series of murderous assaults on Jews. The hungry and unemployed workers everywhere, and especially in Lodz, gathered in mobs and marched on the homes and factories of the Jewish industrialists. They demanded work when there was none; and when there was work, the unemployed demanded it on their own terms. They besieged the Jews in their homes and factories. The police did not interfere; the higher officials shrugged their shoulders. When rioters broke into the Ashkenazi factory, and the weary, half-paralysed old woman applied for protection to the police commissioner, she was thrust from the door.[4]

The critics reacted with particular enthusiasm to Singer's novel *The Family Karnowsky*, a study of intermarriage in Germany. According to one critic, "Singer brings to bear a mastery of psychological insight in describing relationships, in the gradual unfolding of events, in projecting himself into the complicated status of frustration and inferiority feeling besetting the young boy, half-Jewish and half-German."[5]

In the family tradition, Singer's younger brother Bashevis produced novels on a grand scale, *The Sotn fun Gorey* ("The Plots") and *Family Mushkat*.

Ranking high among the poets were J. I. Segal, Menachem Boraisha, né Goldberg (1881–1949), Meilech Ravitch, né Z. Kh Bergner, and J. Glatstein (b. 1896). The works of lyricist N. Gross (1895–1956) reveal his powers of character portrayal. His poems *Bal Agoleh* ("Coachman"), *Dorf Yid* ("Village Jew"), *Maggid* ("Preacher"), *Yosssel Klezmer* ("Joseph the Musician") are all true to life.

The poet Jack Kahan took for his key characters workless men, starving women, and stunted children. Among religious bards was Michael Ber Sokolow (1902–1942), son of a Kozinitzer Chassid, grandson of Rabbi J. J. Weingarten of Kinz, and graduate of the yeshiva of Sochaszew. Ber Sokolow has sought the hidden spark in every human being, below the rugged exterior and the workman's smock. Dr. Ben Zion Pelser, born in 1894 near Kosov in Eastern Galicia, was the son of a Vishnitzer Chassid and

a law student in Vienna. He worked for the Poale Aguda
and even composed the hymn for the movement. He published a book of verse, *Arim Dir* ("Around you"), with
each poem based on a Biblical theme. Other well known
writers and essayists included M. Weissenberg (1881–
1937) and Isidor Elyashew (pseudonym: *Baal Machshovot,*
"A thinking man"), 1873–1924, the founder of modern
esthetic criticism in Yiddish.

JEWS IN POLISH LITERATURE

The Jews made a considerable contribution to Polish
literature. In Warsaw there was one solitary unbaptized
Jew in the Polish press. Nonetheless, in 1932, there were
43 Jews among the 212 registered members of the Polish
Writers' Union.[6]

Lyricist Julian Tuwim (1894–1953) was one of the
leaders of the coterie known as the "Skamander" after
the name of the poetry monthly published by the group.
Tuwim's poetry throbbed with a power and intensity
that classed him with Poland's major poets. His lyrics
were written in harmonious language full of neologisms.
His collection *Czychanie na Boga* ("Lying in Wait for
God") and *Sokrates tanczacy* ("Dancing Socrates") were
widely read. "I have no occupation," avows Tuwim in
Slowo i Cialo ("Words and Body"); "I am a hunter of
words. My blood is in my speech, the hot pulp of the
earth." Tuwim translated into Polish contemporary Russian poets: K. Balmont, W. Briusow and D. Mereżkowski;
and he was awarded the annual 1,000 zloty prize by the
Polish P.E.N. Club for the best translation of Pushkin's
works.

Tuwim's work *Kwiaty Polskie* ("Polish Flowers") is a

powerful indictment of the Germans: "Whether they had a Goethe or not may a bright thunderbolt strike them." "Tuwim has shown the deep sense of the value of his historical inheritance as a Polish poet," evaluated Roman Dyboski, "and it is he, if anybody, who may be singled out as a leading figure among the Polish poets of our generation." Tuwim spent the war years in America and returned to Poland in 1946.

Another award-winner, Josef Wittlin, won an accolade from the Polish P.E.N. Club for his translation of Homer's *Odyssey* in 1924. Wittlin was born at Dmytrow, Austrian Poland in 1896, and was educated at Lwow. A pacifist by conviction, Wittlin's platform was a series of poems entitled *Hymny* ("Hymns") and a book of essays called "War, Peace and a Poet's Soul" (1924). "True Democracy," he wrote,[7] "means a rejection of racial and class hatreds, the union of continents in a common United States of the World." His novel *Sol Ziemi* ("Salt of the Earth"), translated into English in 1939, was dedicated to the unknown "patient foot soldier" of the Imperial Austrian Army. An ascetic who meditated in solitude for days on end, Wittlin was a painstaking craftsman who took ten years to write "Salt of the Earth." He was Poland's official candidate for the Nobel Prize.

Another notable man of letters was Antoni Slonimski (b. 1895), son of a distinguished physician and grandson of Chayyim Selig Slonimski (1810–1904). Slonimski was one of the founders of the "Skamander Group" and his weekly feuilletons in *Wiadmosciach Literackich* ("Literary News") were cosmopolitan in mood and scope. Besides small volumes of verse, Slonimski wrote a number of satirical comedies, among them *Wieża Babel* ("The Tower of Babylon"), 1927, and *Rodzina* ("The Family"), a brilliant satire on Hitlerism and Bolshevism. During the Second World War, Slonimski was active in liberal circles in England. He was known as "The Poet of the New Emigration." In a small collection of poems entitled "Alam," published in Polish by the Minerva press in July, 1940, he records his experiences. "Now you will know," he writes in a poem called "To a French Friend," "the bitterness of remembering the vanity of dreams. Pick your way cautiously now in the darkness. Stretch out your hand. That darkness I know."[8]

THE PRESS

In Poland the Yiddish press was "the first estate" as far as Jews were concerned, a power to be reckoned with and a vociferous champion of Jewish rights. It had more than half a million readers and a yearly turnover of 20,000,000 zlotys. In 1927, 47 per cent of the world's Yiddish press was published in Poland. By August 1939, there were 27 Jewish dailies, over 100 weeklies, 24 bi-weeklies, 58 monthlies, 4 bi-monthlies, 4 quarterlies, 17 bi-annual yearbooks. In all there were 391 publications.[9]

Seventy per cent of the newspapers were in Yiddish, 18 per cent in Polish, 4 per cent in Hebrew, 7.5 per cent in Polish and Yiddish and 0.5 per cent in German.

Jewish papers were published in 45 localities. Vilna had 5 dailies, Bialystok 4, Grodno 2, Lwow 2 and Lodz 2. Seventy per cent of these newspapers appeared in Warsaw.

The greatest Yiddish newspaper in Poland was *Haint* ("Today"). From January 22, 1908, until two weeks after the Nazi invasion, this was the major spokesman of the Jewish people. *Haint* had over one thousand correspondents scattered throughout Poland and was read by Jews the world over. It enlisted the finest Jewish talents and numbered among its contributors David Ben Gurion, Nahum Sokolow and Sholem Asch.

Founded by Samuel Jacob Jackan and Nechemia Finkelstein, *Haint's* circulation grew rapidly and reached a hundred and fifty thousand readers by 1913. On January 1, 1920, it amalgamated with the Zionist paper *Yiddishe Folk,* ("The Jewish People"). It produced two daily editions: a provincial edition at 7.40 P.M. and a Warsaw edition at 4 A.M. For a time, a weekly illustrated edition was also issued. Every Friday, *Haint* put out a literary supplement, "Out of the World of Books," and, in 1929, it began to publish an afternoon paper, "Latest News," under the editorship of Simcha Pietrushka. On special occasions, such as the eve of a festival, it published twelve to sixteen page editions. The reportage was lively and features were enterprising. *Haint* organized contests with sets of Talmuds and Mishnah as prizes. It even sponsored excursions to Israel (1911, 1924 and 1932) in which eight hundred people participated.

Chlodna 8, headquarters of *Haint,* was the scene of hubbub and activity almost twenty-four hours a day. Under the pseudonym "B. Iushzohn" or "Itchele," the contributions of Moses Justman became a national institution. His *Politische Brief* ("Political Letters"), his satirical romance *In Rebben's Oiff* ("In the Rabbi's Court"), and his weekly selections of gems from rabbinical writings (*Fun Undzer Alten Otzer*), were regularly sought by loyal readers. But around the premises of the *Haint,* as in its columns, battle raged. Hoodlums broke windows and wrecked furniture. Crushing taxation caused continual hardships. On October 19, 1938, it was closed down by the authorities and it promptly reappeared under the name *Der Tog* ("The Day"). On January 23, 1939, it resumed its old name for eight more months. The last issue appeared on September 22, 1939, and reproduced *in toto* a whole chapter of the Psalms, a fitting and noble requiem.

Unlike the pro-Zionist *Haint*, its rival *Der Moment*, founded by Zevi Prylucki on November 5, 1910, was an independent daily without political strings, striving to win acceptance among the masses. In 1924, it expanded to issue an afternoon paper *Radio*, and a streamlined, $100,-000 building was erected at Nalewka 38 to become the editorial headquarters. Jabotinsky's articles, "The Eleventh Hour" and "My Diary," proved effective circulation boosters. Among other noted contributors were Hillel Zeitlin, Noach Prylucki, the son of the first editor, and Hirsch David Nomberg (1876–1927). Few copies of the *Moment* survived the holocaust.

The Aguda's *Dos Yiddishe Togblat* ("The Yiddish Daily Paper"), established in 1929, soon built up a circulation of thirty thousand. Resolved that the *Togblat* should not perish as prematurely as its predecessors *Hakol* ("The Voice," 1912–1919), *Dos Yiddishe Vort* ("The Jewish Word," 1912–1919) and *Der Yid* ("The Jew," 1919–1926), the Aguda enlisted the help of the Gerer *rebbe*. Before the sounding of the *shophar* on *Rosh Hashana* 1931, the *rebbe* urged his followers to support the orthodox newspaper. The *Togblat* employed contemporary techniques to reinforce the ancient faith. Among special features were *Torah Kwall* (selections from rabbinic writings) by Alexander Zisha Friedmann, detective stories such as *Der Umbakanter* ("The Unknown") by David Flinker, Chassidic legends by Samuel Rothstein, literary critiques by Dr. Hershel Klepfish, poems by Samuel Nadler and Israel Emmiot (b. 1909). "A stock of flour and sugar is not enough," declared one of the last editorials of the *Togblat*. "We need a stock of faith, courage, strength and endurance. We need stout hearts, iron nerves and plenty of faith and hope."

Folkszeitung ("The People's Paper"), the organ of the Bund, with a circulation of twelve thousand was set up to be the mouthpiece of the masses. The four small rooms at Novolipie 7 were journalistic caves of Adullam for the downtrodden and the destitute. For a time, the Bund also issued an afternoon paper "2 O'Clock," and in March, 1931, it began to appear on Saturdays. Government censors were frequently incensed by editorial outspokenness, and, in 1937, *Folkszeitung* was confiscated no less than eighty times. Doggedly it reappeared under different names. *Nayer Folkszeitung* and *Undzer Folkszeitung* maintained the fight against injustice and oppression.

Other influential newspapers included the non-partisan *Undzer Express* (established in 1927 by Lazar Cohen); *Dos Naye Wort* ("The New Word"), established in 1937 by Zionist socialists; the Zionist *Nasz Przeglad* ("Our Review"), established in 1923 by Jacob Apenszlak; *Nowe Zycie* ("New Life"), edited by M. Balaban (1929); the bimonthly *Jerozolima*; the Revisionist paper *Wyzwolona*; *Miesiecznik Zydowski* ("Jewish Monthly"), edited by Z. Ellenberg (1930–1935); *Glos Gminy Zydowskiej* ("The Voice of the Jewish Community"), published in Warsaw 1937–1939; *Nasz kurjer* (1923–1930); and *Nowa Slowo* (1931), edited by Joseph Davidson.

YIVO

At a five-day conference in Berlin, in August, 1925, a group of Jewish scholars and scientists from various countries decided, under the direction of critic-philologist Nahum Shtif (1879–1933), to establish in Vilna the Yidisher Visenshaftlicher Institut (The Institute for

Jewish Research), known as Yivo. Its objects were three-fold: (1) to collect and prepare material relating scientifically to Jewish problems, (2) to gather historical data and (3) to train new research workers in various domains of Jewish scholarship. Yivo's three storey headquarters in Vilna were dedicated in 1928, and by 1939 the Institute had surpassed the expectations of its founders. It possessed 2,500 periodicals in Yiddish, Hebrew and other languages; a library of more than 100,000 books; a press archive of some 10,000 volumes; a manuscript collection of 100,000; a gallery of several thousand photographs; a museum of pedagogy and ethnography; a bibliography and records of Yiddish book production. In the course of two decades Yivo itself published a total of 60,000 pages of scholarly research. The Asperantur, a graduate school for research techniques, was established in 1935. The undergraduate school was founded three years later. Yivo issued *Historishe Shriften* ("Historical writings") in 1929, 1937 and 1939, the *Ekonomishe Shriften* ("Economic Writings") in 1928 and 1932, and the *Yivo Bletter* ("Yivo Papers").

Apart from the Yivo Library, there were in Poland 251 Jewish libraries with 1,650,000 books.[10]

HEBREW CENTER

In the 1931 census, 243,539 (7.9 per cent) of the Jewish population gave Hebrew as their mother tongue. For this sizable minority the Hebrew printing presses pulsated. The publishing house of "The Widow and the Brothers Romm," established by Baruch ben Joseph Romm in 1789, was famed throughout the Jewish world. It produced prayer books, editions of the Talmud, the Mishnah, the Codes and a large number of secular works.

Abraham Joseph Stiebel (1885–1946), the Maecenas of Hebrew literature, issued translations from Greek, Russian (Pushkin, Turgenev), German (Goethe, Schiller, Heine), and English (Oscar Wilde, Charles Dickens, Mark Twain).

The *magnum opus* of the Stiebel Publishing Company was the compilation of the twenty-three volumes of the *Hatekupha* ("The Age"), edited by David Frischmann (1861–1922) and Jacob Kohen. It was in the Hebrew quarterly *Hatekupha* that poets like Uri Zvi Greenberg (b. 1894) and M. Z. Walopski, writers like Eliezer Steinmann and Isaac Katzenelson (1886–1944), published their first literary efforts. Another publishing firm, Achiasaph (established in 1893), revived suddenly in 1923 and published over a hundred titles in a great burst of activity. It published a literary annual *Luach Achiasaph* (thirteen volumes, 1893–1904), a periodical *Hashiloah* (1896–1921), and a weekly *Ador*. The catalog listed the books of Judah Halevy (c. 1075–1141), Abraham Ibn Ezra (1098–1164), Achad Ha-Am, Moritz Steinschneider (1816–1907), and Moritz Gudemann (1835–1918).

Efforts were made to maintain a daily Hebrew newspaper, first the *Hatzphirah* ("The Dawn") and then *Hayom* ("The Day" 1932). Neither survived very long. Among the sixteen Hebraic periodicals were *Haoved* ("The Worker") 1922, *Tarbut* ("Culture"), *Ofikim* ("Horizons"), *Kolot* ("Voices") 1923–24, and *Tennuatenu* ("Our Movement").

YIDDISH THEATRE

The Yiddish theatre had long flourished in Poland. Star and architect of the Yiddish stage, Esther Rachel

Kaminska (1868–1925), established the Kaminska theatre in Warsaw at the turn of the century and introduced into the Yiddish repertoire the works of European writers, both Jewish and non-Jewish. Yiddish versions of Shakespeare, Chekov and Shaw were performed. And it was for Kaminska that the Yiddish playwright Jacob Gordin (1853–1909) wrote such classics as *Der Yiddisher kening Lear* ("The Jewish King Lear") 1892, *Mirele Efros* (1898), *Gott, Mensh un Taivel* ("God, Man and the Devil") 1903. He translated some of the plays of Lessing, Victor Hugo, Zangwill, Tolstoy and Strindberg.

Banned in Czarist Russia, the Yiddish theatre suffered a twenty-years' eclipse; but in 1919 it blossomed out in the new Poland. During the inter-war period there were from sixteen to twenty active theatre groups, and Warsaw itself had five or six playhouses. Their repertory was keyed to light entertainment, although attempts were made here and there to deal with weightier themes. Many actors, later famous in the New World, like Ludwig Zack, Yitchak Field and Leo Fucks were nurtured in Poland's Yiddish theatre. Efforts to create a professional theatrical organization and a drama school were frustrated by the machinations of the censor, the boycott of the orthodox, and the contempt of the assimilated.

In the 1920's and the 1930's, there was hardly a town without a Yiddish amateur repertory company. Among them were the Vilner Truppe founded by David Hermann (1876–1930) in 1916, modeled after the Stanislavsky's (1865–1938) Russian Art Theatre. The Truppe became a veritable beehive of theatrical adventure, a forum for numerous dramatists and a home for foremost stars of the Polish stage. Sonja Alemis (Lubaka), wife of Alexander Azro, Abraham Morewski and Joseph Buloff

(Bulkin) were its shining lights. In 1926, Zygmunt Turkow and his wife Ida Kaminska established the Wikt (Warshawer Yiddisher Kunst Teater) on Lesna No. 1, with a repertory that ranged from *It is Hard to Be a Jew* by Sholem Aleichem to Moliere's play *"L'Avare"* ("The Miser"), Victor Hugo's *The Bell Ringers of Notre Dame de Paris* and Ben Jonson's *Volpone*.

Dr. Michael Weichert, a pupil of Max Reinhardt, established a School for Dramatic Art in 1927 and among the lecturers were Dr. Isaac Schipper, Noah Prylucki and Dr. Raphael Mahler. Its graduates formed the nucleus of the new Yiddish Yugunt Teater ("Young Theatre"), established in 1933 at Dloga 19 by Clara Segalowicz (1896–1942). Among its outstanding productions was *Motke Ganoff* ("Motke the thief"). There were also a number of vaudeville theaters such as Azazel, Scala and Sambatyon in Warsaw, and Arrarat in Lodz. There was also a Marionette theatre in 1937. From New York came Maurice Schwartz to produce *Yoshe Kalb* and *Brothers Ashkenazi*, and from Palestine came the Habimah and the Ohel theater companies.

Alexander Hertz was one of the pioneers of the Polish film industry. However, his company "Sphinx" produced only Polish nationalistic films. It was Jechiel Baum, yeshiva *bachur* turned producer, who produced the first Yiddish film. The opening venture of Leo Films, headed by Leo Farbert and Jechiel Baum, was *Tekiyat Kaff* ("The Vow"), with Zygmunt Turkow in the leading role. So enthusiastic was the response that Leo Films went on to produce *Lamid Vavnik* ("One of the 36 Saints") and *Polish Woods*, in which scenes were deleted to avoid giving offence to the Chassidim of Kotzk.

JEWS IN ART

"Jews should have no place in the artistic life of Poland," ruled M. Skotinski, Director of the Arts Department of the Ministry of Education. So it was that Jewish participation in the cultural development of the country was spurned and growth of Jewish art forms stunted. Yet, without patrons and without grants, Polish Jewry produced several artists of international repute. The Jewish Art Society, founded in 1920 by Dr. Samuel Goldflamm, held over 125 exhibitions. Joseph Sandal, in his two-volume work *Umgekumene Yiddisher Kinstler in Polin* ("Yiddish Artists Who Perished in Poland"), lists 160 artists who flourished in the inter-war years.

A young painter of rare promise was Maurycy Gottlieb (1856–1879) who died at the age of twenty-three. He was just sixteen when he left his home in Drohobycz, Eastern Galicia, and went to study in Vienna. In seven brief years, he achieved wide recognition. After working with Makart in Vienna, he studied under the Polish painter Jan Matejko (1838–1893), nicknamed "the Great Barbarian." Under his guidance, Gottlieb painted historic scenes, "Boleslaw before the Gates of Kiev," "Casimir the Great admits the Jews into Poland," "The Prussians Paying Homage to King Sigismund." Matejko acclaimed young Maurycy as the "most promising disciple of Polish art" and as his "worthy successor." "The Praying Jew on the Day of Atonement" was Gottlieb's last and greatest canvas. In 1918, it was sold for 300,000 Austrian crowns.

His brother Leopold (1883–1934), born four years after Maurycy's death, was a fashionable portrait painter and Josef Pilsudski was among the famous personalities who sat for him. During the First World War, Gottlieb fought in the Polish Legion. His sketches of action on the Russian front are preserved in the Museum of Cracow. In 1926, he left Poland and settled in Paris where he died in 1934.

The Seidenbeutel family produced three painter sons: Joseph who died at the age of twenty-nine; Ephraim and Menasseh (b. June 17, 1903) whose paintings were exhibited in Italy and England. A painter who led rather a tumultuous life was Moses Appelbaum (1882–1934). Born in Amszynow, near Warsaw, he came to England as a young man and settled in Liverpool. When the First World War broke out he refused to join the army and was for a time imprisoned as a conscientious objector. After the war he moved to London, and in 1920 held an exhibition which was opened by Max Nordau. That year he was deported to Poland on a mere technicality, failure to register change of address.

Portrait painter Leopold Pilichowski (1867–1933) preferred the Paris scene and he there studied under Benjamin Constant (1845–1902). One of Pilichowski paintings, a panorama 16 feet by 8 feet of the opening of the Hebrew University in 1925, has one hundred and thirty recognizable characters. It was displayed in the Throne Room of Buckingham Palace in July, 1937. Another scene, "Yom Kippur," was chosen by the French Government for the Luxembourg Museum.

Lodz-born Arthur Szyk (1894–1951) specialized in book illustrations. He studied in the Académie Jullian in Paris and in the Cracow School of Fine Arts. He painted Jewish minters striking the first Polish coins, and the Jewish physicians sent to the Polish King Sigismund Augustus to heal Queen Barbara by Don Joseph Nasi, Duke of Naxos. He painted the death of Berek Joselowicz and

Bronislaw Mansperl, Jewish heroes in the army of Pilsudski. His thirty-eight studies of George Washington were
presented by the Polish Government to the United
States.[11]

Sculptors included Joseph Gabowitz (1862–1939), born
in Kolna, Lomza. He studied at Warsaw as well as at the
St. Petersburg Art Academy, and in Paris under the
celebrated French sculptor Auguste Rodin (1841–1917).
One of his pieces, "Self-Defence," was awarded a prize in
the Paris Exhibition of 1898. In 1921, Gabowitz returned
to Warsaw.

Henryk Kuna (1893–1945) received a prize for the
memorial of Adam Mickiewicz and Henryk Barczynski,
and was awarded first prize in the International Red Cross
Exhibition in 1924. Among notable women artists were
Natalia Landau (b. 1907), Rachel Sutzkover (b. 1905),
Amelia Menkes (b. 1897) and Hadasa Gurewitz (b. 1911).

Musicians of note included the violinist Bronislaw
Huberman (1882–1947), and the pianist Arthur Rubin-
stein (b. 1886), who spent a short time studying with
Paderewski at Morgesin in Switzerland. Pianist and composer Ignacy Friedman (1882–1948) studied at Vienna
under Leschetizky. When Vienna organized a series of
concerts in 1927 to celebrate the centenary of Beethoven's
death, Friedman, Huberman and Casals were invited to
play the master's trio. Friedman wrote over ninety works,
mainly for pianoforte, but also some chamber music. He
prepared the new edition of Chopin's works for Breitkopf
& Hartel of Leipzig.[12]

Although the medical schools strove to make medicine
a closed shop for Jewry, several Jewish doctors achieved
remarkable results in medical research. Dr. Leon Pines
(1867–1938) known as the "physician of the poor man,"

was a famous opthalmic surgeon. Nephew of Zionist author Jechiel Michael Pines (1842–1912), Pines studied under Marklakoff and Silex of Berlin. "The physician of the poor," he was one of the pioneers in the study of the retina. Dr. Samuel Goldflam (1852–1932) was the acknowledged "father of neurology." Dr. Maksymillian Rose was Poland's outstanding brain specialist.

As early as 1919 Captain Wright reported that "Jewish professors, however able, have been turned out of the university."[13] Among the few Jews who penetrated the scholastic sanctum was Hugo Steinhaus (b. 1887), Dean of the Mathematical Faculty of Lemberg and joint editor of *Studia Mathematica*. Dr. Marceli Handelsmann (1882–1940), a member of the French Academy of Moral and Political Sciences, became editor of the Political Review in 1926. Professor Maurycy Allerhand (1868–1942) of Lwow and Professor Rafal Taubenschlag of Cracow were authorities in the field of law.

In Polish political life Herman Diamand (1860–1931) emerged as a key figure. Born in Lwow, then part of the Austro-Hungarian Empire, he entered the Austrian Parliament as one of the leaders of the Polish Socialist Party. He retained his Socialistic affiliations until the foundation of the Polish Republic. Then he became a member of the Polish Constituent Parliament. Diamand was returned to every subsequent Parliament from 1919 to 1931. In 1928 he was elected President of the Central Council of the Socialist Party as successor to Daszynski, who became President of the Seym. Diamand played an important part in the Second International where he represented the Polish Socialist Party for a number of years. His seventieth birthday was celebrated by the Socialist press on an international scale. The London

Daily Herald published an appreciative editorial, and such notables as Prime Minister James Ramsay MacDonald sent messages of congratulation.[14]

Another prominent labour leader was Herman Lieberman (1870–1941). He denounced the abuses of dictatorship and in September 1930 he was thrown into the military prison of Brest. When Poland fell he became Vice-Chairman of the Polish National Council and in 1941 he was appointed Minister of Justice in the Polish Government-in-exile in London. "The rule of law is essential for freedom," he said, "just as the existence of freedom is essential to the rule of law. . . . People cannot be thrown about like balls nor can inferior elements be dumped into somebody else's national backyard."[15]

At the outbreak of the Second World War there were at least one hundred and fifty thousand Jews in the Polish Army. Thirty-two thousand were killed in action before the downfall of Poland, and sixty-one thousand were captured by the Germans. The only unbaptised Jew to achieve high military rank was Brigadier General Bernard Mond of Cracow.

A handful of Jews were prominent in the realm of finance. Raphael Szereszewski was one of the richest men in Poland. His bank, M. D. Szereszewski, established in 1891, became a symbol of stability. In 1931 a rumour spread that the bank was "in trouble," and depositors flocked there *en masse*, demanding their money back. The bank mobilised its entire staff in the Deposit Department and worked round the clock to meet all demands in full. Complete confidence was restored and after a few days many of the deposits were paid back in to the bank. Szereszewski was a member of the Jewish Agency, a member of the World Jewish Congress, Chairman of the

Jewish Merchant Association, and Chairman of the Anti-Nazi Boycott Committee. There were few Jewish institutions which the Bank did not support and it covered the deficit of the Mirer and Brisker Yeshivot. Yet the founder, rich Raphael, died in New York on April 28, 1948, a poor forgotten man.

As usual, Jewish philanthropy far exceeded Jewish wealth. Hypolit Wawelberg (1843–1901) donated 600,000 rubles to build low-rental homes for workers, both Jewish and Christian. Together with Stanislaw Rotwand (1839–1916), he founded the Technical High School in Warsaw. There were many philanthropists among the men of wealth but most remarkable of all was the way in which the poor gave to the poor. Every street was a social welfare state in miniature where neighbour helped neighbour even when the gift was no more than hot soup or stale bread. So in a hostile hateful climate, the Jews practised charity and loving kindness.

10

Starving Children and Anti-Shechitah Laws

I spent this afternoon in the poorest district. I have seen nightmare-sights that hurt even to remember. Children sit in the gutters begging, singing their pitiful little Yiddish songs. Their tiny half-starved bodies are covered with rags. I am told that begging is becoming the children's profession. They prefer that to going to school where they receive but one scant meal. Their eyes alone reflect a spark of hope, for the rest of their countenances bespeak suffering and privations.

These notes were written by Dr. Boris David Bogen (1869–1929) the American social worker, after a visit to Poland in 1919.[1]

Conditions did not improve. Jewish families spent an average of ten zlotys a week on food.[2] Twenty to 25 per cent of them had no means at all of subsistence.[3] Between 60 and 80 per cent of Jewish workers were out of work. For thousands "seventy *groschen* a day" represented an average wage. The state paid a form of dole, but only to ex-workers discarded by companies employing more than five hands. Since most of the Jews were occupied in tiny workshops or with piecework, only about 10 per cent qualified for government relief.

The employment picture in Brzeziny was typical. In this small industrial town 75 per cent of the Jewish population was engaged in tailoring. Only 10 to 12 per cent had work, and even they were employed only three or four days a week. Their houses were cold, for fuel was too costly. Food was scant, just potatoes and salt. In hundreds of little towns this situation was duplicated, for Poland itself was in sore economic straits.

In 1929, the national income was 600 zlotys per head, as against 2,100 in France, 2,500 in Germany, 4,200 in the United Kingdom and 5,800 in the United States. "The Jews, being an urban element, entered the newly-born Polish republic in much worse state than any other predominately rural national minority."[4] The situation of the power of the peasants brought thousands of Jewish tradesmen to the verge of ruin. For the Jewish masses, bread was the crucial question. Of the 40,000 families in Lodz, 15,488 received food and other aid from the *Kehilla*. Only 11 to 13 per cent of the Jewish population were able to pay their communal taxes.[5] Nor were conditions better in Warsaw where 60,000 Jews appealed for relief and were provided with *matzot*, potatoes, fuel and clothing. Similar provisions were made for 41 per cent of the Jews in Vilna,[6] and 47 per cent of the Jews in Lwow.

Little children were the chief sufferers and the pawns in the painful maneuvers of direst poverty. In many large towns, desperate beggars would "hire" a child or two, and coach them to play only-too-true-to-life roles. "Have pity, Jews!" wailed these tiny tattered waifs. "I have no mother. I have no father. I am hungry. I am barefooted. Give me work. Give me bread." For thirty-five thousand school children, a glass of milk and a slice of bread provided by their teachers constituted the day's main meal. Seven-year-olds would pocket these morsels and take them home to hungry families. Tuberculosis and mental disorders increased alarmingly, and on June 18, 1933, *Toz* reported that forty thousand Jewish children urgently needed medical care. Many children were left in the streets or on a door step in most cases "with a note from the unfortunate mother appealing that it be taken care of until she earned enough to be able to support it herself."[7]

The carefully planned campaign for eliminating Jews from industry and commerce systematically denied them all means of livelihood. Young people were hedged in by ever mounting barricades, without scope, without hope. "I have never seen such poverty," wrote Professor Norman Bentwich, formerly Attorney General for Palestine, "such a struggle for life as I have seen in Warsaw and in the smaller towns of Poland."[8] Even the anti-Semitic Dmowski conceded this fact. "The rapid pauperisation of the small-town Jew who was never excessively rich, is an irrefutable fact."[9] According to the 1931 census, 28.2 per cent of Poland's unemployed workers were Jews.

Suicides were commonplace. Almost every day the newspapers reported two or three such incidents. On the initiative of the rabbi of Zwolen, a league was formed specifically to combat the "suicide philosophy" that was gaining so many adherents among the despairing Jews. Rabbis warned their congregations that the Jewish religion strictly forbade suicide and anyone who committed it forfeited his portion in the world to come.[10]

"The Jew is a thief," was a typical piece of causeless calumny, yet statistics plainly disprove it. Of the 358,036 convicted in the years 1932–1938, only 23,131 or 6.5 per cent were Jews.[11] Jewish youngsters constituted 5½ per cent of the juveniles convicted.[12] One thousand one hundred fifty-one murders were committed in Poland between 1932 and 1934; 19 (or 7 per cent) were committed by Jews.

Convicted for assault were 44 Jews per million inhabitants, whilst the number for non-Jews was 213. In 1931, Polish Jewry numbered 3,113,993. Compared with the census taken ten years earlier, this constituted an increase of 258,615. By the outbreak of World War II, this figure was close to 3,510,000.

As compared with the total population of Poland, the census figures showed a decrease from 10.5 per cent to 9.8 per cent for the period 1921–1931,[13] a decline due to migration and a lowering birth-rate.

In 1931, 2,380,075 Jews were urban-domiciled, comprising 76.4 per cent of all Jews in Poland.[14] There were 808,327 Jews living in Galicia, 1,730,600 in Congress Poland, and 616,150 in the territory recovered from Russia. Every fourth Jew lived in one of the five big towns of Warsaw, Lodz, Vilna, Bialystok and Lublin. Over one-sixth of all Polish Jewry lived in two communities. There were 35 communities of over 10,000 Jews:[15] 25 were located in Polish districts, 10 in districts with a Ukrainian majority, and 5 in districts with a Russian majority.[16] In 1931, there were 352,659 Jews (30.1 per cent) in Warsaw, 202,497 (35.5 per cent) in Lodz, and 99,595 (31.9 per cent) in Lwow.

Early marriages were a thing of the past. Thirty-four and five-tenths per cent of the females married before the age of twenty-five years, 39.9 per cent married between twenty-five and twenty-nine, while only 3.5 per cent married under the age of nineteen.[17] Inter-marriage was hardly known in Poland; in 1927, it accounted for 21.33 per cent of marriages in Germany, 12.4 per cent in Hungary, but a mere 0.15 per cent in Poland.[18] Infant mortality, too, was low:[19] in 1937, this was 136 per 1,000 live births for the total population, but only 46 for the Jews.

RELIEF MEASURES

A quarter of Polish Jews made a comfortable living. A half managed with difficulty to support themselves and the remaining quarter suffered fearful privations.[20] To cope with the desperate shortage of medical facilities, the American Joint Distribution Committee set up some five hundred hospitals and clinics. Between 1915 and 1939, American Jews sent 53 million dollars through the Joint Distribution Committee, while an additional 4 million dollars streamed in from private sources. In 1937 alone, the American Joint Distribution Committee & Ort granted $945,000 for Poland.[21]

To a lesser degree British Jews, too, sent relief to Poland. In 1935, the Board of Deputies of British Jews launched a united appeal for Polish Jewry signed by Chief Rabbi Hertz, Haham Gaster, Neville Laski, Avigdor Goldsmid, Nahum Sokolow: "Utter destitution has for many years overwhelmed the Jewish population in Poland. That destitution has often been described but in the opinion of competent observers never adequately. The short and terrible fact is that nearly one million Jews are given over to actual starvation."[22]

"Credit would be issued by the state banks to state institutions," declared Bartel, "without any question being raised of religion or nationality." This affirmation of credit equality was as meaningless in Poland as political guarantees. Two government banks—Bank Polski and the Bank of Agriculture—extended credit. Yet of the 70,-000,000 zlotys advanced by the Bank of Poland in 1931, the Jews received less than 2,000,000 zlotys. So they struggled valiantly to help themselves. Backed by the Joint Distribution Committee of banks, free loans were organized. With a capital of 250,000,000 dollars, and a yearly turnover of 4,500,000 dollars, they granted 185,-000 loans amounting to 3.5 million dollars in 1937.[23] Everyone in Poland used *Wekslech* ("Letters of Exchange"). Eighty per cent of the Jewish workers received *Wekslech* in lieu of payment, and these became almost a second currency which could be sold below cost in moments of crisis.

Expediency spurred the phenomenal development of the Jewish co-operative movement. In 1922, there were 158 co-operatives with 65,751 members. By 1933, there were 545 co-operatives and a capital of 66,000,000 zlotys.[24] On December 19, 1934, all Jewish co-operatives in Poland united in self-protection. They were ill-equipped to meet the competition of the non-Jewish co-operatives which received extensive credit from the government. The union that Polish Jewry could not achieve politically was to some extent achieved in economic terms. By 1939, the Co-operative Union owned 702 co-operative people's banks, 42 merchant's banks, 17 agricultural co-operatives and 13 producers co-operatives, a total of 774 co-operatives.[25]

WELFARE AGENCIES

The *Toz* (*Tow. Ochrony Zdrowia Ludnosci Zydowskiej w Polsce*) was a welfare agency formed by the American Joint Distribution Committee in 1921. In 1939, it had branches in 50 towns, 368 medical institutions, 43 polytechnics, 41 dental clinics, 18 tuberculosis clinics, 8 x-ray clinics, as well as maternity and child welfare clinics, 30 summer camps for school children and 15 day nurseries. This was a time when 60 per cent of the Polish Jews needed more than subsidies—they needed bread. The basic elements of nutrition were lacking and increasing demands were made upon Toz to supply free meals, especially to school children. Of the 14,216 children sent by Toz to holiday homes, 56.5 per cent were severely under-nourished, 47 per cent were in poor physical condition, 11 per cent suffered from scurvy, 41 per cent were anaemic and 44 per cent suffered from glandular irregularities. Only 3.5 per cent had received adequate nourishment at home.

"The cure of the sick is a great *Mitzvah* ["good deed"], but the prevention of sickness is a greater one," was the motto of the Toz. In 1928, Toz organized a Jewish medical congress and also held a national health week. It arranged lectures for adults and talks for children. It published two journals, one for general readership the other for physicians. It also issued tens of thousands of popular booklets on different aspects of health and hygiene. In the course of fifteen years it organized 2,730 lectures on medicine for 424,227 listeners. On November 29, 1937, *Toz* celebrated fifteen years of fruitful activity, and Dr. Leon Wulman, the secretary, reported that 19 million zlotys had been ploughed back in investments, an annual average of 1,400,000 zlotys. A Joint Distribution Committee subsidy met 15 per cent of this budget.

Twenty-seven thousand Jewish children were maintained by *Centos* (*Zwiazek Tow. Opieki nad Sierotami Żydowskiemi*, "The Union of Societies for the Protection of Jewish Orphans"). Founded in 1923, Centos had a budget of over 3,000,000 zlotys in 1936. Paying regular dues, 45,000 patrons contributed more than 75 per cent. In 1938, Centos controlled 105 orphanages, 21 specialized schools and 177 holiday camps.[26] It published a monthly *Dos Shutzloze kind* ("The Helpless Child") and *Undzer Kind* ("Our child"), edited by Abraham Levinson.

A sister organization, the Central Organization for the Protection of Jewish children in Poland (*Organizacja Centralna Opieki nad Dzieckiem Zydowskiem w Polsce*) was founded in 1926, to provide summer camps for under-privileged youngsters.

Ort (initials of Russian *Obstchestvo Resemeslenovo Truda*, "Society for the Encouragement of Handicraft"), established in Russia in 1880 by Baron Horace de Günz-burg, branched into Poland in 1921. Setting up industrial schools and vocational courses and model workshops, it trained some fifty thousand Jewish artisans. Products of Ort's carpentry and locksmith schools were displayed at the All Polish Industrial Exhibition in Vilna, and were awarded first-class prizes.

There were 47 Jewish hospitals in Poland. The largest was the Warsaw hospital at *Czyste* Street with 1,490 beds, and an annual budget of 2,200,000 zlotys. It employed 147 physicians, 59 interns, 119 nurses and 6 pharmacists.[27] The country as a whole was desperately in need of hos-pitals. Yet even here the Jewish community suffered from governmental interference. Arbitrarily, a physician of mediocre calibre was set at the head of the great Warsaw hospital. Elsewhere, on pretext of "interchange," non-Jews replaced Jews in Jewish hospitals, while Jewish doctors were debarred from non-Jewish hospitals.

The various Jewish political parties developed departments for physical culture. The largest sports organization was the Maccabi which was affiliated to the World Union of Jewish Athletic Organizations founded in 1894. Under Maccabi auspices, international Jewish sports festivals were held in Czechoslovakia (1929), Holland (1930) and the Holy Land (1932 and 1936). The Hapoel ("The Workman") flourished under the wings of the Poale Zion, the Morgenstern ("The Morning Star") under the Bund and the Gwiazda ("Star") under the Poale Zion left.

Through the gloom glowed kindly lights—societies for helping the poor, the sick, the orphan, the widow, the aged and the disabled. Every town had its Linat Hazedek ("Charity Loans"), a Jewish "Red Cross" which provided medicines free of charge and surgical appliances on loan. Bikkur Cholim ("Visiting the Sick") societies ministered to the sick and carried these ministrations right into the sufferer's home. In Warsaw the Bet Lechem ("House of Bread") society distributed parcels of fish, meat, bread and eggs. The Vaad Hazalah ("Jewish Rescue Committee") helped to rehabilitate impoverished artisans and businessmen by means of interest-free loans.

Unique was the society known as Gut Shabbas Yiddelech ("Good Sabbath, Jews"). Its leaders were labourers, porters and drivers. All week long, they struggled to piece together a few inadequate pence. But on the sabbath they dedicated themselves to even less fortunate ones. In groups of three they would enter the Jewish courtyard every sabbath morning. Placing the huge empty baskets on the ground they would exclaim: "Gut Shabbas Yiddelech." Instantly windows opened and householders responded generously. Soon the baskets were heaped high with bread, cakes, meat and fish which were promptly

distributed to hungry families. Few hearts remained un-
moved at the cry "Good Sabbath, little Jews."

ANTI-SHECHITAH LEGISLATION

Kashrut is one of the major pillars of traditional Judaism and at the very heart of *kashrut* lies *Shechitah*, the
law that regulates with meticulous detail the slaughter
of animals for human consumption. Throughout the ages,
enemies of Israel have attacked *Shechitah* in the attempt
to prove it barbaric. Yet a large body of experts attest, to
this day, to the speed and humanity of the method of
slaughter prescribed by Jewish law.

Predictively, the Seym, too, seized upon this ideal ve-
hicle for harassment and in May, 1923, deputy Dymowski
and Father Wyrebowski introduced a motion prohibiting
Shechitah. "The method of ritual slaughter," they asserted, "is only a pretext to collect unjust tribute from
Christians for the benefit of Jews. It has nothing in common with the principles of hygiene and scientific sanitary
inspection; on the contrary, it is opposed to them."[28] The
motion was defeated yet the anti-*Shechitah* propaganda
was maintained, motivated not by humanitarianism but by
the fact that "the meat and cattle trade is in Jewish hands
and that is not a desirable state of affairs."

On February 7, 1936, a bill of so-called humane
slaughter was introduced by deputy Janina Prystor, wife
of the Senate speaker and former Prime Minister
Aleksander Prystor (1874–1941). Article I stated in part:
"When slaughtering in public or private slaughterhouses,
horned cattle, swine, sheep, goats, horses, asses, mules, or
dogs, they shall be stunned before being bled."[29] Prystor
based her case on a booklet *Ubój rytualny w swietle Biblji*

i Talmudu ("Ritual Slaughtering in the Light of the Bible and Talmud"), written by Father Stanislaw Trzeciak and published in Warsaw in 1935. "It is not my business to care for the Jewish religion or for *kosher* meat for Jews," declared Madame Prystor. "I want, however, to make it clear that the Jewish *Shechitah* is against my religion. It is against the honour of my people, against our ethical conceptions and against our pockets."[30]

Prystor's supporters alleged that the non-Jews had hitherto been required to subsidize *Shechitah* to the extent of millions of zlotys a year. They disregarded the unpalatable fact that wide spread boycott and anti-Jewish legislation had so impoverished Jewry that the entire annual income of all the 817 communities did not amount to more than £1,500,000.[31] The Prystor bill, a near replica to an earlier Nazi-sponsored Bavarian anti-*Shechitah* law, was adopted almost unanimously.

Yielding to pressure by the Jewish community and other minorities, the government grudgingly permitted *Shechitah* for a limited quantity of meat "for groups in the population whose religion requires a special method of slaughtering." *Shechitah* was prohibited in areas where Jews numbered less than 3 per cent of the general population.[32] In permitted areas, special abattoirs were to be used, and licences for Jewish butchers were only to be issued to qualified persons possessing an artisan's card, which few Jews were able to acquire.[33]

On January 1, 1937, the *Shechitah* Law became effective, "a new year present for the Jews," as the Endek press laconically reported.[34] The Warsaw quota of *kosher* meat for January was fixed at 1,900,000 kilograms, which would ordinarily have meant 5 kilograms of meat per head. Since certain portions of slaughtered animals are not consumed by Jews, and a certain number of animals are on diverse grounds disqualified as *trefa* (ritually unfit), the ration was more realistically interpreted as amounting to 2 kilograms per person.[35] Of cattle killed in 1937, 23.1 per cent were slaughtered according to Jewish ritual. In the following year the figure was 20 per cent.

Still, even now, the anti-Semites were not satisfied. On March 9, 1937, Andrzej Wierzbicki complained in the Senate that the Jews were still in control of the meat industry. In vain, Minister of Agriculture Juliusz Poniatowski pleaded for patience:

... why are you so disturbed? The law has been in force only two months, and you are already certain that no benefit will accrue from it! . . . I am convinced that in a little while longer, you will be able to see that the meat business has come into Polish hands and ritual slaughter has been restricted to the limits required by those who need a special method of slaughter.[36]

On January 31, 1938, Deputy Dudzinski introduced a bill calling for the abolition of *Shechitah*.[37] Polish Jewry protested. At a meeting of three hundred rabbis, a "Fortnight Without Meat" was proclaimed. From March 14 to March 30, Jews were required to refrain from all meat (except poultry which was not affected by the bill) even on the Sabbath, and to observe a day of fasting. Polish Jewry complied to the letter. All Jewish butchers and meat factories remained closed. During the specified sixteen days, meat was absent from every Jewish home and restaurant. Even the Bund joined the ranks of the meatless ones, and Jewish newspapers published special meatless menus.

These demonstrations did not deter the Seym. On March 25, 1939, it adopted the bill outlawing *Shechitah* by the progressive reduction of the *kosher* meat quota over the next three years. "We desire," declared Dudziński, "to plunge a knife into the vital nerve of Polish Jewry and to make their lives unbearable."[38]

Only the dissolution of the Seym during the Czechoslovakian crisis on September 13, 1938, prevented the endorsement of the bill. *Shechitah* was abolished by the Nazis on October 26, 1939, a sinister step in their calculated program of total annihilation.

11

"Get Thee Out of Thy Father's House"

"If my country can do without me, I can do without her. The world is large enough," declared Huig van Grotius (1583–1645), the Dutch jurist who founded international law; and there were actual times when the Jews could have echoed these proud words. During the second half of the nineteenth century and the first decade of the twentieth century, the world was actually "large enough" to provide new homes for the tempest-tossed Jews of Eastern Europe. Between 1830 and 1930, a total of 4,-215,000 Jews emigrated from Eastern Europe. Some two-thirds, about 2,900,000, reached the United States, while 800,000 were received by South America, 260,000 by England and 140,000 by France.[1] Between 1901 and 1914 the number of emigrating Jews from Russia, Rumania and Galicia reached 1,602,441; 84 per cent of them headed for the United States, 5 per cent for Canada, 5.5 per cent for Argentina and the remaining 4.6 per cent scattered around the globe.[2]

The Poles, whom Israel Zangwill termed "beggars on horseback," regarded the Jews as "outsiders," "aliens," "surplus citizens." An editorial in the *Gazeta Warszawska*[3] reflected this attitude with brutal clarity. "All Poland's troubles are the result of the centuries of Jewish invasion. If we want to be a great independent nation, we must get rid of the Jews as the Spaniards did in the fifteenth century.[4]

This policy was proclaimed from every political platform. It was endorsed by the General Council of the Polish Labour Party, by the Radical Party of Tytus Filipowicz, by the General Council of the Polish Conservative Party, by the All Polish Congress of Peasants, and by the Council of the Camp of National Unity.[5] On December 31, 1938, 116 of the 208 deputies of the Polish Seym, headed by General Skwarczynski, demanded that the government take "instant measures to increase the emigration of the Jews from Poland." "The Government of the Polish Republic," replied the Premier, General Slawoj-Skladkowski on January 23, 1939, "agrees to the interpellation to the effect that one of the most effective measures of solving the Jewish question in Poland is a considerable reduction in the number of Jews through emigration." He assured the deputies that the government would use its influence to obtain outlets for emigration by international action, and would not accept the notion that new outlets will be opened only "as a result of catastrophes from which the Jewish people suffer."[6]

The government needed little persuasion. According to Deputy-Speaker Colonel Buguslaw Miedzinski, "Poland has room for only fifty thousand Jews. The remaining three million must emigrate."[7] "The Jewish question can be solved only by the emigration of the Jews from Poland," echoed the pro-government paper *Czas*.[8] "This surplus of Jews," declared *Polska Zbrojna*, mouthpiece of Generalissimo Smigly-Rydz, "hangs like a millstone round

the neck of Poland and exercises a most fatal influence on
the economic development of our country."[9] "The Jewish
problem is one of the most important questions in
Poland," expounded the Camp of National Unity, "primarily because of the excessive number of Jews. It is for
this reason that the Jewish problem can be solved prin-
cipally by emigration."[10]

The crisis over Poland's "surplus Jews" received
world-wide ventilation. At a meeting of the economic
committee of the Assembly of the League of Nations on
5 October, 1936, the Polish representative, Adam Charles
Rose, proposed the convocation of an International
Emigration Conference under the auspices of the International Labour Office "to deal with this problem."[11]
Early in July, 1938, the Polish League of Nations Society
submitted a resolution to the League's International
Federation Conference at Copenhagen reiterating its demand for a special convention on the Jewish question. At
the Political and Legal Commission, the Polish representative passionately urged Europe's six million Jews to
emigrate *en masse*. He proposed the creation of a Jewish
State or Dominion in Palestine or in some other territory.[12]

The League of Nations was not Poland's only international platform. An official communique on November
18, 1938, recorded that Poland had informed the American government on several occasions of the need for the
emigration of Polish Jews, and that instructions had been
given to Polish diplomatic representatives in London
and other capitals to relay this message to the heads of
state.[13]

Poland sent observers to the Evian Refugee Conference
convened by President Roosevelt on July 6–12, 1938, at
which 32 countries and 39 private organizations were

represented.[14] Dr. Stephen S. Wise, president of the Executive Committee of the World Jewish Congress, urged the Conference "to reaffirm the principle of equality for Jews in all countries and to remind the states of Eastern Europe that they have no right to create new masses of refugees through driving their Jewish citizens out of their boundaries."[15]

Poland could not induce the Evian Refugee Conference to study Polish-Jewish emigration,[16] and the conference was a dismal failure. "If the thirty-two nations that call themselves democracies cannot agree on a plan to rescue a few hundred thousand refugees," deplored the *New York Times*, "then it is futile to hope that it can cooperate in anything." The Inter-Government Committee set up in London under the chairmanship of Lord Winterton could do little to help in a world "divided into countries in which the Jews cannot remain and countries which they must not enter."

Jewish emigration became one of the main responsibilities of Colonel Beck who enlisted Rumanian cooperation. After a three-day visit to Warsaw, Rumanian Foreign Minister Gafencu "authorised Colonel Beck to discuss Jewish emigration on behalf of his country as well." In London, Beck stressed the Polish government's anxiety that Palestine be kept open to Polish Jews. The British government replied with a counter promise to urge Dominion governments, particularly Australia, to open the doors to Polish Jewish immigrants.[17]

A statement issued in London on April 6, 1939, used terms characteristically noncommittal:

In the course of recent conversations in London, M. Beck expressed the desire that any international effort for the treatment of the Jewish problem should be extended to that of the Jews in Poland, and that the Jewish emigrants from Poland should have their due share in any opportunity of settlement which may be found. Monsieur Beck at the same time, at the request of the Rumanian Government, drew attention to the similar problem existing in Rumania. Monsieur Beck was assured that His Majesty's Government fully appreciated the difficulties to which he had referred, and would at any time be ready to examine with the Polish and Rumanian Governments proposals arising in Poland and Rumania which are part of a larger problem.[18]

In the years 1926–1935, a total of 186,365 Jews emigrated from Poland, nearly 100,000 settling on the American continent and 68,142 heading for Palestine.[19] Between 1921 and 1937, Jewish emigrants numbered 400,000, a proportion five times higher than among the total population.[20] From 1931 to 1935, the average fell to only 17,000, a mere trickle, while in 1937 and 1938, the figure declined to 8,900 and 9,200 respectively. The Jewish immigration of 30,000 in 1934 and 1935 cost the Bank of Poland from 45,000,000 to 50,000,000 zlotys,[21] a financial commitment Poland was not prepared to accept. It demanded that the cost be defrayed by sympathizers outside.

Woahin zoll ich gein? ("Where shall I go?") is a popular song that reflects a harrowing and humiliating dilemma. One after another, the great democracies of the world set up selective emigration policies which totally debarred the Eastern European exiles. The world grew smaller as liberal traditions proved themselves illiberal after all. The years after the First World War saw the promulgation of the American Immigration Quota Act. This set the limit for annual immigration at 3 per cent of the total population of the United States on the basis of the census of 1910. In 1921, America restricted the

Polish quota to 40,000. In 1926, this figure was diminished to 6,000 per year. In human terms, the results were catastrophic—despair, rejection, suffering. The courtyard of the American consulate in Warsaw was thronged with Jewish applicants averaging 700 to 1,000 a day. Most of them were turned away. Other countries were quick to follow this convenient American precedent and even improved upon it. A Canadian Order in Council, dated February 23, 1923, inaugurated a closed-door policy debarring all immigrants from Eastern Europe.[22] Similarly, the South African Immigration Act of May 1st, 1930, put an end to Jewish immigration.

Woahin zoll ich gein? comes the plaintive refrain. In the third decade of the twentieth century, Palestine was the only country in the world to which the Jew came with International sanction "as a right and not on sufferance." Under the Mandate, it was the duty of the Administration, "while ensuring that the rights and position of other sections of the population are not prejudiced to facilitate Jewish immigration under suitable conditions."[23]

The resettlement of Palestine as a Jewish national home had been one of the objectives of Polish foreign policy, in one of its few redeeming features. Poland had never placed obstacles in the way of the Zionist organizations, and new statutes legalizing Zionism were eventually formulated.[24] On March 31, 1926, Prime Minister Count Aleksander Skrzynski (1882–1931) wrote to Nahum Sokolow: "The Polish Government is following with interest the progress made by the Zionist organization in its effort to resurrect the national individuality and culture of the Jews in Palestine."[25]

As a practical expression of sympathy, Poland concluded an agreement with the Jewish Agency facilitating the transfer of funds on behalf of settlers.[26] On an international level, Poland frequently championed Jewish rights in Palestine and expressed vehement opposition to the British White Paper of May 17, 1939, which restricted Jewish immigration to ten thousand a year for the next five years. "Palestine is today the only outlet for the Jewish masses in Eastern Europe," reasoned Tytus Kormarnicki, Polish delegate to the League of Nations. "The Polish Government therefore supports the proposal to establish a Jewish State in Palestine provided that it is large enough to absorb a large and compact Jewish immigration."[27] In reinforcement, Beck promised Polish support for the Jewish claim to "as large a part of Palestine as it is possible to give them."[28]

For the most part, Polish Jewish immigration to Palestine during the 1920's showed a steady upsurge: 2,552 (1920), 1,800 (1921), 2,631 (1922), 2,175 (1923), 5,670 (1924). Peak years were 1925 (17,115), 1934 (16,-829) and 1935 (29,407).[29] In all, Poland provided 132,203 of the 358,900 Jews who entered Palestine between 1919 and 1942.[30]

Jabotinsky, passionate advocate of Jewish emigration from Poland, became *persona grata* with the Polish Government. He regarded Eastern Europe as a "zone of Jewish distress," and a "danger zone." "Several million Jews must in the nearest future evacuate the main centres of Eastern Europe," Jabotinsky declared at the Fifth World Revisionist Conference in Vienna in August, 1932, "and set up a national Jewish State in Palestine."[31] He broadcast these views on April 28, 1933, on the Polish government-controlled radio in Warsaw,[32] and urged Beck to bring up the Jewish problem at the League. On September 10, 1936 Jabotinsky recommended that Poland take the inita-

tive in summoning an international conference of governments interested in the mass emigration of Jews from their
respective countries.[33] In 1934, a Revisionist petition to
the government signed by 217,000 Polish Jews declared:
"The only way of normalising our existence is for us and
our families to settle in Palestine. We ask the Polish
Government to intervene with the Mandatory Power so
that the unjust immigration restrictions may be revised."[34]

Many Jewish leaders condemned Jabotinsky's attitude
because it pandered to Polish intolerance. At a time when
every avenue was closed, and when the position of Polish
Jews grew daily more desperate, Jabotinsky was rein-
forcing Poland's premise that the Jewish masses were fit
only for expulsion. "Mr. Jabotinsky and other Jews who
advocate similar views are apostates," accused Dr. Stephen
Wise.[35] "What Jabotinsky is now doing in Poland goes
beyond all limits," thundered Sholem Asch. "One has to
have a heart of stone to be devoid of any feeling for
human sufferings, to be so brazen as to come to Poland
with such proposals at such a terrible time. Heaven help
a people with such leaders."[36] The Jewish press was
especially outspoken. "The Premier of Poland," wrote
Dr. Samuel Margoshes, editor of *Der Tog* ("The Day"),
one of New York's foremost Yiddish dailies, "wishes to
throw out three and a half million Jews as if they were
so much rubbish."[37]

This Polish obsession with Jewish emigration was seriously frustrated by the restricted quotas of the Western
world and the difficulties of settlement in Palestine. In
desperation, Poland sought out new territories on which
to unload her hapless repudiated citizens.

Most important of the abortive and ill-sorted attempts
to find them "a place under the sun" was the Madagascar
scheme. This island in the Indian Ocean, under French

suzerainty since 1896, had a population of 3,797,796 in 1936. The possibility of dispatching thither "a considerable number of compatriots" was first mooted in 1926 by Count Chlapowski, Polish Ambassador in France to M. Marcel Olivier, Governor-general of Madagascar.[38] Whilst the Polish Peasant Party reacted violently to the idea of peasant emigration to Madagascar, it was most favorably disposed to sending Jews there.[39]

In the autumn of 1936, Colonel Beck discussed the issue with Premier Leon Blum (1872–1950) who agreed in principle. "We are in favour of colonization in Madagascar," conceded French Minister for Colonies, M. Marius Mouter, "because of our liberal attitude towards friendly nations who have no colonial possessions in which to settle their own citizens. But this should not be interpreted to mean that we wish to provoke an exodus of people."[40]

In April, 1937, the Polish government, with the acquiescence of the French Colonial Ministry, sent to Madagascar a group of experts headed by Major Mieczyslaw B. Lepecki, president of the International Colonization Society, Solomon Dyk, an agricultural engineer, and Leon Alter, executive director of Jeas (Polish branch of *Hicem*). Their official report was never published. Yet, according to a statement of Major Lepecki published in the *Gazeta Polska* on January 9, 1938, the commission agreed that the Central District, an area of about 170,000 square kilometers, was climatically suitable for settlement by Jewish emigrants from Central Europe.[41] In a later newspaper interview, Lepecki maintained that "from five thousand to seven thousand peasant families could be settled in that region making a total of twenty-five to thirty-five thousand people. It would cost 30,000 francs to establish each family."[42]

In a book entitled "Madagaskar, Kraj, Ludzie Kolonizacja" (published in Warsaw in 1938), the Major proposed Ankaizina, a district of North Central Madagascar, for immediate settlement. He estimated total tillable land at 240,000 acres, enough to provide a livelihood for forty to sixty thousand people.

The two Jewish members of the commission did not, however, share his optimism. "The colonization of the Jews," reported Leon Alter, "will be particularly difficult since they consist of an urban element which is not bound to the soil and which requires a long period of instruction and assistance to prevent them overrunning the whole island which could eventually lead to their being deported from Madagascar." He also noted that any attempt to settle Jews on the island would meet with wide opposition from its current inhabitants. A sinister footnote was the fact that, in spite of the high birth rate, the native population had dwindled by more than 14 per cent in twenty years, primarily because of endemic diseases.[43] Similar misgivings were expressed by Solomon Dyk in his personal report to the American Jewish Committee.[44]

Warmest support for the Madagascar plan came from Nazi Germany which even attempted to float an international loan to finance the scheme. On May 15, 1940, Himmler wrote: "I hope that, thanks to the possibility of a large emigration of all Jews to Africa or some other colony, I shall live to see the day when the concept of Jew will have completely disappeared from Europe." A blueprint was prepared by the chief of the Jewish division in the Foreign Office, Dr. Franz Rademacher, but by then Europe was aflame with the fires of World War II and the Madagascar project was doomed.[45]

By the end of 1938, three committees had been formed under the sponsorship of the Polish Government to work

for Jewish emigration: the Committee for Jewish Colonization (*Zydowskie Tow. Kolonizacyjne*) headed by Professor Schorr; the Committee for the Promoting of Jewish
Pioneering and Colonization in Madagascar and Kenya,
and the Committee for Promoting Emigration to Africa
and Australia. These new associations reinforced the
activities of the *Hias* (Hebrew Sheltering and Immigrant
Aid Society), the Jewish Central Emigration Association,
founded in 1923, and its Polish counterpart Jeas, established in 1925, with headquarters in Warsaw and branches
in eleven towns. The Bund, too, opened its Emigration
Bureau in 1925, concerned mainly with re-settling workers
in France and Argentina. In a rare display of unity, all
Zionist groups in Poland dissociated themselves from these
committees. "The fight for a Jewish national home," they
declared, "must be combined with the fight for the equal
civil and national rights of the Jewish masses in Poland."
Moreover, the Zionists could not conceive of successful
Jewish settlement in any territory other than Palestine.

"Give me your tired, your poor, your huddled masses
yearning to break free, the wretched refuse of your teem-
ing shore. Send these, the homeless, tempest-tossed to me,"
proclaims the Statue of Liberty in ringing tones of tender
compassionate humanitarianism. Yet these words had become a fantastically empty invitation. In a veiled reprimand to Poland, President Franklin Delano Roosevelt
underlined the responsibility borne by a state towards its
people. "We are determined to make every American
citizen the subject of his country's interest and concern;
and we will never regard any faithful law-abiding group
within our borders as superfluous."[46] The reprimand remained unheeded.

The final demoniacal "solution" of Poland's Jewish

problem was conceived by the Nazis and accomplished almost in its entirety. The number of Jews in Poland on September 1, 1939 amounted to about 3,474,000. Ninety-eight per cent perished and only 55,509 were left in 1945.

"Never would Hitler," wrote Sholem Asch,[47] "have dared to select one people for annihilation had not the road been prepared for him by all kinds and degrees of anti-Semites. A person's constitutional rights are secured only when his social standing in a community is secure. If a people is singled out for hatred, as a group, if the fact of just belonging to this group is considered enough to count as a crime, that people loses, in the eyes of its persecutors, the dignity and mysticism of a human being. Then justice is warped and animal instincts are brought forth. All who have prepared this ground of hatred towards the Jews and other races are exactly as responsible for the bestial slaughter in Poland as Hitler and his clique. Hitler only gathers the fruit of their well-planted seed."

12

Pillars of Polish Jewry

Many bright stars illumined the constellation of Polish Jewry, for this was no *dor yatom* ("orphaned generation"). This was the birthplace of leaders, lay and religious, who brought arts and ethics and assorted talents to the Jewish communities of the world.

THE CHOFETZ CHAYYIM

As in the middle ages, twentieth century Poland was primarily an *achsania shel Torah* ("home of Torah"). "High priest" was Rabbi Israel Meir Kahan (1838–1933) known throughout the Jewish universe as the *Chofetz Chayyim*. This was the title of his famous book, published in 1873, based on Verses 13 and 14 of Psalm xxxiv. "He who desires life . . . keep thy tongue from evil and thy lips from speaking guile."

The Chofetz Chayyim studied at Yeshivot in Vilna and soon revealed a remarkable intellectual potential. At the age of seventeen the young *illui* ("Talmudical prodigy") married Frieda, his step-sister. Unwilling to make Torah "a crown wherewith to aggrandize himself" the Chofetz Chayyim declined rabbinical positions. "He who hates gifts shall live,"[1] was one of his favourite sayings. He earned his living as a teacher in Minsk and at Washilishok (1864–1869).

In 1869 he established the Yeshiva Chofetz Chayyim at Radin where he began to exert tremendous influence over his students. Yet he called himself a "simple Jew" and led a simple life, refusing all honours and all honoraria. He opened a grocery store and all the Jews of the town became his customers. When the modest rabbi realized that other shopkeepers were suffering as a result of this clerical competition, he shut up shop and began to travel up and down the country selling his books. Eventually he accepted a rabbinical post in Radin on two conditions: firstly, that he was not to receive a salary, and secondly, that his decisions in religious matters were to be final.

The most momentous work of the rabbi of Radin was *Mishnah Berura* ("Lucid Learning"), a commentary on the Code *Orach Chayyim* ("Way of Life"). This was published in six volumes (totalling 1,800 pages) between 1884 and 1907. It was immediately accepted as a standard work of reference and established the Chofetz Chayyim as a great codifier, a worthy successor of Rabbi Moses Isserles. "The *Mishnah Berura* is authoritative and its rulings are binding on everyone," declared Chief Rabbi A. I. Kook. Other notable works on cognate themes are: *Shemirat Halashon* ("The Guarding of the Tongue"), a moral and ethical treatise, and *Likute Halachot* ("Condensed Laws").

In his book *Ahavat Chesed* ("Lovingkindness") the Choftez Chayyim deals with the interrelating obligations of employer and employee. "I have seen fit to include here the laws about the payment of wages to the hired man," writes the rabbi of Radin, "since this matter is of supreme importance and it involves a number of expressed Biblical precepts. In the sinfulness of our age, people have grown indifferent to it and they take it lightly to postpone payment on the smallest pretext."

Certainly he could bring new clarity to obscured enmeshed areas of *Halachic* disputation. But he could also clarify the everyday problems of the man in the street. His manual *Machne Yisrael* ("The Camp of Israel," 1881) was specifically designed for Jewish soldiers, *Nidchei Yisrael* ("The Dispersed of Israel," 1893) was written to help Eastern European immigrants to adjust themselves to the New World; and *Geder Olam* ("Eternal Fence," 1890) on *Taharat Hamischpacha* ("Family purity") illuminates the Judaic concept of marital relations.

Unassuming, unassertive, this uncrowned leader of Polish Jewry chose to live in a remote hamlet, absorbed in his studies. But when religious Jewry turned to him for guidance he readily responded. It was he who opened the Aguda *Knessiya* in Vienna in August, 1923. In his memorable opening address he said:

Why did you bestow upon me the privilege of opening this Torah Parliament? It was surely because you think I am a scholar. Yet in truth I am an ignoramus. Nor am I of priestly descent. Some sages hold that priestly genealogy is somewhat suspect. The only reason for this great honour is my old age. On that basis let me address you, my beloved brethren.

It was the Chofetz Chayyim who led a delegation consisting of the rabbis of Ger, Belz and Alexander to Prime Minister Bartel, Minister of the Interior and Minister of Education, seeking support for orthodox education. In

1925, he addressed an assembly of five thousand women urging them to safeguard the institutions of Judaism. A house awaited him in Petach Tikva, yet although he yearned for the Holy Land, he could not desert his followers. With overwhelming compassion he viewed their sufferings and suffered with them.

On one occasion he said:

I recall the horrors of about seventy years ago when the Russian Cossacks dragged in shackles those Polish patriots who rebelled against the Czarist yoke, banishing them to Siberia and to other isolated sections. I remember how heart-broken I felt. In tears I retired to my room and prayed to the Almighty, saying: "O, Father of mercy and justice, have not these Poles a right to live their own lives as freely and as independently as their oppressors?" . . . So God granted me the privilege of seeing a resurrected independent Poland. Do you wish to cause me to shed tears again? Remember that God always intervenes in favour of the oppressed! Then why be the oppressor?[2]

CHAYYIM OZER GRODZENSKI

A close associate of the "Chofetz Chayyim" was Chayyim Ozer Grodzenski (1863–1940). Born in Ivia, near Vilna, one of nine children, he studied at the celebrated seats of learning at Eishishok and at Volozhin where he sat at the feet of Naphtali Zevi Judah Berlin (1817–1893) and Raphael Shapiro.[3] At the age of twenty, the *illui* of Ivia married the granddaughter of Rabbi Israel Salanter (1810–1883), founder of the *Musar* movement. On the death of his father-in-law Rabbi Elijah Eliezer on *Rosh Chodesh Sivan*, 1887, Chayyim Ozer, at the age of twenty-four, was appointed one of the rabbis of Vilna, the Jerusalem of Lithuania.

The newly appointed rabbi founded a group for advanced studies, the Kibbutz of Rabbi Chayyim Ozer, and among its elite were Rabbi Moses Avigdor Amiel (1882–1945), chief rabbi of Tel-Aviv, Rabbi Ezekiel Abramski (later *Dayan* in London), and Rabbi Isaac Halevy Herzog of Israel. Chayyim Ozer's *responsa*, *Achiezer*, published in 1922 and 1933, were at once concise and comprehensive, placing him in the foremost rank of Torah authorities. "Even the light which shone for us from the East, from the land of our venerable ancestors has become obscured of late," lamented the author in his introduction, "and we do not know what tomorrow will bring. Distress, troubles, killing, murder, expulsion, evil decrees surround us on all sides. The entire Jewish people is sinking in the rivers of blood and oceans of tears of innocent victims of oppression. Oh, what has become of us!"

The tragedy of his life was the death, after a four-year illness, of his only daughter, a gifted, beautiful girl, whom he adored. She was twenty years old. "Unless Thy Torah had been my delight," wept the broken-hearted father, "I should then have perished in mine affliction." (Ps. cxix : 92.)

Faithfully, he ministered to his community for fifty-six years. He participated at the Aguda Conference at Katowice. He organized *kosher* kitchens for soldiers and diligently sought solutions for the pressing problems of the day. At a conference for the support of yeshivot in July, 1924, he established the *Vaad Hayeshivot* ("Central Committee of Yeshivot"), a medium for obtaining support from home and abroad, particularly from American Jewry. In the winter months of 1939–40, Vilna became the home of sixteen yeshivot with 1,907 students in addition to innumerable *kolelim* (groups). A dedicated student,

Rabbi Chayyim Ozer set aside his beloved studies in order to dedicate himself wholeheartedly to the salvaging of the refugees. "Years ago," he wrote, "I thought that writing books was the most desirable and honorable occupation. As I advance in years, I begin to realize that such work is insignificant in comparison with the job of helping Torah scholars, orphans, widows, and other unfortunates."[4]

To meet the needs of yeshiva students Chayyim Ozer urged every Jew to donate one dollar every six months. With justification, Rabbi Yerucham Levovitch, spiritual head of the yeshivah of Mir, wrote to Chayyim Ozer: "You are the greatest treasure of our generation." Rabbi Chayyim Ozer died on August 8th, 1940.

MENACHEM ZIEMBA

Warsaw, "the new Jerusalem," was the home of many famous rabbis and scholars. Among them were Solomon Zalman ben Isaac, author of *Chemdat Shlomo*, Dob Baer Meiseles and Jacob ben Isaac Gesundheit (1814–1878), author of *Tiferet Yaacov* on *Hoshen Mishpat* (the code of civil law administration). Warsaw had no chief rabbi and jurisdiction over religious affairs was exercised by the Warsaw rabbinate. Its incumbents in the inter-war years were Rabbis David Shapiro, Samson Stochmacher, Solomon David Kahana, Chayyim Joshua Gutschechter, Ezekiel Michelson, author of twenty *halachic* works, and Gerer Chassid Menachem Ziemba of Praga, one of the greatest intellects that Poland has ever produced.

Menachem Ziemba was born in August, 1882, in Praga, suburb of Warsaw. His father, Elazer Lippa, died when the boy was barely nine years old and he was brought up

by his grandfather Abraham Ziemba. A frail, ailing child
he possessed a phenomenal memory and a most incisive
mind. At eighteen, he married Mindele, daughter of
Chayyim Isaiah Zederbaum, a wealthy iron merchant.
Relieved of financial worries, Menachem Ziemba could
now dedicate twenty hours daily to his studies. For five or
six hours a day he shared his Talmudical "discoveries"
with a small group of students. He did not believe that
the master should prepare his daily lectures in advance
because he felt that it was more profitable if the students
participated in the actual preparations.

The death of his father-in-law compelled him to attend
to business but even ironmongery did not distract him
from his studies. He did not work in a vacuum. He kept
in close touch with the intellectual giants of the era and
Talmudist Rabbi Meir Simcha Hakohen of Dvinsk,
author of *Or Someah*, referred to him as "a beautiful
vessel."

In 1919, Ziemba published *Zera Abraham* ("The Seed
of Abraham") and two years later *Tozaout Chayyim*
("Offsprings of Life"), a compendium on the "39 categories of labour" prohibited on the Sabbath. For his work
on Maimonides (*Machezh Lemelech*, novellae on *Yad
Hachazakah*) he was awarded a literary prize by the Warsaw community. In 1930, he contributed to the periodical
Degel Hatorah ("The Banner of the Torah"), edited by
Rabbi Menachem Kasher, director of the *Mesivta* yeshiva
in Warsaw. When Kasher left for the United States,
Ziemba himself published the last two issues. Every
Sabbath evening he delivered a *Midrashic* discourse and
every afternoon, from twelve o'clock to two, he gave a
Shiur (discourse) to selected young men. He received
many "Calls" to distant pulpits. When Joseph Chayyim

Zonnenfeld died, Moses Blau was delegated to offer Ziemba a rabbinical post in Jerusalem, but Ziemba refused to leave his beloved Warsaw. To the end he remained a devoted disciple of Ger and the Gerer *rebbe* loved him dearly. "Come, let us ask our Menachem," the rabbi of Ger would say.

Ziemba was the author of twenty published works. Among unpublished manuscripts, destroyed in the holocaust, were a four-volume set of *responsa,* a thousand-page commentary on the Palestinian Talmud, *Menachem Yerushalayim* ("Comforting Jerusalem"), and a work on Maimonides. When he lost his son Yehuda at the age of eighteen, he wrote *Gur Arye Yehuda* ("Judah is a Lion's Whelp") in memoriam. In 1935, Ziemba was elected to the Vaad ha-Rabbanim in Warsaw and associated closely with Rabbis Jacob Meir Biderman and Abraham Weinberg.

During the Nazi occupation, Ziemba inspired the fighters of the Warsaw Ghetto. At the memorable council of war on January 14, 1943, Ziemba spoke out with characteristic fire:

Of necessity, we must resist the enemy on all fronts. . . . We shall no longer heed his instructions. Henceforth we must refuse to wend our way to the Umschlagplatz which is but a blind and a snare, a veritable stepping-stone on the road to mass annihilation. . . . Had we lived up to our presumed status of "a people endowed with wisdom and understanding" we would have discerned *ab initio* the enemy's plot to destroy us as a whole, root and branch, and would have put into operation all media of information in order to arouse the conscience of the world. As it is now we have no choice but to resist. We are prohibited by Jewish law from betraying others, nor may we deliver ourselves into the hands of the arch-enemy. . . . Our much vaunted prudence—not to be identified with genuine wisdom and true understanding—blurred our vision and turned out to be more devastating than folly and stupidity. To paraphrase the words of our Sages, Korah of old accentuated his innate aptitude for providence to such an extent that it blurred his vision and, in the end, it was his folly that brought his ultimate doom. In the present, however, when we are faced by an arch foe, whose unparallelled ruthlessness and total annihilation knows no bounds, *Halachah* demands that we fight and resist to the very end with unequalled determination and valor for the sake of the Sanctification of the Divine Name.[5]

He was murdered on the 19th of *Nisan* 1943, while crossing Kupieca Street.

RABBI MEIR SHAPIRO

A colourful personality, Rabbi Meir Shapiro (1887–1934),[6] born near Czernowitz, Bukovina, traced his descent to Rabbi Phinehas ben Abraham of Koretz (1726–1791). At the age of nine, he was known as the *illui* of Shatz. An outstanding student, young Meir knew by heart the Code *Yoreh Dea* (dealing with dietary laws) together with its massive commentaries. Rabbi Solomon Ha-Kohen, author of *Dat Torah* ("Knowledge of the Torah") applied to him the benediction: "Blessed be He the creator of Lights," a punning play on the name "Meir," which means "Light" in Hebrew. Ordained by Rabbi Eliezer Steinberg of Brody and Rabbi Meir Arak, Meir married the daughter of the wealthy Jacob David Breitmann of Tarnopol.

In 1910, Meir Shapiro became rabbi in Gline, then in Sanok (1920), and later in Piotrkow (1924–1930). He was an excellent educator and devoted most of his attention to young people. He was an innovator, too, and among his far-reaching innovations was the *Daf Yomi* which he proposed at the *Knessiya Gedola* in *Elul,* 1923. This was a simple scheme of amazingly vast, in fact, universal scope. It required the study each day by each Jew of one page of the Talmud, so that in seven years the entire Babylonian Talmud would be covered in a cycle of studies which would bind the scattered Jewries of the world in spiritual bonds. *Daf Yomi* caught the imagination of both scholar and layman, and it was inaugurated on *Rosh Hashana,* 1924. On that day the rabbi of Ger told his followers: "I am now going to study each day a page of the Talmud," and many followed his example. The first *Siyyum* ("Completion") of the entire Talmud was celebrated on 15th of *Shevat,* 1931.

Rabbi Shapiro's second great achievement was the establishment of *Yeshivat Chachmei Lublin.* At that time, yeshiva students in Poland and Lithuania lived a Spartan life. Few yeshivot had dormitories or even kitchens. Spiritual food was dished out in great abundance, but little provision was made for physical welfare. To keep threadbare body and soul together, a student often ate "days," which meant that each day he would be a "guest" in a different home, often a humiliating experience. Many had difficulty in finding lodgings. In Warsaw, it was not uncommon for Yeshiva students to serve as night watchmen in shops and factories. "We should be grateful for the existence of thieves," jested Shapiro ironically, "were it not for them, shopkeepers would not employ watchmen, and were it not for the need of watchmen where would Yeshiva students find accommodation?" Shapiro grieved at the sufferings of these diligent, unworldly young men.

A man of action, Rabbi Meir Shapiro quickly translated dreams into blueprints. He chose as his site Lubertovska 57, Lublin. Aware that poverty-stricken Polish Jewry was incapable of financing such a costly venture, he set out for the United States in *Elul*, 1924. There, in thirteen months he delivered 242 discourses and collected $56,000. He also visited England, France, Germany and Switzerland. In addition, collection boxes were placed in the homes of pious Jews. The number of students increased from a hundred and fifty in 1932, to five hundred in 1939.

A day after the dedication of the *Yeshivat Chachmei Lublin* on the 28th of *Sivan*, 1930, Shapiro was appointed Rabbi of Lublin. Now he turned to new and distant fields. "I hope to establish a Yeshiva in Jerusalem which will put to shame the buildings of the Hebrew University," envisaged this rabbinic builder. Three years later he fell ill. He took loving leave of his students and drank *Lechayyim* ("To Life") with them. His dying words were "Only with joy," and he died on the 7th of *Heshvon*, 1934, at the age of forty-six.

Shapiro's students were orphaned. They sat *shiva* ("seven days of mourning") and recited the mourner's *kaddish* for their spiritual father. The proceeds of his life insurance went to the yeshiva. "Some pay with money," he once remarked "and some pay with their life." It was said of him, "From Rabbi Meir (a Palestinian teacher of the second century) to Rabbi Meir, there was no one like him." His yeshiva shared the fate of Polish Jewry. The *Deutsche Jugendzeitung* in February, 1940, gives a painfully vivid account of the wanton destruction of this beloved citadel of learning. "It was a matter of special pride to us," exults the Nazi narrator, "to destroy this Talmudic Academy, known as the greatest in Poland. We threw out of the building the large Talmudic library, and brought it to the market place. There we kindled a fire under the books. The conflagration lasted twenty hours. The Jews of Lublin stood about weeping bitterly. Their outcries rose above our own voices. We called up a military band and the cries of triumph of the soldiers drowned out the noise of the Jewish wailing."[7]

In 1959, Rabbi Meir was reburied in the Holy Land.

RABBI AARON LEWIN

The rabbi-statesman of the middle ages re-emerged in twentieth century Poland. Wresting leadership from the secularists and assimilationists, the clergy raised impassioned voices on political platforms.

Among these declamatory divines was Aaron Lewin, born on the 14th of *Heshvon* (October 31), 1879, in Przemysl, Galicia. His father, Rabbi Nathan Lewin, son-in-law of the community rabbi Isaac Shmelkes, was a descendant of Rabbi Isaac Schorr (d. 1776), author of *Tevuot Shorr*, and David ben Samuel Halevi (1586–1667), known as the *Ture Zahav* ("Rose of Gold"), a commentary on the *Shulchan Aruch*. In 1902, Aaron married Doba, daughter of Elias Hirsch Friedmann from Wieliczka, near Cracow. His first rabbinical post was in Sambor, with a Jewish population of ten thousand. In his inaugural address, the twenty-four-year-old rabbi expressed a deep sense of vocation. He expounded

Elijah is destined to deliver three things to Israel: the container of manna, the dish of oil and the dish of water. Some say also the staff of Aaron. The rabbi's duties are characterised by these items. "The container of *Manna*" symbolizes charitable activities providing sustenance for the poor. "The dish of oil" stands for educational activity, teaching of the people. "The dish of water" represents purification, pointing out the purpose of life; and "Aaron's Staff" is the symbol of peace to which every rabbi must aspire in his community.[8]

Aaron devoted eight years to *Birkat Aaron* ("The Blessing of Aaron," Drohobycz, 1913), a compendium of 310 essays on assorted themes. In 1913 he was appointed Crown Councillor (*Kaiserlicher Rat*) by the Emperor of Austria. A dedicated Agudist, he was elected president of the Aguda's Central Council in 1923. Three years later he accepted the rabbinate of Rzeszow (Reisha). From 1930 to 1935, when his two Agudist colleagues (Leib Mincberg and Asher Mendelsohn) were integrated into the Government Bloc and forced to accept government discipline, Lewin boldly took the lead. "The terrible incidents that took place in Warsaw and Cracow Universities bring disgrace upon their good name," he thundered in the Seym. "Is this the Polish intelligentsia of the future, destined eventually to supply the nation with its leaders, which now so brutally attacks its Jewish colleagues? . . . Repetition of such incidents in the Universities must be prohibited. If these 'strong arm' men feel that they have excess energies, let them utilize them for worthwhile purposes, for the benefit of science and the state and not against unarmed Jews."[9]

Early in 1939, he was one of the delegates sent to London to discuss Polish-Jewish immigration with Lord Winterton. "The land of Israel," he told the third *Knensiya*, "is today the focal point of our nation's problems. The eyes of the house of Israel are directed to our land and soil."[10] His book *Hadrash Vehaiiun* became the preacher's *vade mecum*. He was murdered on the 6th of *Tammuz*, 1941, at Lwow.

SARAH SCHENIERER

"We do not erect sepulchres for the righteous, their work is their memorial," say the rabbis. Every girl who graduated from a Bet Jacob school is a tangible, living tribute to the little seamstress who managed almost single-handed to revolutionize the education of women in Poland. This was Sarah Schenierer.

Sarah was born in *Tammuz*, 1883. Her father, Bezalel ha-Kohen of Tarnov, a devoted Chassid of Belz, was a descendant of Rabbi Shabbetai ben Meir ha-Cohen known as *Shach* (after the initials of his book *Siphte Kohen* on *Yoreh Deah*). She herself attended a state school but even as a child her piety and idealism singled her out. Jestingly, schoolmates nicknamed her "Chassida" ("the pious one"). She devoted the entire sabbath to Jewish studies. She read *Zeenu Urennu, Nachlat Zevi* and other works specially written for the edification of women. As her father grew poorer and poorer, Sarah became a dressmaker to support the family. As she cut her paper patterns, she reflected on the patterns of education prevailing in her day. For boys there were many educational establishments, ranging from *Chedarim* to yeshivot, but there was no provision at all for the religious education of girls. She observed the care which women lavished upon fashions and their indifference to spiritual furnishings.

Sarah spent the war years in Vienna and was greatly influenced by the teachings of Rabbi Dr. Flesch of the Stumpergasse Synagogue.[11] In 1917, she returned to her native Cracow and the dressmaker's fantasy became a fact. With the blessing of the Belzer *rebbe* Isaac Dov Rokeach, she started a school for twenty-five girls in a tiny room at Katarzyna, in the Cracow Jewish quarter. This was the foundation of the Bet Jacob Movement, whose alumni were to become the anti-assimilationists, the upholders of Jewish tradition, the opponents of the subversive new socialism that was spreading among Jewish youth. Although Sarah Schenierer did not marry, she had hundreds of thousands of "Children." This is her epitaph, written by one of her "daughters": "We have lived under the influence of the Torah and Judaism. . . . Here the very walls were breathing that spirit; the atmosphere was filled with it. . . . We must create among Jewish children the type of atmosphere we have been living in. Till now we have been the recipients; now it is time for us to be the givers."[12]

In her last will and testament, Sarah wrote: "Be strong and of good courage. Do not tire. Do not slacken your efforts. You have heard of a Chassid who came to his *rebbe* and said joyfully, 'Rabbi, I have finished the whole Talmud.' 'What has the Talmud taught you?' asked the rabbi. Your learning is commendable but your actions are the main thing." She died on the 7th of *Heshvon*, 1935, but her spirit inspired the 93 Bet Jacob girls in the Warsaw Ghetto who committed suicide rather than fall into Nazi hands.

JANUSZ KORCZAK

A legend in his lifetime Dr. Henryk Goldsmith, popularly known by his literary pseudonym Janusz Korczak, was born in 1878 (or 1879) to a prosperous lawyer in a cultured, thoroughly assimilated family. As a student of medicine at Warsaw University, he was imprisoned for a short term for his socialist views. Later he did clinical work in Berlin and Paris, and in London he studied methods of rehabilitating deprived or maladjusted children. In 1903, he returned to Warsaw to work as a child specialist in a small slum clinic. He devoted himself to under-privileged children and, in 1909, became the director of a Jewish orphanage. A fatherly warm-hearted man, Korczak cared passionately for his little charges and in a very real sense he turned the institution into a loving home.

His pedagogical system was far in advance of his time. With unstinted affection, a sense of humor, and a fairy-tale imagination he won the hearts of the children. His first novel, *Street Urchin* (1901), shows his intimate knowledge of the child's small, tangled world. This sympathy is shown in *Child of the Drawing Room, How One Should Love a Child, King Macius the First* and *Confessions of a Butterfly*. In 1926, he founded a children's newspaper, *Maly Przeglad*, with the aid of Stefania Wilczinskia. Both Hebrew and Yiddish were foreign to him and he read the Bible in a Polish translation. He visited Israel and was deeply impressed by the achievements of the *yishuv*. The Nazi occupation shattered the careful edifice he had built for his fledglings and the orphanage was transferred to the ghetto. Under hopeless conditions, he fought to the last to comfort his children and he died among them.

MOSES SCHORR

Notable contributions to *Jüdische Wissenschaft* were made by Polish Jewry, and among key contributors were Nachman Krochmal (1785–1840), Rabbi Solomon Rapoport (1790–1867) of Lwow, Samuel Abraham Poznanski (1864–1921) and Moses Schorr. Poznanski was an eminent scholar whose command of Hebrew was equalled by his mastery of Arabic. A prolific writer, his works comprised seven hundred titles. Yet his appointment as rabbi of the Great Synagogue, Warsaw, in 1921, aroused much indignation among the orthodox elements. Numerous meetings were held and on one occasion demonstrators stormed the Communal Council.[13]

Poznanski's successor as Rabbi of the Tlumacka Synagogue, Warsaw, was Moses Schorr, native of Przemysl, Galicia. He studied philosophy at the University of Vienna, concentrating on Assyriology and Polish Jewish history. His first study, "Biography of Don Joseph Hanassi," appeared in 1896. After six years as a secondary school teacher, he became a lecturer at Lwow in 1910. In 1915, he was promoted professor, and, in 1928, he was made a member of the Academy of Sciences in Cracow. Schorr was eventually appointed professor of Sumerian languages and ancient oriental culture at the University of Warsaw.

Among Schorr's great works were "Jewish Communal Organization in Poland until 1772" (*Organizacja Zydów w Polsce*), and "Jews in Przemysl up to the End of the Eighteenth Century" (*Żydzi w Przemyslu*). He was Chairman of the *Bnai Brit* in Poland, chairman of the Friends of the Hebrew University in Jerusalem, and president of the Relief Committee for Polish Jewish sufferers from German persecution.

Spokesman of Polish Jewry, Schorr was nominated senator by the government in 1936. "The Jews do not demand privileges," stated Schorr without equivocation, "but they object to curtailment of their rights as citizens." Fearlessly he denounced government treatment of the Jewish minority. "The Premier said that the Government will punish those who are responsible for the anti-Jewish excesses," reasoned the senator, "but a modern State is more than a policeman. The only way of combating the excesses is to prevent their occurrence." During the war, he was seized by Russian troops and died in Uzbekistan.[14]

MEIR BALABAN

Historian Meir Shmuel Balaban, born in Lwow in 1867, started his literary career under the pseydonym *Emet* ("Truth"), with articles in the Zionist weekly paper *Przyszlosc*, in Galicia. During World War I, he lived in Vienna where he acted as an Austrian Army Chaplain 1915–1918.

For his work on *The Jews of Lwow at the Turn of the Sixteenth and Seventeenth Centuries*, he received the Wawelberg prize. Balaban believed that monographs of individual communities are the mortar of history. To him history was an art as well as a science, and he painted the Jewish scene with careful objectivity, making extensive use of material from the Polish archives. In forty-five years he published over three hundred books and studies.[15] His range was enormous and he had a vivid narrative style. The Sabbetian and Frankist movements (followers of the pseudo-messiahs Shabbetai Zevi, 1626–1677, and Jacob Frank, 1726–1791) were treated by Balaban in his *Zur Geschichte der frankistischen Bewegung in Polen* ("Studies and Sources for the History of the Frankist Movement in Poland"), in S. Poznanski's *Memorial Volume* (Warsaw 1927), and in his *Letoledot hatenuah hafrankist* (2 vols., Tel-Aviv: 1934–5). He quotes a transcript of the minutes of the two disputes which took place between the Frankists and the Jews in 1757 and 1759, as well as the correspondence between the papal nuncio in Warsaw and the Vatican regarding the Frankists.

He wrote a two-volume history of the Jews in Cracow, and monographs on the Jewish communities of Lwow and Lublin.[16] Hundreds of his essays are scattered through Hebrew, Yiddish, Russian, Polish and German periodicals. His *Bibliografia historii zydow w Polsce i w Krajach osciennych za lata 1900–39*, published in Warsaw in 1939, lists three thousand items. Among unpublished material are a history of the Blood Libel, a history of Poznan, and a history of Jewish mysticism in Poland. His teachings were the inspiration of many young historians.[17]

An eye witness in the Ghetto recorded that

in December 1942, Balaban was visited by a delegation of professors from Cologne who had known him before the war and respected him greatly. During the course of the visit, the German scholars assured him that they would visit him again after six weeks. Professor Balaban expressed doubt as to whether they would still find him alive since the Ghetto would almost probably have been liquidated by then. The Germans could not believe it. Such an end, they declared, might at most be meted out to the "raw masses" but not to men of science.[18]

Balaban died three weeks later.

DR. ISAAC SCHIPPER

Dr. Isaac Schipper (1884–1943) was a man of many parts: Zionist, parliamentarian, publicist, president of the Writers' Union, director of the *Keren Hayesod* ("Foundation Fund") in Poland. A noted historian, he wrote on the participation of the Jews in the Polish uprising of 1831, on Jewish commerce in Polish territory (*Dzieje Handlu Zydowskiego na Ziemiach Polskich*, Warsaw: 1937), on Jewish economic life (*Yidishe Virtshaftsgeshichete*, four volumes, Warsaw: 1930), on the Yiddish theatre, arts and drama from the beginning to 1750 (*Geshichte fun der Yidisher teatrkunst,* 4 volumes, Warsaw: 1923–1928).

It was Schipper's thesis that the Jewish community in Poland originated with the *Chazars* and he maintained that the "Council of Four Lands" was born of economic expediency. His life was largely concerned with setting down and analysing the treasure-house of information which he had amassed in his younger days. His great strength lay in the popularization of knowledge in the form of highly readable history books.

No less impressive is the vast number of articles, sketches and critiques scattered in countless journals. He was the master of the brief essay as well as the long narrative. He represented the Poale Zion in the Seym from 1919 to 1922.

SZYMON ASKENAZY

Szymon Askenazy (1866–1935) laid the foundation for the modern study of Polish history. His self-allotted task was to demonstrate that the partitions of Poland were the result of external factors. *The Polish Prussian Alliance,* published in 1890, and *Danzig and Poland,* published in 1919, became standard works. He discovered a short story, written by Napoleon as a young man, and it appeared in the *London Evening Standard* in the series of "Great Short Stories."[19] He was the only Polish historian represented in the *Cambridge Modern History of Poland,* and two chapters were his contribution. He modelled himself on Thomas Carlyle, Lord Macaulay and Hippolyte Adolphe Taine, and wrote in a style that was elegant if overly ornate. His special interest in the Napoleonic period produced the *magnum opus, Napoleon and Poland.* The rich bibliography and the abundant footnotes testify to the author's acquaintance with the monumental literature on this subject. Yet each page proves him an original and independent thinker.

Appointed assistant professor at the University of Lwow in 1897, Askenazy occupied the Chair of Polish History until 1914. In 1917, he moved to Warsaw, and, from 1920 to 1923, he acted as Poland's Minister Plenipotentiary and Chief Delegate at the League of Nations. His assimilationist views were attacked by the Polish Jewish press, for Askenazy believed, an incredibly naïve belief, that the Jewish provisions of the Minority Rights Treaty were unnecessary. Such provisions, he feared, might lead the world to suspect Poland of not treating her Jewish minority with fairness.

Askenazy tasted Polish "fairness" when the university senate rejected his application for professorship. He died on June 22, 1935 at the age of sixty-eight, disillusioned with the spirit of the new Poland that he had helped to create.

ISAAC GRUENBAUM

Isaac Gruenbaum (b. 1879) was a medical student who switched to law and later found his vocation in journalism and politics. In 1914, he went to Petrograd (Leningrad) where, after the May Revolution, he edited the Petrograd *Togblatt* until it was suppressed by the Bolsheviks. In 1917, at the Zionist Conference in Petrograd, he campaigned for the establishment of an autonomous Jewish community and official recognition of Yiddish. Returning to Poland in 1918, he edited the Zionist daily newspaper and for a time the Hebrew daily. Later he headed the provisional Jewish National Council. He was appointed a member of the constituent Seym and a member of the commission which drafted the Polish Constitution.

Father of the Minority Bloc and president of the Club of Jewish Deputies, Gruenbaum paid highly for his principles. Leaving a meeting of the Zionist organization one night, he was savagely attacked by hooligans.[20] He opposed Dr. Weizmann's Jewish Agency policy and formed a party, Al Hamishmar, to conduct the opposition. He visited England in 1924 and the United States in 1927, where he was received by President Coolidge. He resigned the presidency of the Club of Jewish Deputies when the Club refused to oppose the Bartel Government. Whilst Leon Reich fought for individuals, Gruenbaum championed the masses. Yet his unfortunate declaration, "There are a million too many Jews in Poland," quoted out of context, provided ammunition for numerous opponents. In 1933, he was elected to the Jewish Agency Executive and settled in Paris. In 1948–49 he was appointed Minister of the Interior in the Israel provisional government.

DR. OSIAS THON

Dr. Osias Thon (1870–1936) was a dominant figure in Polish Zionism. A Seym deputy (1919–1935) and for many years president of the Club of Jewish Deputies, Thon played a leading role in parliamentary activities. He believed that compromise was possible and practical, the only way of making "Jewish equality" into at least a partial reality. "Nobody in Poland," he once asserted, "pays the slightest attention to the plight of the Jews. If the Government considers certain social reforms necessary, they are always carried into effect across the bodies of Jews economically ruined. It has become a dogma that economic salvation is to be found in the elimination of the Jewish middle man."[21]

Life-long Zionist, member of the Council of the Jewish Agency and president of the Zionist organization of West Galicia, vice-president of the Comité des délégations juives at the Paris Peace Conference, Thon was an active writer for over forty years. His Hebrew works include a dissertation on Herbert Spencer. His German books include studies of Herzl and essays on Zionist ideology. Together with Chayyim Nahman Bialik (1873–1934), he was one of the founders of the Tarbut.

LEON REICH

Jewish politics in Poland in the 1930's became a tussle between the rival policies of Gruenbaum and Leon Reich (1875–1926), one of the vice-presidents of the Comité des délégations juives at the Paris Peace Conference. President of the Eastern Galicia Zionist Federation and a staunch supporter of Chaim Weizmann, Reich advocated collaboration with the Polish government. In 1925, Lucien Wolf paid tribute to Reich's moderation, patriotism and patience. Yet the Reich-Gruenbaum conflict continued after the Pilsudski rising of 1926 when the Reich camp declared that "there is no longer reason for opposition by the Club of Jewish Deputies to the present Government."[22] He was a brilliant speaker and he represented Poland in the Inter-Parliamentary Union. He died while presiding at a conference of the East Galician Zionist Federation.

HENRYK ERLICH

The history of the Bund is the history of Henryk Erlich, (1882–1941). As a Socialist, as a Pole and as a Jew, he found fulfilment in the movement. Erlich, son-in-law of the historian Simon Dubnow, came from a Chassidic background. He studied first in Warsaw, then in St. Petersburg (now Leningrad). As a student he participated in a demonstration against the anti-Semitic play "The Golden Calf." The result was three months imprisonment and dismissal from the university. Returning to Poland, he was elected member of the Warsaw municipality and was the only one of the 120 members who spoke out in 1920 against the Polish-Soviet War.

Erlich edited the Bundist *Folkszeitung*, spicing his editorials with Hebrew and Talmudical phrases. He was arrested five times by the Czarist government, once by Poland and twice by Soviet Russia. He represented the Bund at Socialist conferences in Hamburg (1923), Marseilles and Vienna (1931), where he attacked the German Social Democratic party for its apathy in fighting Nazism. He was executed by the Soviets in 1941.

VICTOR ALTER

"The only man in the Town Hall who worked conscientiously was Bundist Victor Alter," attested City Mayor Stefan Starzynski. Alter was a true servant of the people. Instinctively, the homeless, the unemployed, the injured, turned to him for help and he rarely failed them.

Born in Mlawa, Poland, Victor Alter (1890–1941), son of a rich timber merchant, studied engineering and later edited a weekly Polish paper. He was conversant with mathematics, economics, literature, and seven languages were at his fingertips: Yiddish, Polish, Russian, French, English, Italian, German. He was the author of ten books, written in Yiddish, Polish and French. Though regularly a candidate for the Seym, he never managed to get elected. He was a member of the Executive Committee of the Second International and, together with Erlich, represented the Bund at International conferences. "We are plain Jews," he maintained, "without pride or shame. There was no need for us to discover Judaism because of anti-Semitism. We are Jews *sans* nationalism who combine first of all their fate with Socialism. To them one fatherland is adopted—where they live—that is Bund."

The Man in the Community, (Warsaw: 1938), the best of Alter's Polish books, gives his credo.

Humanism means a certain human attitude towards life and reality and comprises all the spheres of intellectual activity. It is a struggle against all wrongs and an endeavour to achieve a maximum of justice for all. It means the pursuit of truth, spurning all the chains that fetter it. It means solidarity with all oppressed and opposition to all oppression. It means genuine friendship and tolerance towards every individual irrespective of his origin, faith and colour. Humanism is a faith in the possibility of shaping a really beautiful and really humane world.[23]

He was executed by the Russians in December, 1941.

HILLEL ZEITLIN

Author, philosopher, Cabbalist and journalist, Hillel Zeitlin (1872–1943) exercised tremendous influence over the Jewish intelligentsia. Born in Russia, he settled in Homel in the early 1890's. At first he was an active Zionist. Then he became a keen supporter of the Jewish Territorial Organization (a body devoted to finding suitable territory, not necessarily in Palestine, for Jewish settlement on an autonomous basis). For a time he lived in Vilna and finally this "*litvak* from the land of the *litvaks*" made his home in Warsaw. Equally at ease in Hebrew and in Yiddish, he published a monograph on Spinoza. His controversial articles in the Yiddish paper *Der Moment* ranged from the *Tanya* of Rabbi Shneur Zalman of Lyady, to the stories of Nachman of Braclaw, from Seym elections to anti-Semitism.

He was an impassioned writer who preached religion, a one-man party with his own individual philosophy. Zeitlin was a heretic to the ultra-orthodox, a hypocrite to the *Maskilim* ("The Enlightened"). Yet to his home at Sliska 60, Warsaw, flocked Chassidim, *Mitnaggdim*, writers, politicians, Agudists, Bundists and Zionists to listen and to learn from this modern "prophet." He was no demogogue. He spoke quietly, eyes closed, oblivious of the people around him. Yet every public appearance brought eager crowds to his feet.

On the road to Treblinka extermination camp, Hillel Zeitlin heard the footsteps of the Messiah. He went to meet Him on 10th *Elul*, 1943, wearing *Tallit* and *Tephillin*, and reciting passages from the Zohar, engaging on the fringes of earthly hell in mystical, esoteric speculation. This was Hillel Zeitlin and this, personified, was the indestructible soul of Polish Jewry.

In the words of Professor Abraham Joshua Heschel:

The masses of East European Jews repudiated emancipation when it was offered at the price of disloyalty to Israel's traditions. Both pious and freethinking Jews fought for a dignified existence, striving to assure the rights of the community, not only those of the individual. They manifested a collective will for a collective aim. With lightning rapidity, they straightened their backs and learned to master the arts and sciences. Gifts for abstract dialectical thinking, developed in the course of generations, were carried into scientific research. Chassidic enthusiasm was sublimated in the noble profundity of musical virtuosos. Three thousand years of history had not made them weary. Their spirits were animated by a vitality that often drove them into opposition to accepted tenets.[24]

Abbreviations Used in the Notes

AJYB.   *American Jewish Year Book, The,* ed. by Cyrus Adler, Harry Schneidermann. Philadelphia.

Ency.   Encyclopedia

J.C.B.   Jewish Correspondence Bureau.

J.C.   The Jewish Chronicle, London.

J.T.A.   Jewish Telegraphic Agency.

The full titles of the books quoted in the notes, and the facts of publication, will be found in the Bibliography, if not given in the notes.

Notes

CHAPTER 1

1. J. C., February 26, 1932, p. 18.
2. Friedlaender, *The Jews of Russia and Poland*, p. 32.
3. Adam Vetulani, "Jews in Mediæval Poland" in *Jewish Journal of Sociology* Vol. IV, No. 2 (London, December, 1962), pp. 280–1.
4. *Ibid.*, p. 283.
5. *Ibid.*, p. 282.
6. Moses Isserles, *Responsa* Nos. 63, 64 (Amsterdam, 1711).
7. Yeven Metzula (Venice, 1653), quoted by Dubnow, *History of the Jews in Russia and Poland*. Vol. I, p. 111.
8. M. S. Lew, *The Jews of Poland*, p. 91.
9. I. Schipper, "The Share of the Jews in the Freedom Movement in Poland," in *Ten Years of Poland's Independence in the Polish Jewish Press* (Warsaw, 1931), p. 41.
10. Dubnow, *op. cit.*, Vol. I, p. 295.
11. *Ibid.*, p. 299.
12. R. L. Leslie, *Polish Politics and the Revolt of November 1930* (London, 1956), p. 185.
13. Schipper, *op. cit.*, pp. 41–42.
14. *Yidn Algemeyne Entziklopedie*, Vol. I, p. 192.
14. Elbogen, *A Century of Jewish Life*, p. 217.
15. Dubnow, *op. cit.*, Vol. III, p. 167.
16. S. J. Paprocki, *Minority Affairs and Poland*, p. 152.

CHAPTER 2

1. Lawton Kessler, "American Jews and the Paris Conference," p. 234. O. I. Janowsky, *The Jew and Minority Rights 1888–1919*, pp. 266–7.

2. *La Question Juive devant la Conférence de la Paix*, Alliance Israelite Universelle (Paris, 1919).

3. Nathan Feinberg, *La Question des minorités à la Conference de la Paix dès 1919–1920 et l' action juive en faveur de la protection internationale des minorités* (Paris, 1929). Kazimiersz Kierski, *Ochrona praw mniejszosci w Polsce* (Poznan, 1933).

4. Komarnicki, *Rebirth of the Polish Republic*, p. 294. Joseph S. Roucek, *The Working of the Minorities System under the League of Nations* (Prague, 1928), pp. 28–42. *Europe between the Two World Wars 1919–1939*, The American Jewish Committee (New York, 1943), p. 8.

5. S. Segal, *The New Poland and the Jews*, p. 190. H. M. V. Temperley (ed.) *A History of the Peace Conference of Paris* (London, 1920–1924), Vol. V, pp. 132–141, 437–442.

6. AJYB, Vol. 23 (5682), p. 186.

7. S. J. Paprocki, *op. cit.*, p. 23.

8. *The Times* (London), December 23, 1918. J. C., December 27, 1918, p. 8.

9. Samuel, *Report*, p. 9.

10. Mongenthau, *All in a lifetime*, p. 412.

11. Israel Cohen, *Vilna*, p. 379.

12. Mongenthau, *op. cit.*, p. 414.

13. *The Times* (London), February 8, 1919.

14. Samuel, *op. cit.*, p. 15.

15. J. C., April 18, 1919, p. 8.

16. Samuel, *op. cit.*, p. 15.

17. *Jewish National Council* (Bericht der Tatigkeit d. National rat und Saim Klub) ed. I. Gruenbaum (Warsaw, 1923), p. 57.

18. *The Jewish World*, July 2, 1919, p. 12.

19. Morgenthau, *op. cit.*, pp. 359–360.

20. AJYB (5681), Vol. 22, p. 256.

21. *The Jewish World*, October 1, 1919.

22. Morgenthau, *op. cit.*, p. 430. Also *New York Times*, January 19, 1920. I. Cohen, *op. cit.*, p. 512.

23. *New York Times*, December 15, 1919.

24. Komarnicki, *op. cit.*, p. 302.

25. House of Commons, May 11, 1920: *Parliamentary Debates*, Vol. 129, Col. 215.

26. J. C., December 19, 1919, p. 12.
27. Samuel, *op. cit.*, pp. 6 and 8.
28. *Ibid.*, p. 8.
29. *Ibid.*, p. 16.
30. *Ibid.*, p. 34.

CHAPTER 3

1. Prov. XXX : 22.
2. Isaac Schwartzbart, *Zwischen Beide Welt Milchomot*, p. 226.
3. J. C., September 7, 1934, p. 32.
4. I. Schwartzbart, *op. cit.*, p. 208. Paprocki, *op. cit.*, p. 153.
5. *Ibid.* F. B. Czarnomski, *The Polish Handbook, 1925.* (London, 1925) , p. 42.
6. Schwartzbart, *op. cit.*, p. 269.
7. AJYB (5687) , Vol. 28, p. 52.
8. Segal, *The New Poland and the Jews*, p. 47.
9. Schwartzbart, *op. cit.*, p. 242.
10. *Ibid.*, p. 238.
11. William L. Shirer, *The Rise and Fall of the Third Reich.* (London, 1960) , p. 458.
12. "The Nazi International," in *The Quarterly Review*, October, 1935, p. 228.
13. Buell, R. L., *Poland Key to Europe*, p. 109.
14. Israel Cohen, *op. cit.*, p. 418.
15. *Nazi Przeglo*, June 9, 1938; in Cang, "The Opposition Parties in Poland," *Jewish Social Studies*, Vol. I, p. 245.
16. A. Balcikowska, *Stronnictwa i Zwiazki Polityczne w Polsce* (Warsaw, 1925) , p. 731.
17. *Kalendarz Wyzwolenia* (1922) , in Cang, *op. cit.*, p. 248.
18. *Biuletyn Wszytkich stronnictw*, December 19, 1935, No. 51/439, in Cang, *op. cit.*, p. 249.
19. *Sprawa Zydowska a Socjalizm* (Warsaw, 1937) , in Cang, *op. cit.*, p. 253.
20. Bruell, *op. cit.*, p. 98.
21. *Daily Herald*, June 1, 1936.
22. Segal, *op. cit.*, pp. 85–86; Buell, *op. cit.*, p. 299.
23. Segal, *op. cit.*, pp. 79–80.
24. AJYB, Vol. 40 (5699) , p. 241.
25. *Manchester Guardian*, April 23, 1937, p. 16; in Segal, *op. cit.*, p. 74.

26. J. T. A., June 5, 1937.
27. *Manchester Guardian*, December 13, 1937.
28. *Czenstochower Yidn*, p. 186.
29. Schwartzbart, *op. cit.*, pp. 208 and 259.
30. A. Tartakower and K. R. Grossmann, *The Jewish Refugee*, p. 32. The AJYB (5700), p. 302, gives the figure as "over 12,000."
31. *Ibid.*, p. 489.
32. House of Commons, Vol. 347, p. 445–446; Waclaw Jedrzejewicz, *Poland in the British Parliament*, Vol. I, New York, 1946, p. 53.
33. *Ibid.*, p. 50.
34. *Haint*, April 25, May 2 and 5, 1939.
35. AJYB, Vol. 41 (5700), p. 294.
36. J. T. A., August 30, 1939.
37. J. T. A., August 29, 1939.
38. J. T. A., September 5, 1939.

CHAPTER 4

1. Roman Gorecki, *Poland and Her Economic Development* (London, 1935), p. 21.
2. *American Joint Reconstruction Report*, May 15, 1924.
3. *Report on Financial Conditions in Poland*, presented by the Rt. Hon. E. Hilton on February 10, 1924 (London, 1924), p. 9.
4. Jack Taylor, *The Economic Development of Poland 1919–1950* (New York, 1952), p. 70.
5. *Ibid.*, p. 128.
6. *Ibid.*, p. 130.
7. *Report on Financial Conditions in Poland*, p. 7.
8. S. Bronsztejn, "The Jewish Population in Poland in the Light of the General Census of Population of December 9, 1931" (fragments of a statistical study), p. 26; in Taylor, *op. cit.*, p. 103.
9. Bronsztejn, *loc. cit.*, p. 26.
10. Segal, *op. cit.*, p. 138.
11. Jacob Lestschinsky, "The Industrial and Social Structure of the Jewish population in Inter-bellum Poland," p. 246.
12. J. T. A., December 5, 1938.
13. Lestschinsky, *op. cit.*, p. 256.
14. *Ibid.*, p. 256.
15. Segal, *op. cit.*, p. 109.
16. J. C., July 8, 1927, p. 22.
17. Duker, *The Situation of the Jews in Poland*, p. 19.

18. J. H. Retlinger, *All About Poland* (London, 1940), p. 178.

19. Lestschinsky, *Oifn Rand Fun Opgrunt*, p. 103.

20. AJYB, Vol. 40 (5699), p. 256.

21. Israel Cohen, "Jews in Poland," in *Review of Reviews*, January, 1937, p. 75.

22. Lestschinsky, *op. cit.*, p. 103.

23. Boris Smoler, "What Polish Jews are Facing," in *The Nation*, CXXXIV (January 27, 1932), p. 106.

24. J. Taylor, *op. cit.*, p. 92; Buell, *op. cit.*, p. 170.

25. Apenszlak (ed.), *The Black Book of Polish Jewry*, p. 254.

26. J. C., February 23, 1934, p. 18.

27. AJYB, Vol. 39 (5698), p. 397.

28. *The Times* (London), May 22, 1919.

29. *Sixtieth Annual Report of the Anglo-Jewish Association, 1931*, p. 10.

30. *The Manchester Guardian*, September 14, 1937.

31. *Warsaw Weekly*, January 16, 1937.

32. R. Mahler, "Jews in Public Service and the Liberal Professions in Poland," p. 294.

33. *Ibid.*, p. 305.

34. Eccles., XXXVIII : I.

35. Mahler, *op. cit.*, p. 325.

36. Lestschinsky, "Industrial and Social Structure," p. 267.

37. Bruell, *op. cit.*, p. 315. Mahler, *op. cit.*, p. 331.

38. Bruell, *op. cit.*, p. 305.

39. Mahler, *op. cit.*, p. 320.

40. Nasz Przeglad, March 8, 1939, quoted by Mahler, *op. cit.*, p. 321.

41. Mahler, *op. cit.*, p. 323. *Nasz Przeglad*, November 22, 1938; April 8, 1939.

42. Exod. III:9.

43. *Warszawski Dzienny Narodowy*, March 23, 1938. Mahler, *op. cit.*, p. 339.

44. Bruell, *op. cit.*, p. 316.

45. *Der Moment*, May 10, 1937.

46. Friedlaender, *op. cit.*, p. 50.

CHAPTER 5

1. Segal, *op. cit.*, pp. 189–190.

2. Duker, *op. cit.*, p. 12. Elbogen, *op. cit.*, p. 535.

3. *Ibid.*, p. 535. Segal, *op. cit.*, p. 193.

4. J. C., December 14, 1934, p. 26.

5. J. C., January 10, 1930, p. 25.

6. *Concise Statistical Year Book of Poland, 1938*, p. 28.

7. Eisenstein, *The History of Jewish Education*, Vol. II, p. 139.

8. AJYB, Vol. 28 (5687), p. 26.

9. A. J. Heschel, "The Eastern European Era," in *Yivo Annual of Jewish Social Studies*, Vol. I (New York, 1946), p. 103.

10. Scharfstein, *The History of Jewish Education*, Vol. II, p. 139.

11. XXXIV : 12.

12. J. T. A., March 12, 1935.

13. *Report of Activities, 1930–1938*, (Haffkine Foundation for the Benefit of Yeshivot [Lausanne, 1938]), p. 20.

14. *Mishnah Abot* VI : 4.

15. *Sotah*, 20a.

16. *Jerushalmi, Sotah* III : 4.

17. Scharfstein, *op. cit.*, p. 152.

18. "In the Forge of the Beth Jacob Seminary," *Beth Jacob* (March, 1937); in Eisenstein, *op. cit.*, p. 85.

19. Judith Grunfeld-Rosenbaum "Sara Schenierer" in *Jewish Leaders*, Leo Jung (ed.), p. 432.

20. A. Drayanow, *Zionism in Poland* (Tel-Aviv: Masadah, 1932), p. 59. Eisenstein, *op. cit.*, p. 42.

21. AJYB, Vol. 31 (5688), p. 31.

22. Eisenstein, *op. cit.*, p. 19.

23. *Ibid.*, p. 21.

24. I. Rubin, "The Tasks of the New School," in *The New School*, June 15, 1921, p. 30. Eisenstein, *op. cit.*, p. 21.

25. "Report of Cysho Committee on School Budget" in *School and Life*, July, 1922. Eisenstein, *op. cit.*, p. 38.

26. N. Eck, "The Educational Institutions of Polish Jewry" in *The Jewish Social Studies*, IX, No. I (1947), p. 27. Eisenstein, *op. cit.*, p. 67.

CHAPTER 6

1. *Parliamentary Debates*, March 8, 1873.

2. *Ency. Warsaw*, Vol. II, p. 303. Also Lestschinsky, "Yiddishe Students noch der Weltmilchomoh" in *Yivo Bleter*, Vol. VIII (1933), pp. 4–26. In 1930–31 there were 8,923 Jewish students, i.e., 18.5 per cent.

3. Mahler, *op. cit.*, p. 341.

4. *Ibid.*, p. 343. Stephan Horak, *Poland and Her National Minorities, 1919–39*, p. 114. Paprocki, *op. cit.*, p. 107.

5. Samuel, *op. cit.*, p. 34.

6. J. C. B., July 7, 1922.

7. Notes on June 29, July 2 and 6, 1923.

8. AJYB, Vol. 25 (5684), p. 99.

9. Manfred Kridl, *The Democratic Heritage of Poland*, p. 173.

10. *Report to the League of Nations, 1926*, presented by the Board of Deputies of British Jews (London, 1926).

11. Shatzky, *History of the Jews in Warsaw*, p. 82.

12. J. T. A., May 30, 1939.

13. J. C., December 6, 1929, p. 24.

14. AJYB, Vol. 40 (5699), p. 264. Also Vol. 39, pp. 416–25.

15. *The Manchester Guardian*, March 1, 1939.

16. *Ibid.*, October 12, 1937.

17. *The Daily Express* (London), October 16, 1937.

18. *Manchester Guardian*, March 1, 1939.

19. Israel Cohen, *Vilna*, p. 420.

20. Horak, *op. cit.*, p. 118.

21. Kridl (ed.), *For Your Freedom and Ours*, p. 264. Buell, *op. cit.*, pp. 288–91; Kridl, *Democratic Heritage of Poland*, p. 173. AJYB (5698), p. 271.

22. Horak, *op. cit.*, p. 117.

23. Megillah, 12b.

24. J. C., March 3, 1939, p. 26.

CHAPTER 7

1. *Address delivered by the Fifth Conference of the Polish Zionists* (Lodz, 1921), pp. 14–17, quoted by M. Eisenstein, *op. cit.*, p. 17.

2. *Report of the Executive of the Zionist Organisation to the XII Congress* (London, 1921), p. 159.

3. *Report of the Executive, to the XXI Congress* (Jerusalem, 1939), p. 80.

4. *Report of the Executive to XX Congress, 1937*, p. 195.

5. *Haint*, August 6, 1939, p. 2.

6. *Report of the Executive to XX Congress*, p. 195.

7. *Report of the Executive to the XV Congress* (London, 1937), p. 103.

8. S. Levenberg, *The Jews and Palestine* (London, 1945), p. 103.

9. Israel Cohen, *The Zionist Movement* (London, 1945), p. 132.

10. *Ency. Warsaw*, Vol. II, p. 158.

11. Lewin, *Late Summer Fruit*, p. 16.

12. *Jewish Social Studies*, July, 1945, p. 263.

13. AJYB, Vol. 40 (5699), p. 278.

14. *Nayer Haint*, No. 3, 1923.

15. AJYB, Vol. 39 (5698), p. 273.

16. J. T. A., February 5, 1930.

17. I. Bernstein, "The Structure of the Budget of the Jewish Kehilloth in Poland," in *Dos Wirshaftlekhe Lebn*, No. 182 (Warsaw, 1934). J. Lestschinsky, "Economic Aspects of the Jewish Community Organisation in Independent Poland," in *Jewish Social Studies*, Vol. IX (New York, 1945). *Glos Gminy żydowskiej* (Warsaw, 1938).

18. Lestschinsky, "Jewish Community Organization in Poland," p. 329.

19. *Ibid.*, p. 330.

20. *Ibid.*, p. 322.

21. D. Flinker, *Ency. Warsaw*, Vol. I, p. 294.

22. Lestschinsky, *op. cit.*, p. 322.

23. *Ibid.*, p. 327.

24. *Ency. Warsaw*, Vol. II, p. 266.

25. J. T. A., February 26, 1931.

26. Levinson, *Toledot Yehudi Varshaw*, p. 219.

27. *Nayer Haint*, June 17, 1924. Levinson, *op. cit.*, p. 220.

28. D. Flinker, *Ency. Warsaw*, Vol. I, p. 294. Levinson, *op. cit.*, p. 223.

29. AJYB, Vol. 39 (5698), p. 431. Flinker, *op. cit.*, pp. 294–5.

30. AJYB, Vol. 40 (5699), p. 276.

31. *Contemporary Jewish Record*, Sept.-Oct., 1939 (New York, 1939), p. 75.

32. Levinson, *op. cit.*, p. 218.

CHAPTER 8

1. Samuel, *op. cit.*, p. 18.

2. Algemeyne Entizklopedie, p. 394.

3. I:5.

4. Minz, Benjamin, *Rabbenu Miger* (Tel-Aviv, 1950), p. 57.

5. J. T. A., February 2, 1925.

6. J. T. A., September 9, 1927.

7. A. I. Bromberg, *Admurei Neschiz, Lechowich, Koidenov, Novominsk* (Jerusalem, 1963), p. 155.

8. Edited by H. Rabinowicz (London, 1948).

9. D. M. Rabinowicz (ed.), *Tiferet Avot* (Jerusalem, 1961), p. 121.

10. J. T. A., April 10, 1928.

11. J. T. A., March 12, 1928.

12. J. T. A., December 30, 1927.

CHAPTER 9

1. Num. XXIII : 9.

2. A. A. Robak, *Contemporary Yiddish Literature* (London, 1957), p. 54.

3. Joseph Leftwich, *The Golden Peacock*, p. 537.

4. A. A. Robak, *op. cit.*, p. 65.

5. *Ibid.*, p. 69.

6. Mahler, *op. cit.*, p. 348.

7. Kridl, *op. cit.*, p. 212.

8. *New York Times Book Review*, December 22, 1940, p. 14.

9. *Ency. Warsaw*, Vol. I., p. 503. Flinker, *op. cit.*, p. 193. "Tentative List of Jewish Periodicals in Axis-occupied countries," 1947 supplement to *Jewish Social Studies*. Vol. IX, No. 3, p. 30.

10. Friedman, Philip, "The Fate of the Jewish book during the Nazi Era," in *Jewish Book Annual* 5718 [1957–8], Vol. 15 (New York, 1957), p. 4.

11. J. C., March 31, 1939, p. 28.

12. Grove's *Dictionary of Music and Musicians*, Vol. III (London, 1954), p. 503.

13. Samuel, *op. cit.*, p. 34.

14. J. T. A., February 28, 1931.

15. Kridl, *op. cit.*, p. 196.

CHAPTER 10

1. Boris D. Bogen, *Born a Jew* (New York, 1930), p. 137.

2. S. Bornstein, "The Problem of Pauperization of the Jewish Population in Poland," in *The Jews in Restored Poland*, Table II (Warsaw, 1934), p. 407.

3. J. Lestschinsky, *Resettlement and Regrouping of the Jews in the last Century* (Warsaw, 1933), p. 14.

4. Apenszlak, *The Black Book of Polish Jewry*, p. 260.

5. Segal, *op. cit.*, p. 179.

6. Cohen, *op. cit.*, p. 405.

7. J. Lestschinsky, *Crisis, Catastrophe and Survival* (New York, 1948), p. 21.

8. J. T. A., August 3, 1934.

9. Dmowski, *The Post War World and Poland* (Warsaw, 1931), p. 322.

10. Lestchinsky, *op. cit.*, p. 263. Levinson, *op. cit.*, p. 369.

11. L. Hersch, *Jewish and non-Jewish criminality in Poland,* p. 183.

12. Hersch, *op. cit.*, p. 191.

13. S. Fogelson, "The Natural Increase of the Jewish Population in Poland" in *Problems of Nationality* (Warsaw, 1937), p. 4.

14. Lestschinsky, "Jews in the Cities of the Republic of Poland," in *Yivo Annual of Jewish Social Sciences,* Vol. I (New York, 1946), p. 159.

15. *Ibid.*, p. 160.

16. *Ibid.*, p. 164.

17. H. S. Halevi, "The Demography of Jewish Communities in Eastern Europe" in *The Jewish Journal of Sociology,* Vol. II (1960), p. 107.

18. Halevy, *op. cit.*, p. 46.

19. *Ibid.*, p. 46. J. Lestschinsky, *Encyclopedia of the Jewish Diaspora, Warsaw,* I. Gruenbaum (ed.), Vol. I, p. 138. Dr. Z. Schabad, "Mortalitaet und Natalitaet der Juden in Wilna," *Ose-Randschau*, 1927, Nos. 3–4.

20. D. Kiss, "The Jews in Eastern Poland," *Foreign Affairs*, XV, 330 (January, 1937). Horak, *op. cit.*, p. 124.

21. H. Agar, *The Saving Remnant,* p. 254. *Aid to Jews Overseas, Report of the Activities of the American Joint Distribution Committee for 1937,* p. 27.

22. J. C., May 10, 1935, p. 15.

23. Sacher, *Sufferance is the Badge,* p. 188.

24. Apenszlak, *op. cit.*, p. 262.

25. *Ibid.*, p. 261.

26. Levinson, *op. cit.*, p. 357.

27. Apenszlak, *op. cit.*, p. 38.

28. Isaac Lewin (ed.), *The Right to Practice Shechitah,* p. 46.

29. *Ibid.*, p. 85.

30. J. T. A., March 6, 1936.

31. J. C., April 3, 1936, p. 21.

32. Isaac Lewin, *op. cit.*, p. 85.

33. J. C., March 13, 1936, p. 24.

34. J. T. A., September 21, 1936.

35. J. T. A., January 4, 1937.

36. *Senat Rzeczypospolitej Polskiej, Kadencja IV.* Sprawozdanic Stenograficzne 80, pp. 119–150. Lewin, *op. cit.,* p. 89.

37. Moses Moskowitz, "Anti-Shechitah Legislation" in *Contemporary Jewish Record,* Vol. II, No. 3 (May-June, 1939), p. 39. AJYB, Vol. 40 (5699), p. 255.

38. Moskowitz, *op. cit.,* p. 41.

CHAPTER 11

1. *The Times* (London), February 2, 1937.

2. Mark Wischnitzer. *To Dwell in Safety,* p. 151.

3. November 23, 1933.

4. J. C., April 12, 1935. *Gazeta Warszawska,* April 19, 1935. I. Cohen, *Vilna,* p. 418.

5. J. T. A., May 31, 1938; J. C., June 3, 1938, p. 23; J. T. A., January 29, 1936; J. C., July 1, 1938, p. 31; J. T. A., June 22, 1937; J. C., May 27, 1938, p. 33.

6. J. T. A., December 22, 1938; AJYB, Vol. 41 (5700), p. 299; *Contemporary Jewish Record,* March-April, 1938, p. 72; *Nasz Przeglad,* January 24, 1939.

7. J. T. A., February 22, 1937. Segal, *op. cit.,* p. 88.

8. *The Times* (London), October 10, 1936.

9. J. T. A., October 14, 1936.

10. AJYB, Vol. 39 (5698), p. 387.

11. J. T. A., October 12, 1936; J. C., October 16, 1936, p. 29. Segal, *op. cit.,* p. 86.

12. J. T. A., March 1, 1939.

13. AJYB, Vol. 41 (5700), p. 300.

14. Tartakower, *The Jewish Refugee,* p. 412.

15. *Ibid.,* p. 531.

16. AJYB, Vol. 41 (5700), p. 299.

17. J. C., April 14, 1939, p. 27.

18. Wacław Jedrzejewicz, *op. cit.,* p. 53.

19. *The Times* (London), February 2, 1937.

20. Tartakower, *Yiddishe emigrazie,* pp. 30–32.

21. Bruell, *op. cit.,* p. 227.

22. Wischnitzer, *op. cit.,* p. 163.

23. *The Mandate for Palestine, 1922,* Article 6.

24. J. T. A., October 18, 1926; J. C., October 29, 1926, p. 27.

25. Paprocki, *op. cit.,* p. 149. *Warsaw Weekly,* No. 22 (May 29, 1937), p. 1.

26. J. T. A., May 3, 1937.

27. J. T. A., September 23, 1937. *Minutes of the Sixth Committee* (Records of the Eighteenth Assembly, Official Supplement No. 14), p. 27.

28. Ninety-eighth Session, Official Journal (December, 1937), p. 909. *Warsaw Weekly,* September 18, 1937.

29. I. Cohen, *The Zionist Movement* (London, 1943), p. 319.

30. *Ibid.,* p. 320. Between 1918–1938, 149,770 Polish Jews entered Palestine: *Ency. Warsaw.* Vol. I, p. 434.

31. Joseph B. Schechtman, *Fighter & Prophet,* Vol. II, p. 338.

32. *Ibid.,* p. 214.

33. AJYB, Vol. 39 (5698), p. 386.

34. J. B. Schechtman, *op. cit.,* p. 34.

35. J. T. A., March 2, 1937.

36. J. B. Schechtman, *op. cit.,* p. 341.

37. January 26, 1937. AJYB, Vol. 39 (5698), p. 229.

38. M. Marcel Olivier, *Raisons, difficultés et moyens d'une solidarité europèene en Afrique* (Rome, 1940). Eugene Hevesi, "Hitler's Plan for Madagascar," *Contemporary Jewish Record,* Vol. IV (New York, August, 1941), p. 392. Egon van Winghene in a pamphlet published in 1931, *Arische Rasse, Christliche Kultur und das Juden-problem,* stated, "the entire Jewish people must, sooner or later, be confined to an island."

39. J. Cang. *op. cit.,* p. 250. Philip Friedman, "The Lublin Reservation and the Madagascar Plan" in *Yivo Annual of Jewish Social Studies,* Vol. VIII, p. 165, note 50.

40. J. T. A., May 11, 1937; *The Manchester Guardian,* December 31, 1937, and January 1, 1938.

41. AJYB, Vol. 40 (5699), p. 244.

42. J. T. A., December 16, 1937.

43. J. T. A., January 18, 1938; Eugene Hevesi, *op. cit.,* p. 386.

44. *Ibid.,* p. 391.

45. *The Wiener Library Bulletin,* September/December, 1955. Hilberg, *The Destruction of European Jews* (Chicago, 1961), pp. 260–1.

46. AJYB, Vol. 39 (5698), p. 229.

47. Elbogen, *op. cit.,* p. 677.

CHAPTER 12

1. Prov. XV : 27.

2. Moses M. Yosher, "Israel Meir ha-Kohen, the Hafetz Hayyim" in *Jewish Leaders* (ed. by Leo Jung), p. 471. M. M. Yosher, *Saint and Sage* (New York, 1937), p. 256.

3. J. L. Kagan and H. B. Perlman, "Hayyim Ozer Grodzenski (1863–1914) " in *Jewish Leaders* (ed. Leo Jung), p. 436.

4. J. L. Kagan, *op. cit.*, p. 441.

5. Israel Elfenbein, "Menahem Ziemba of Praga" in *Guardians of Our Heritage* (ed. Leo Jung), p. 612. *Ele Ezkero* (ed. I. Lewin), Vol. II, p. 61.

6. Isar Frankel, *Rabbi Meir Milublin* (Tel-Aviv, 1952), p. 12.

7. Lewin, *Israel of To-morrow*, p. 396; *Late Summer Fruit*, p. 19.

8. I. Lewin, "Aaron Lewin," in *The Guardians of Our Heritage*, p. 585.

9. *Minutes of the Seym*, November 7, 1931, p. 58. Lewin, *Late Summer Fruit*, p. 48.

10. *Ibid.*, p. 38.

11. Judith Grunfeld-Rosenbaum," Sara Schnerier," in *Jewish Leaders* (ed. Leo Jung), p. 431.

12. Eisenstein, *op. cit.*, p. 85.

13. J. C., December 8, 1921.

14. *Bulletin of the Polish Institute of Arts and Science in America*, Vol. I (1943), p. 650.

15. P. Friedman, "Major Balaban," in *Miesiecznik Zydowski*, Vol. III (1933), pp. 346–51.

16. *Dzieje zydow w Krakowie i na Kazimierzu 1304–1868* ("History of the Jews in Cracow") (Cracow, 1912). *Zydzi Lwowscy na przelomie xvigo i xviigo wieku* ("The Jews of Lwow about 1600") (Lwow, 1906). *Studja historyczne* ("Studies of the Jews in Poland") (Warsaw, 1927). *Die Judenstadt von Lublin* (Berlin, 1919). *Dzieje zydow w Galicyi i w Rzeczypospolitej Krakowskiej 1772–1868* ("A History of the Jews in Galicia and the Republic of Cracow, 1772–1868") (Lwow, 1914). *Zabytki historyczne Zydow w Polsce* ("Historical Remains of the Jews in Poland") (Warsaw, 1929).

17. Friedman, "Polish Jewish Historiography," p. 374.

18. *Ibid.*, p. 403.

19. J. T. A., January 19, 1935.

20. J. C., November 25, 1927, p. 21.

21. J. T. A., November 11, 1936.

22. *Ibid.*, December 2, 1929.

23. Kridl, *op. cit.*, p. 184.

24. A. J. Heschel, *The Earth is the Lord's* (New York, 1956), pp. 104–105.

Glossary

Ab	The fifth month of the Jewish calendar.
Adar	The twelfth month of the Jewish calendar.
Aggadah	(Lit. "tale.") Sections of Rabbinic literature containing homiletic expositions of the Bible.
Aliya	(Lit. "going up.") Emigration of Jews to the Holy Land.
Amora	(pl. *Amoraim*; lit. "to speak.") Sages from c. 200 A.C.E. to c. 500 A.C.E. whose teachings constitute the Gemara.
Ashkenazim	(Lit. "Germans") Jews of Central and Eastern European origin.
Baale Batim	Householders
Bachur	(Lit. "Youth.") An unmarried youth or a yeshiva student.
Bagel	A donut-shaped hard roll, whose dough is first boiled, then baked.
Baraita	(Lit. "External.") *Tannaitic* sayings not included in the Mishnah.
Ben	Son.
Bet Hamidrash	(Lit. "House of Study.") Term applied also to a synagogue.

Bikkur Cholim	Visiting the sick.
Cabbala	(Lit. "Tradition.") Jewish mysticism.
Chalutz	(Lit. "Vanguard.") A pioneer in modern Israel.
Chanukah	Eight-day festival which occurs on the 25th of *Kislev* and commemorates the triumph of Judaism over Hellenism in the revolt against Antiochus Epiphanes in the year 165 B.C.E.
Chassidism	A pietistic movement founded by Rabbi Israel Baal Shem Tov (1700–1760).
Cheder	(Lit. "room.") A private Hebrew school so called because the locale was originally the teacher's house.
Elul	The sixth month of the Jewish calendar.
Gaon	(pl. *Geonim*; lit. "Illustrious.") Title of the head of the Babylonian academies seventh to eleventh centuries. Also a title conferred upon a great rabbinical scholar.
Gemara	(Lit. "learning.") The part of the Talmud which is the *Amoraim's* exposition of the Mishnah.
Groschen	A German silver coin with a value of about two cents.
Gulden	An Austro-Hungarian silver coin with a value of about forty-eight cents.
Hachsharah	(Lit. "Preparation.") Training for settlement in Israel.
Halachah	The legal part of rabbinic tradition and literature.
Heshvon	The eighth month of the Jewish calendar.
Hurban	(Lit. "Destruction.") The Nazi massacres of the Jewish communities in Europe.
Iyar	The second month in the Jewish calendar.
Kaddish	(Lit. "Sanctification.") Doxology in Aramaic. Recited at the conclusion of each

service, and by the bereaved at the time of mourning.

Kapote
From the French word *capote*, a coat. The long frock-coat worn by pious Jews.

Kosher
(Lit. "fit," "permitted.") Food prepared according to Rabbinic dietary regulations.

Kehilla
Community.

Kislev
The ninth month of the Jewish calendar.

Kol Nidre
(Lit. "All vows.") Opening words of the formula preceding the religious service on the Eve of the Day of Atonement.

Krone
Coinage of Austria-Hungary (1892–1925).

Lag Ba'Omer
The thirty-third day of the counting of the *Omer*. Known as the scholar's feast because according to legend the plague which had carried off many disciples of Rabbi Akiva ceased on that day.

Litvak
A Lithuanian Jew.

Maskilim
(Lit. "Enlightenment.") Men of the Haskalah, the movement which spread modern European culture among Jews (1750–1880).

Matzah
(pl. *matzot*.) Unleavened bread, eaten on Passover.

Midrash
(pl. *Midrashim*; lit. "Exposition.") Homiletic exposition of the Scriptures.

Mishnah
(Lit. "Repetition.") The authoritative code of Jewish oral law compiled c. 200 A.C.E.

Mitnaggdim
(Lit. "Opponents.") The antagonists of Chassidism.

Musar
Ethics. The moralist movement among Lithuanian traditionalists of the late nineteenth century.

Nisan
The first month of the Jewish calendar.

Numerus clausus
(Lit. "Closed number.") The restriction of

Jewish students admitted to educational institutions.

Purim
(Lit. "Lots.") The festival of lots celebrated on the 14th of *Adar* in commemoration of the overthrow of Haman.

Rav
A rabbi.

Rebbe
A Chassidic leader, not necessarily the rabbi of a community.

Responsa
Opinions (written replies) by religious authorities on questions of Jewish Law.

Rosh Hashanah
The beginning of the civil Jewish year, on the first and second of *Tishri*.

Ruble
Silver coin with a value in Czarist Russia of about fifty-one cents. (2/1½d.)

Sephardim
Originally, the Jews of Spain and their descendants; later, those who adopted the liturgy of the *Sephardim*.

Sepher Torah
Scroll of the Law.

Seym
Polish parliament.

Shalosh Seudot
(Lit. "Three meals.") The Chassidim, like the Cabbalists, found mystical meaning in the "third meal" eaten on the Sabbath. Rabbi Isaac Luria wrote special Aramaic hymns for this meal.

Shechina
The Divine Presence, often used as a synonym for God.

Shechitah
The term applied to the Jewish ritual method of slaughtering animals and fowl for food.

Shekel
A silver unit of weight, later an accepted coin among the Jews. The concept of the Shekel was revived by the Zionists, the members of which pay a small annual levy called a Shekel which entitles them to participate in elections to the Zionist Congress. It was introduced in 1897 at the First Zionist Congress.

Shevat	The eleventh month of the Jewish calendar.
Shophar	Ram's horn sounded on *Rosh Hashanah* (q.v.).
Shtetl	(Yiddish.) A Jewish town or village.
Shulchan Aruch	(Lit. "Set Table.") The code of law compiled by Rabbi Joseph Caro of Safed in mid-sixteenth century.
Sivan	The third month of the Jewish calendar.
Tallit	A prayer shawl used by males during prayers.
Talmud	(Lit. "Learning.") Comments and discussions on the text of the Mishnah by Palestinian and Babylonian scholars of the third to the fifth century A. C. E., which constitute the Palestinian Talmud and the Babylonian Talmud. The Babylonian Talmud contains nearly 3,000 pages and was edited by *Rav* Ashi (352–427). The Palestinian Talmud was completed in the fifth century and is only one seventh as long as the Babylonian version.
Talmud Torah	A Hebrew school.
Tammuz	The fourth month of the Jewish calendar.
Tanna	(pl. *Tannaim.*) The sages whose teachings constitute the Mishnah.
Tephillin	Phylacteries. Small cases, containing biblical verse, donned by male worshippers during weekday morning prayers.
Tevet	The tenth month of the Jewish calendar.
Thaler	A large silver coin issued by various German States with a value of 72 cents.
Tishri	The seventh month of the Jewish calendar.
Torah	(Lit. "Teaching," "Instruction.") Primarily the Five Books of Moses. By ex-

tension of the whole body of Jewish religious literature.

Tosaphot   (Lit. "Additions.") Critical glosses on the Talmud by French rabbis of the twelfth and thirteenth centuries.

Tregers   (Yiddish.) Porters.

Tzizits   Fringes attached to the four corners of a *tallit* (Num. XV (9-unit): 37–41).

Vaad   Council.

Yeshiva   Institute of high learning for the study of the Talmud and rabbinical literature.

Yishuv   A settlement, more specifically the Jewish communities of Israel.

Yom Kippur   Day of Atonement, tenth of *Tishri*, a fast day.

Zaddik   (pl. *Zaddikim*). (Lit. "Righteous man.") A Chassidic teacher.

Zloty   A monetary unit of Poland minted on May 1, 1924, with an approximate value 11¼ cents (10d). Before World War II it was equivalent to $0.18.

Bibliography

Agar, Herbert. *The Saving Remnant*. London, 1960.

Algemeyne Entsiklopedie, I. New York, 1950.

Apenszlak, Jacob (ed.), *The Black Book of Polish Jewry*. New York, 1943.

Apenszlak & Polakiewicz, Isaac. *Armed Resistance by the Jews in Poland*. New York, 1944.

Bader, Gershon. *Draisig Dorot Iden In Poilen*. New York, 1927.

Balaban, M. *Bibliografia Historii Żydów w Polsce (1900–1930)*. Warsaw, 1939.

Bornstein, I. *Rzmiosło Żydowskie w Polsce*. Warsaw, 1936.

Bruell, Raymond Leslie. *Poland: Key to Europe*. New York and London, 1939.

Cang, Joel. "The Opposition Parties in Poland and their attitude towards the Jews and the Jewish problem," *Jewish Social Studies*, Vol. I. New York, 1939, pp. 241–257.

Cohen, Israel. *A Report of The Pogroms in Poland*. London, 1919.

———. *Vilna*. (1943 Jewish Community Series.) Philadelphia, 1943.

Concise Statistical Year Book of Poland, 1938. (Chief Bureau of Statistics of the Republic of Poland.) Warsaw, 1938.

243

Dmowski, Roman. *Polityka Polska i odbudowanie Panstwa.* Warsaw, 1926.

Dubnow, S. M., *History of the Jews of Russia and Poland.* Tran. by I. Friedlaender. 3 vols. Philadelphia, 1916–1920.

Duker, A. G. *The Situation of the Jews in Poland.* With an Introductory Statement by M. R. Cohen and S. W. Baron. New York: Conference on Jewish Relations, 1936.

Eck, Nathan. "The Educational Institutions of Polish Jewry 1921–1939," *Jewish Social Studies* (New York), Vol. IX (1947), pp. 3–32.

Eisenstein, Miriam. *Jewish Schools in Poland 1919–1939.* New York, 1950.

Elbogen, Ismar. *A Century of Jewish Life.* Philadelphia, 1946.

Elfenbein, Israel. "Menahem Ziemba of Praga," Leo Jung (ed.). *Guardians of Our Heritage.* New York, 1957, pp. 605–617.

Encyclopaedia of the Jewish Diaspora (Heb.)

  Brest-Litovsk, Eliezer Steinmann (ed.). Jerusalem-Tel-Aviv, 1954.

  Lwow, Dr. N. M. Gelber (ed.). Jerusalem-Tel-Aviv, 1956.

  Lublin, N. Blumenthal and M. Korzen (eds.). Tel-Aviv, 1957.

  Mir, N. Blumenthal (ed.). Jerusalem, 1962.

  Tarnopol, Dr. Ph. Korngruen (ed.). Jerusalem, Tel-Aviv, 1953.

  Warsaw, Vol. I Itzhak Gruenbaum (ed.). Tel-Aviv, 1953.

  Warsaw, Vol. II Itzhak Gruenbaum (ed.). Tel-Aviv, 1959.

Filipowicz, T. *Poland Past and Present.* New York, 1933.

Finkielstein, Leo. *Megillat Poilen.* Buenos Aires, 1947.

Flinker, David. *Encycloplaedia of the Jewish Diaspora,* "Warsaw." Jerusalem, 1946.

Friedlaender, Israel. *The Jews of Russia and Poland.* New York, 1920.

Friedman, Philip. "Polish Jewish Historiography between the two wars 1918–1939." *Jewish Social Studies* (New York), Vol. XI, no. 4 (1949), pp. 373–409.

"The Lublin Reservation and the Madagascar Plan," *Yivo Annual of Jewish Social Sciences*, (New York), Vol. VIII (1953), pp. 151–177.

Fun Noenten Ovar (The Jewish Press in Poland.) New York, 1956.

Gliksman, G. *L'aspect économique et la question juive en Pologne*. Paris, 1929.

Goodhart, Arthur L. *Poland and the Minority Races*. London, 1920.

Grunfeld, Judith. "Sara Schenierer," in Leo Jung (ed.), *Jewish Leaders, 1750–1940*, New York, 1953, pp. 407–432.

Haftka, Alexander. *The Activity of the General Aid Committee for the Refugees from Germany in Poland*. Warsaw, 1939.

Halecki, O. A. *History of Poland*. New York, 1943.

Halevi, Haim Shalom. *The Influence of World War II on the Demographic Characteristics of the Jewish People* (Thesis for the degree of Doctor of Philosophy submitted to the Senate of the Hebrew University on May 25, 1960).

Henryk, Erlich and Victor Alter. New York, Unser Tsait, 1951.

Hersch, Liebman. "Jewish and Non-Jewish criminality in Poland 1932–1937," *Yivo Annual of Jewish Social Science* (New York) Vol. I (1946), pp. 178–194.

Hertz, Aleksander. *Zydzi W. Kulturze Polskiej*. Paris, 1961.

Horak, Stephen. *Poland and Her National Minorities 1919–39*. New York, 1961.

Janowsky, Oscar I. *Poland at Bay: The Jewish Problem in East-Central Europe*. New York, London and Toronto, 1938.

The Jew and Minority Rights 1898–1919. New York, 1933.

Jews in Poland. Vol. I. (Committee for the publication of Jews in Poland). New York, 1941.

Jung, Leo. (ed.). *Guardians of our Heritage*. New York, 1958.

———. (ed.). *Jewish Leaders 1750–1940*. New York, 1953.

Kajdan, Ch. S. *Destruction of Yiddish Culture in Poland.* Buenos Aires, 1943.

——. *History of the Jewish School System in Independent Poland.* (Yiddish) Buenos Aires, 1947.

Kessler, Lawton. "American Jews and the Paris Peace Conference," *Yivo Annual of Jewish Social Science.* (New York) Vol. II–III (1947–48), pp. 222–243.

Klub Poslow i Senatorow Zydowskiej Rady Narodowej, Biuletyn 1–5. Warsaw, 1928–1930.

Komarnicki, Titus. *Rebirth of the Polish Republic.* London, 1957.

Kridl, Manfred; Wittlin, Jósef; Malinowski, Wladyslaw. *Democratic Heritage of Poland.* London, 1944.

Kridl, Manfred (ed.). *For Your Freedom and Ours.* New York, 1943.

Levinson, Abraham. *Toledot Yehudi Varshaw.* Tel-Aviv, 1953.

Lestschinsky, Jacob. "Economic Aspects of Jewish Community Organisation in Independent Poland," *Jewish Social Studies,* (New York), Vol. IX (1945), pp. 319–362.

——. "Der Yidisher proletaryat in polyn," *Yivo Bleter* (New York), Vol. XV (1940), pp. 12–27;

——. "The Jews in the Cities of the Republic of Poland," *Yivo Annual of Jewish Social Science,* (New York), Vol. I (1946), pp. 156–177.

——. *Der Wirtschaftliche Zusammenbruch der Juden in Deutschland und Polen.* Paris, 1936.

——. *Di Ekonomishe Lage fun Yidn in Poyln.* Vilna, 1932.

——. *Oifn Rand Fun Opgrunt.* Buenos Aires, 1947.

——. "The Industrial and Social Structure of the Jewish Population of inter-bellum Poland," *Yivo Annual of Jewish Social Science* (New York), Vol. XI (1956–57), pp. 243–270.

——. *Probleme der Bevoelkerungs Bewegung bei den Juden. Metron* Vol. VI. Padua, 1926.

——. *La Situation économique des juifs depuis la guerre mondiale—Europe orientale et centrale.* Paris, 1934.

Lew, Myer. S. *The Jews of Poland.* London, 1944.

Lewin, Isaac. "Religious Judaism in Independent Poland," in Leo Jung (ed.), *Israel of Tomorrow*, New York, 1946, pp. 389–397.

———. *Late Summer Fruit*. New York, 1960.

———. *Contributions to the History of the Jews in Poland*. Lwow, 1935.

———. "Aaron Lewin," in *Guardians of our Heritage*, New York, 1958, pp. 583–601.

———. (ed.). *Ele Ezekero*. Biographies of leaders of religious Jewry in Europe who perished during the years 1937–1945. 5 vols., New York, 1957–1963.

Lewin, Isaac, Michal L. Munk and Jeremiah J. Berman (eds.). *Religious Freedom: The Right to Practice Shechitah*. New York, 1946.

Machray, Robert. *Poland 1914–1931*. London, 1932.

Mahler, Raphael. "Jews in Public Service and the Liberal Professions in Poland, 1918–1939," in *Jewish Social Studies* (New York, 1944), Vol. VI, No. 4, pp. 291–351.

———. *Zydzi w dawnej Polsce w swietle cyfr*. (Yiddish.) Warsaw, 1957.

———. (ed.). *Czenstochover Yidn*. New York, 1947.

Mark, Bernard. *Di Geschichte Fun Yidn in Polyn-Bizn Soph Fun XV Y.H.* Warsaw, 1957.

Mirski, Samuel, K. (ed.), *Mosdot Torah Beirope* (Jewish Institutions of Higher Learning in Europe: their development and destruction). New York, 1956.

Morgenthau, Henry. *All in a Lifetime*. London, 1923.

Paprocki, S. J. *Minority Affairs and Poland*. (Nationality Research Institute). Warsaw, 1935.

Parkes, James. *The Emergence of the Jewish Problem 1878–1938*. London, 1948.

Peace Conference, The, Paris 1919: Report of the Delegation of the Jews of the British Empire on the Treaties of Versailles . . . and the Annexed Minority Treaties. London, Joint Foreign Committee, 1920.

Polish Jew—Eleventh Year Book Published on the Occasion of the Thirty-fifth Convention of the American Federation. New York, 1944.

Reports of the Executive of the Zionist Organization to Zionist Congresses, (Zionist Organization Publications), 1921–1939.

Sacher, Abraham Leon. *Sufferance is the Badge.* New York, 1940.

Samuel, Sir Stuart. *Report by Sir Stuart Samuel on his Mission to Poland.* (Cmd. 674. Miscellaneous No. 10.) London, 1920.

Sandal, Joseph. *Umgekumene Yidisher Kinstler* Jewish Artists who perished in Poland. 2 Vols. Warsaw, 1957.

Scharfstein, Zevi. *The History of Jewish Education* (Heb.). Vol. II. New York, 1960.

Schechtman, Joseph B. *Fighter and Prophet.* New York and London, 1961.

Schmeltz, O. (ed.). *Jewish Demography and Statistics, Bibliography for 1920–1960.* Jerusalem, 1961.

Schneidermann, Harry; Adler, Cyrus (ed.). The American Jewish Year Book, Philadelphia, 1899.

Schorr, Moses, *Organizacja Żydów w Polsce.* Lwow, 1899.

———. *Zydzi w Przemyslu.* Lwów, 1903.

Schwartzbart, Isaac. *Szwischen Beide Welt Milchumot.* Buenos Aires, 1953.

Shatzky, Jacob. *Di Geshichte Fun Yidn in Varshe* ("The History of The Jews in Warsaw") Vol. III, 1863–1896. New York, 1953.

Segal, Simon. *The New Poland and the Jews.* New York, 1938.

Spizman, Leib. (ed.). *Chalutzim in Poiln* Anthology of the *Hechalutz* Movement. Vol. I. New York, 1959.

Tartakower, Arieh. "Das Jüdische Schulwesen in Polen," in *Monatschrift Fuer die Geschichte und Wissenschaft des Judentums.* (Frankfurt), LXXV (1937), pp. 292–306.

———. *A History of the Jewish Labor Movement.* (Hebrew.) 3 vols. Warsaw, 1929–31.

———. "Jewish Emigration from Poland in Post-War Years,"

in *The Jewish Social Service Quarterly*, New York, 1940, pp. 272ff.

Kurt R. Grossman, *The Jewish Refugee*. New York, 1944.

I. Schipper, A. Hafftki, *Zydzi w Polsce Odrodzonej*. ("The Jews in Renewed Poland") 2 vols. Warsaw, 1934–1935.

Tenenbaum, Joseph. *La Question Juive en Pologne*. Paris, 1919.

Weichert, Michael. *Memoires*. Tel-Aviv, 1961.

Wischnitzer, Mark. *Die Juden in der Welt: Gegenwart und Geschichte des Judentums in Allen Landern*. Berlin, 1935.

——. "Yiddisher historiker in Poyln" in *Zukunft* (New York), Vol. XLVIII (1943), pp. 483–487.

—— *To Dwell in Safety*. Philadelphia, 1948.

Zeidman, Hillel. *Diary of the Warsaw Ghetto* (Yiddish.) Buenos Aires, 1947.

Zylbercwajg, Z. and J. Mestel (eds.). *Lexicon of the Yiddish Theater* (Yiddish.) 2 vols. New York and Warsaw, 1931–1934.

Index